Images of Me

Images of Me

A Guide to Group Work with African-American Women

Sherlon P. Pack-Brown
Bowling Green State University

Linda E. Whittington-Clark
Whittington-Clark and Associates

Woodrow M. Parker
University of Florida, Gainesville

Allyn and Bacon

Boston   London   Toronto   Sydney   Tokyo   Singapore

Series editor: Carla F. Daves
Series editorial assistant: Susan Hutchinson
Manufacturing buyer: David Suspanic

Copyright © 1998 by Allyn & Bacon
A Viacom Company
Needham Heights, MA 02194

Internet: www.abacon.com
America Online: keyword: College Online

Library of Congress Cataloging-in-Publication Data

Pack-Brown, Sherlon P.
    Images of me : a guide to group work with African-American women /
Sherlon P. Pack-Brown, Linda E. Whittington-Clark, Woodrow M.
Parker.
       p.   cm.
    Includes bibliographical references and index.
    ISBN 0-205-17184-2
    1. Afro-American women—Counseling of. 2. Social work with women—
United States. 3. Cross-cultural counseling—United States.
4. Social group work—United States. 5. Group psychotherapy—United
States.   I. Whittington-Clark, Linda E. II. Parker, Woodrow M.
III. Title.
HV1445.P33   1998
362.83'54'08996073--dc21   97-37714
                                                        CIP

Printed in the United States of America
10 9 8 7 6 5 4 3 2 1   01 00 99 98 97

Contents

Preface

The influence of racism and sexism in the lifespan development of African-American women has been well documented in the United States over the past 200 years (Brown, 1993; Evans & Herr, 1991; Jackson & Sears, 1992). The consequences of gender and race discrimination commonly include anger and confusion related to personal identity, difficulty in relationships, and achieving meaningful success in the workplace. In today's diversified society, helping professionals and professional associations are challenged to reevaluate the efficacy of traditional Eurocentric interventions and to identify and prescribe interventions which embrace varied lifestyles, life experiences, and important issues that people face as they increasingly encounter diverse cultures and changes in the social environment. Multicultural counseling has been identified as the fourth force in the counseling profession. A benefit of the multicultural movement has been an increase in efforts to design services that are more consistent with and sensitive to various dimensions of African-American females' worldview. Although efforts to design services have increased and several journal issues and articles on enhancing the mental health of African-American women have been published, a book that addresses cultural competency and training was needed. This book, *Images of Me: A Guide to Group Work with African-American Women*, has become a reality and is a "spin off" of past and present Images of Me support/therapy groups.

Dr. Sherlon Pack-Brown was suggested as senior author because of her history, vision, and commitment to providing services to African-American female groups, initially on predominantly White university campuses. Dr. Pack-Brown and Dr. Linda Whittington-Clark recognized that the issues of Black females extended beyond academia and actually emerged from the realities of their essence as African-Americans and females in a racist and sexist society. For more than six years they have co-led numerous groups for African-American women within the private sector. Dr. Woodrow Parker, an author who writes about multiculturalism and is an expert in group counseling, was invited to join in writing this book to share his expertise on issues and interventions that helping professionals must become aware of, comfortable with, and knowledgeable about as they develop skills and provide services to African-American females.

The book promotes and is written from an Afrocentric theoretical orientation. It underscores assisting group members to live within specific Nguzo Saba principles of *Kwanzaa* (KWAH-nzah)—to identify, appreciate, and empower their collective as well as individual strengths. Six of the seven principles are emphasized: *Nia* (NEE-ah), purpose and direction; *Umoja* (oo-MOH-jah), harmony and unity; *Kujichagulia* (koo-ji-chah-goo-LEE-ah), authenticity, self-esteem, and empowerment; *Ujima* (oo-JEE-mah), collective work, responsibility; *Imani* (ee-MAH-nee), faith; and *Kuumba* (koo-OO-mbah), creativity, a new reality. The reader is advised to think of the application of these principles in circular rather than linear time. All six principles can occur simultaneously or they can occur nonsequentially. Phillips (1990, p. 65) states: "The principles of Nguzo Saba can be universally applied"; that is, they are equally applicable to European-Americans, Latino-Americans, and others because the concepts are based on a spiritual connection that human beings have with the life force.

This book has three basic themes—the culture of African-American women, African-American female issues, and group practices with African-American women. Relevant information is drawn from psychology, sociology, education, economics, spirituality, and personal life experiences to form a comprehensive base of knowledge. Counselors build their work on a foundation of two primary structures. The first structure is a multicultural orientation that actualizes differences, moves beyond monoculturalism, advocates social responsibility and activism, and promotes cultural competency. The second structure is the culture of African-American women, African-American female issues, and group practices with African-American women. The interaction of the multicultural orientation and the three themes promotes the efficacy of group work. Culture, values, and lifestyles are upheld as valid worldview components and are believed to have an impact on life experiences, interpretations, and problems of African-American women, particularly those women who:

1. Have been (within the last two to three years) or are currently employed in a predominately European-American work environment;
2. Desire to address issues related to them as African-American and female;
3. Desire to participate in a support/therapy group offered to African-American women, designed for African-American women, and primarily facilitated by African-American women; and
4. Are working with African-American women.

A unique feature of this book is that the reader is invited into group sessions to learn how to effectively work with African-American women. A culturally competent helping professional needs to be (1) aware of personal biases, stereotypes, and prejudices; (2) knowledgeable about her or his clientele; and (3) able to practice skills that are sensitive to clients' life experiences. Participation in group sessions allows the reader to tap personal "isms," gain knowledge about African-American women, and observe the application of culturally appropriate skills. The book is written in a clear and simple style so that readers in various settings and at different levels of multicultural development can readily comprehend the concepts. The content is realistic, practical, and critical to what counselors should know and what they might do to assist African-American women in living with dignity and respect in the context of those groups and environments with which they identify. It is an "action-oriented" Afrocentric group approach to enhancing the development of personal and racial identity as well as the professional advancement and maturation of African-American women. The book's core philosophy is based on awareness, confidence, and freedom to be "ME: black, female, and empowered." This philosophy enables personal, professional, psychological, emotional, and spiritual maturation to be more readily realized.

The book is a comprehensive, broad-based text and manual for group work with African-American women. Practitioners working with the younger person may also find it helpful in fulfilling their responsibility to prepare young African-American females to more effectively cope with and handle issues of race and gender as they mature into womanhood. *Images of Me: A Guide to Group Work with African-American Women* is unique in that it espouses an Afrocentric approach to helping.

Theoretical Foundation

The Afrocentric, or African, worldview emerged from a need created by deficiencies in the mental health profession to offer suitable services to people other than those of traditional European-American culture. To more appropriately meet the needs of the often misdiagnosed and frequently underserved, this approach presents a set of philosophical constructs that formulate the lenses through which African-Americans tend to view the world and to structure reality. Thus, *Images of Me: A Guide to Group Work with African-American Women* reflects an Afrocentric approach to group counseling and provides a set of therapeutic tools and culturally appropriate knowledge critical to diagnosing worldview and reality as seen through the lenses of African-American female clients. The tools and knowledge shared throughout the book may be used to enhance the quality of life for all clients. Of significance is that the Afrocentric approach is effective in group counseling and in individual and family counseling; however, to successfully use the Afrocentric approach, basic information on the foundation of the philosophy and constructs is warranted.

African-centered psychology (Afrocentric psychology), as defined by the Western Region Retreat of African-American psychologists in 1993, is a dynamic manifestation of unifying African principles, values, and traditions. It is the self-conscious "centering" of psychological analyses and applications in African reality, culture, and epistemology. African-centered psychology examines the process that allows for the illumination and liberation of the Spirit. Relying on the principles of harmony within the universe as a natural order of existence, African-centered psychology recognizes: the Spirit that permeates everything so that everything in the universe is interconnected; the value that the collective is the most salient element of existence; and the idea that communal self-knowledge is the key to mental health. African psychology is ultimately concerned with the systems of meaning of human beingness, the features of human functioning, and the restoration of normal/ natural order to human development.

Major proponents of the Afrocentric approach to mental health include Niam Akbar, Marimba Ani, Molefi Kente Asanté, Thomas Parham, Linda James Meyers, and Wade Nobles. In general, these scholars agree that the Afrocentric concept represents a worldview, philosophical orientation, set of social standards, and codes of conduct that reflect core African values. These values are essential to the total person and particularly to the spiritual and communal nature of African-American people. Thematic values commonly observed in years of group work with African-American females include collective survival (we/sisterhood), emotional vitality (an animated-feelings approach to life), and a being orientation to time (self-validation due to personal birth and existence). Of significance is that many of the Afrocentric values, such as interdependence and collective behavior, parallel values inherent in effective group work. Thus, these values are widespread and universally applicable.

General Audience

The primary purpose of *Images of Me: A Guide to Group Work with African-American Women* is to teach the reader how to responsibly and competently, within an African-American cultural context, provide group counseling services for African-American women. The book is written for (1) practitioners such as human services counselors, elementary and secondary school counselors, college counselors, rehabilitation counselors, mental health counselors, pastoral counselors, psychologists, psychiatrists, and social workers; (2) students (undergraduate and graduate) aspiring toward the previously identified professions; and (3) educators and supervisors of students in the previously identified fields. Teachers in disciplines outside the mental health fields listed before also may benefit from the material. Some of the specific courses for which this book may be used are: Multicultural and Cross-Cultural Counseling, Social and Cultural Foundations, Women's Studies, Comprehensive Introduction/Orientation to Counseling and Human Services in Today's Society, Social and Cultural Issues in the Work of Counselors, Group Psychotherapy, and Group Counseling.

Images of Me: A Guide to Group Work with African-American Women is not an introductory text on multicultural counseling. The requisite behaviors and knowledge for the reader to fully understand, appreciate, and apply the concepts and interventions shared in the book include: (1) a basic theoretical background in multicultural counseling and introductory psychology; (2) a willingness to engage in learning opportunities designed to enhance personal and professional awareness, knowledge and skills related to working with diverse populations and, in particular, with African-American women; and/or (3) access to resource materials promoting the development of multicultural competencies such as the 1996 monograph by The Association for Multicultural Counseling and Development (AMCD), a division of the American Counseling Association (ACA), entitled *Operationalization of the Multicultural Competencies*. The book is designed to assist the reader in meeting the following three objectives while working with African-American females:

- To empower African-American women who question their racial and gender identities.
- To increase understanding of and appreciation for the Afrocentric worldview throughout the African-American female lifespan.
- To promote the value of collective behavior via embracing "sisterhood."

Organization of the Book

The book is divided into three parts. Throughout the book, we have incorporated thematic excerpts from actual group sessions highlighting clinical issues which, based on years of group work, we have found to be common to African-American women. These include racial and gender issues such as anger and relationships. Many chapters incorporate a clinical segment excerpt from a sample group which highlights common issues (e.g., anger and relationships) among gender and racial groups. Following the excerpt is a discussion of group process and dynamics. Included in this discussion are strategies and techniques frequently employed, the strengths and weaknesses of these methodologies, and recommendations for more appropriate methodologies.

Part I introduces the reader to the relationship of identity to race and gender. This means becoming familiar with the emotional and cognitive world of African-American women. Similarities and differences exist between African-American and European-American women; however, our purpose is to provide a brief overview of those that are relevant to issues of both race and gender. Some would say women are women, thus experience similar struggles because of and related to gender. Although, in part, there is truth in this statement, African-American women experience additional struggles related to race. For instance, an African-American woman might say directly or indirectly, "If you do not see my color, then you don't see me and the positive aspects of my race." Failure to recognize both gender and race as significant factors in the identity of African-American women can create psychological and emotional conflicts. One could describe the experience as that of being discounted. Many who struggle with the experience of being discounted seek therapeutic help.

The group therapy experience is an environment that nurtures and offers professional assistance for African-American women who experience psychological and emotional conflicts. Some African-American women are better able to address their racial and gender issues in therapeutic settings comprised only of African-American women. For those women, an opportunity to unite in the privacy of their own racial and gender group needs to be afforded. To facilitate understanding the influence of race and gender on identity development, the reader is invited to follow various group members. These members are a composite of women who have participated in *Images of Me* groups.

Throughout the book, these women take on different characteristics such as age, employment, and so on. A consistent theme is the influence of race (Black) and gender (female) on life experiences. Additionally, African-American female cotherapists for *Images of Me* groups share their personal and professional experiences with the group by writing in the first person.

Chapter 1 profiles the role of race, gender, and class for African-American women in a racist society. The concepts of feminism, race, and class are explored in Chapter 2. Chapter 3 examines the role and efficacy of group work with African-American women.

Part II introduces the process of group work with African-American women. Beginning with Chapter 4, the reader joins the group and experiences being a part of the group as well as a part of the change process. By doing so, the reader learns appropriate methods of group facilitation with African-American women from an Afrocentric worldview. Chapters 5 through 7 present an organized and concrete approach to working with African-American women using the group process—Chapter 5 describes the initial stage of group formation, Chapter 6 addresses the working stage, and Chapter 7 discusses the termination stage. The reader is invited into sessions as a means to facilitate learning, understanding, and employment of methodologies. Chapter 8 offers a summary of the major constructs of group work from an Afrocentric worldview.

The reader is challenged, from an Afrocentric perspective, to help clients define race and gender as bicultural assets. Furthermore, the book should help professionals empower African-American women by encouraging them to confront the realities of their experiences in a new context. This can be done by asking group members, when contemplating the meaning of specific personal scenarios, to consider evaluating these situations in light of two specific questions: "Am I crazy or is this what's happening?" and "Is this for real?" Drs. Pack-Brown and Whittington-Clark observed that these two questions, or their facsimiles, were commonly raised in *Images of Me* groups and that they served a specific purpose—see Chapter 4 for a more complete analysis of these questions.

Part III introduces the reader to therapeutic support for group facilitators. Chapter 9 discusses facilitators' support for "self" as they lead the group. Examples of support that facilitate both personal and professional growth include: (1) co-facilitator planning and processing after and/or before each group meeting, (2) personal journaling, and (3) embracing the principles of Kwanzaa.

Acknowledgments

The authors of this book are indebted to a number of individuals for their contributions to and assistance with the development of this book. First are the typists, Mrs. Judy Maxey and Mrs. Sherry Haskins. Without their patience, advice, technical skills, and keen eyes, this book would not have been possible.

We are also indebted to Dr. Rose Johnson-Kurek for her thorough and comprehensive review of the book. Her support and feedback is greatly appreciated. Thank you to Ms. Laura Hulse for her keen eye and feedback.

Special thanks also go to the numerous members of the *Images of Me* groups. We are extremely grateful for your insights, bonding, and fortitude as you worked to enhance your psychological, emotional, and spiritual growth as the beautiful, visible, and viable African-American females that you, your ancestors, and your daughters are.

We give praises to the Lord God for Her/His love, strength, wisdom, and guidance during the development of this book. We thank God for making and molding African-American females and for validating and protecting the sisterhood. We are also thankful to God who has anchored our knowledge with the wisdom of our ancestors, parents, and the everlasting spirit.

We give praises to our families who endured some neglect while the book was in preparation. Thank you for your love, support, and understanding. We hold in high esteem the foundation of the African-American community, the African-American females of yesterday, today, and tomorrow.

Grateful acknowledgment and love from Sherlon Pack-Brown to my daughter, Allison Sherlon, a beautifully blossoming African-American woman and sister, for carrying on the legacy. For the three precious men in my life, my husband Al, and sons, Scott and Tony, I love you and thank you for allowing me to "be."

A very special thank you from Linda-Janiaba Enid Whittington-Clark to my husband, Larry C. Whittington-Clark, for endless support, and to our son, Marcus C. Whittington-Clark, who graciously allowed me to make up my periods of absence to contribute to this book by enhancing the "quality" of our time together.

Deepest appreciation, love, and respect, from W. M. Parker, to his daughter, Farha, for her kindness, sensitivity, and maturity in her development toward womanhood.

Our appreciation also to the following reviewers for their comments on our manuscript: Pamela Shipp, Denver University, and Robin Young Porter, Young-Rivers Associates.

1

A Profile of African-American Women

Many women say that race and gender are two separate issues. That's not my experience. I know that who I am includes dimensions of myself, such as my age, culture, religion, educational background, socioeconomic status, and lifestyle orientation. Yet, over and over again my race and gender contribute to my everyday life experiences and both are inseparable for me. From the time I was born, my Blackness and my femaleness have influenced my life. Even today, as an adult, I know that race and gender are influencing my life. I can cope better with my experiences in life and the thoughts and feelings that arise in me when I understand that race and gender are important to who I am. Yet, at times I'm confused as to which is more powerfully influencing my life—my race, my gender?

A case in point—I recently applied for a job but did not get it. The interviewer apologetically informed me that I did not get the job but said my qualifications were exemplary. I was praised for the quality of my credentials and work history, yet, was told they had chosen someone else. I found out that they hired a White male who was far less qualified than I. I immediately began to question myself. Since I'm so qualified, did my race or my gender influence their decision? Maybe they didn't hire me because I'm Black. Though they advertised as an equal opportunity employment company, they may have preferred a man over a woman. Perhaps it's a combination of both. It's during these times that I find myself asking (me or others) one of two questions: "Am I crazy or is this what's going on?" or "Is this for real?"

These words reflect a theme communicated by numerous twentieth century African-American women. The words reflect the message of thousands of African-American women who have, for centuries, lived in the United States. They also reflect generation after generation of African-American women's voices transmitted directly or indirectly throughout the years. Soujourner Truth voiced similar words as she spoke during a women's rights convention in Akron, Ohio, in 1851. As a woman and a freed slave, Ms. Truth stood before an audience whose primary focus was women's rights and addressed her gender and her race. Among other powerful words, she shared, "Dat man ober dar say dat women needs to be helped into carriages, and lifted ober ditches, and to have de best place everywhere. Nobody eber helped me into carriages or ober mud puddles, or give me any best places!" And she asked, "Ain't I a woman?"

In this chapter, we introduce the relationship of identity to race and gender by discussing the role of race and gender for African-American women in a racist and sexist society. To accomplish this task, we discuss women in the American society and the role of race in America; present a portrait of the African-American female; and discuss the influence of racial and womanist identity development on the perceptions of life experiences and struggles of African-American women.

In 1994, Mary, a member of an *Images of Me* support therapy group for African-American females, shared with the group: "I feel like I'm not recognized for who I am. When I'm at work, I hear and see people talking about women's rights, but I feel isolated. I know that part of my feeling of isolation is because I'm the only African-American in the office." Sometimes African-American women are blatantly aware of the implications of words that include or exclude their gender and race. Other times, they are oblivious to the implications of the words but experience the impact of the words in their lives. The threads of what some refer to as "the double whammy" of both gender and racial discrimination continue to be woven throughout the lives of African-American females. These threads are often oppressive and influence how she sees herself, how she imagines herself, and her relationships with others (Robinson & Howard-Hamilton, 1994). Some African-

American women see themselves as powerful; others see themselves meeting the needs and desires of important people (children, parents, and so on) in their lives. Some desire only to associate with African-Americans. Still others value the multiculturalism and diversity among women.

The realities and influence of racism and sexism on the growth and development of African-American women suggest that mental health professionals counsel to empower and free these women from any psychological, emotional, or spiritual chains (Jackson & Sears, 1992; Robinson & Howard-Hamilton, 1994). The Afrocentric worldview is espoused as a foundation for an effective counseling approach, which is consistent with the life experiences and cultural values of African-Americans (Jones, 1991; Parham, 1993). *Reality*, as seen through the Afrocentric worldview, is both spiritual and material; places value on interpersonal relationships; explains self-knowledge as the basis of all knowledge; and asserts that knowledge is gained through symbolic imagery and rhythm (Meyers, 1991; Parham, 1993). Nobles (1990a) proposes that Afrocentricity and an Afrocentric helping approach are tools to assist in the identification and employment of interventions that are consistent with the cultural images and interests of African people. These tools promote self-affirmation and generate a reawakening and a revival of personal beliefs and behaviors emanating from a shared African heritage, experience, and history, all of which constitute the core of analyses (Nobles, 1990a). Asanté (1992) suggests that Afrocentricity is a philosophy and perspective representing a strong connection to one's spirituality and kinship culminates in a shared belief that "I am because we are, we are therefore I am." Karenga (1995) offers seven principles of Nguzo Saba as indicative of the African value system which promotes direction and meaning in life.

The Nguzo Saba: An Overview

Asanté (1980) refers to Dr. Maulana Karenga as a leading theoretician of the twentieth century known for reconstructing African-American life and history. In the 1960s, Dr. Karenga proposed a set of principles (*Nguzo Saba*) as guides for African-Americans to live by. The principles are Umoja, Kujichagulia, Ujima, Ujaama, Nia, Kuumba, and Imani. Each principle has a specific guide for living as follows:

1. *Umoja* (unity) encourages striving for unity in family, community, nation, and race.
2. *Kujichagulia* (self-determination) encourages self-identity as a people and an individual.
3. *Ujima* (collective work and responsibility) encourages collectively building and maintaining the African-American community and making the burdens of African-American males and females those of the African-American people and community.
4. *Ujaama* (cooperative economics) encourages building and maintaining African-American businesses and profiting from those businesses.
5. *Nia* (purpose) encourages collective work for the building and developing of the community.
6. *Kuumba* (creativity) encourages doing whatever possible to create beauty in the community.
7. *Imani* (faith) encourages belief in African-American people, parents, teachers, leaders, righteousness, and the victory of the African-American struggle.

Dr. Karenga's ideology was systematic, based on these principles of nationhood, and believed to be routed in African history and tradition.

The Nguzo Saba also serves as the founding principles of Kwanzaa (an African-American ritual celebration of identity, purpose, and direction). The term *Kwanzaa* is Swahili for "first fruit" and proposes a cultural, religious, and political holiday. Kwanzaa is cultural in that African-Americans unite to celebrate their heritage; it is religious in that African-Americans collectively offer thanks for their blessings. Kwanzaa is political in that through a formal celebration African-Americans are reminded of their past and present political struggles.

The symbolism, strength, creativity, and faith inherent to the principles of Nguzo Saba and Kwanzaa provide a physical, psychological, emotional, and spiritual connection for those who comprise the African-American family. *Images of Me*, the group, draws from this symbolism, creativity, faith, and strength by promoting a recognition and appreciation for the collective and individual cultural, religious, and political realities of African-American female group members.

Table 1.1 presents selected thematic gender and racial worldview factors for African-American and European-American females. These worldview factors are to be considered dur-

TABLE 1.1 Selected Gender and Racial Worldview Factors

Worldview Factors	African-American Females	European-American Females	European-American Males
Axiology (What is valued)	Cooperation Emotional vitality Community Self-in-relation Direct/Open Nonverbal and verbal expression	Cooperation Open emotions Community Self-in-relation Direct/Controlled Verbal and nonverbal expression	Competition Controlled emotions Individualism Self as individual Direct/Open Verbal expression
Ethos (Guiding beliefs)	Interdependence Collective behavior Harmony	Interdependence Collective behavior Harmony	Independence Separateness Mastery/Control
Epistemology (How one knows)	Feelings Experience (African-Americans and women)	Feelings Experience (other women)	Thoughts Count/Measure
Logic (Reasoning process)	Diunital (both/and) Employment (survival/ fulfillment) Relational Connectedness	Dichotomous (if/then, either/or) Employment (fulfillment/ survival) Relational connectedness	Dichotomous (if/then, either/or) Employment (survival/fulfillment) Self as individual
Concept of time	Event-focused Present/Future–focused Cyclical	Precise Future/Present–focused Cyclical	Precise Future-focused Measurable
Concept of self	Extended self (I am because we are. Racial and gender factors are significant.)	Extended self (I think, therefore I am. I am because we are. Female factors are significant.)	Individual (I think, therefore I am.)
Critical needs in relationships	"We" care (relate) "We" understand (connect) "We" appreciate each other	"We" care (relate) "We" understand (connect) "We" appreciate each other	"I" can do/am trusted "I" am accepted "I" am appreciated

ing general discussions of race and gender and, in particular, from this point on throughout *Images of Me*—this book. Information for the content of Table 1.1 was gathered from numerous works—Brown, Sanders, and Shaw (1995); Jackson and Sears (1992); Lewis, Hayes, and Bradley (1992); Ossana, Helms, and Leonard (1992); Robinson and Howard-Hamilton (1994); Surrey (1984/1991); and Tucker (1994). Please keep in mind that this table is not meant to be comprehensive. We suggest that more time and energy is invested in looking at the female factor in the movement to provide culturally sensitive and competent helping services to multicultural and diverse populations.

Women in American Society

That women tend to experience themselves primarily in connection with others is fundamental to women's personal experience of self as a living being. Surrey (1984/1991) refers to women's relational nature as a self-in-relation, suggesting that for a woman the self exists in a relational context that is necessary to define her identity. A product of this relational connectedness is a sense of empowerment which provides energy for women to take action in the world. Women's support for each other often clarifies their understanding of what gender is in their lives. Women see themselves both in each others' experiences and when they hear and see experiences influencing other women's lives (Hall, 1992). To illustrate the power of the relational connectedness among African-American women as they encounter other African-American women, define personal experiences as members of the African-American community and the female gender, and sculpture psychological images of African-American women, Vy, a member of *Images of Me*, shares this recent experience:

Vy: I went to a faculty meeting last night and I saw this Black administrator share her expectations of the team for the rest of the year. I felt so proud and empowered. All I could think was "Go on, Sista!" Let them listen to us for a while. It renewed my determination to stay focused on my goals, no matter what the obstacles might be in the future. I know there will be barriers but I will remember my sista. She has passed on an image that I will carry with me. No one can take that image from me.

Because of these gender factors, gender is one of the most important elements shaping a woman's existence from birth throughout her life (Doherty & Cook, 1993). Gender role socialization begins in infancy and females are assumed to have gender-specific roles, philosophies, and approaches to life. Because of the patriarchal nature of American society, the impact of gender-specific expectations is felt across the spectrum of women's lives. Women, for example, have less political and economic power than men. Women are expected to be caretakers and keepers of the home and family. A thread woven throughout the fabric of the female experience is a personalized approach to life in which women care, feel, and value relationships (Cook, 1993; Corey & Corey, 1993; Hayes, 1992; Lewis, Hayes, & Bradley, 1992).

It is not uncommon for participants of the *Images of Me* group to uniquely, yet collectively, reveal this clearly visible thread woven throughout the female experience. Examples include:

Latifa: It is so important for me to know what my husband is feeling. I love him and I would never hurt him. I'm his "soul mate" and that's what I want to be! I remember when we were dating, he told me that I was a part of him (I was one of his ribs), you know, like Eve was taken from Adam's rib. I value that type of relationship. Hell, I like the idea of being a part of him. I want to take care of him. If I take care of him, I am taking care of myself. We are "one" in God.

Marie: My mother and I are very close. I am the strong and confident Black woman that I am today because of her. She put up with a whole lot while I was growing up. Now, I know what it must have been like to raise me. I wasn't always the easiest person to live with, let alone raise. In fact, I was pretty independent and determined to do what I wanted and how I wanted to do it. Don't misunderstand, Mama could bring me back to earth when I was too far gone. Though she allowed me to try new things, she also taught me to respect my elders. In no uncertain terms she'd let me know who was in charge. Even today she reminds me when I'm forgetting who the mother is. She's the mother and I'm her daughter. I don't always like to be reminded of that and, at the same time, I love her for it.

Lillie Mae: My parents taught me the importance of family and that includes my extended family. For example, I have several nephews and nieces that are like my own children. I'm very involved in their lives. Their parents and I relate well and share a desire to raise healthy Black men and women who also value family. I help with their financial demands such as buying clothes for the beginning of school. They spend a lot of time with me during vacations. Several, who live near me, view my home as their second home and see me as their second mother. My nieces and nephews mean so much to me that I use them to gauge the woman that I portray.

I constantly ask myself questions such as, "Am I the kind of woman I would like Tony, my nephew, who's better known as Tee, to date?" When I think of Allison, one of my nieces, I ask myself if the image of Black womanhood I portray reflects the kind of woman I want her to be. Scott is very much like me in personality and he is a significant part of my world. He needs a little more attention and touches my heart as he struggles with life. For example, the relationship he has with his father (my brother) and mother sometimes is rocky and he'll come to me sharing his confusion. I wonder what I, as a strong Black woman who values family and African heritage, ought to do to help him recognize and share his love with my brother and sister-in-law during his times of confusion and struggle with them. I want to help him find the same peace that I have found in the Lord and to embrace God and seek His wisdom and strength during times of struggle in life.

As young girls mature into womanhood, they are defined by the contexts and expectations that accompany rules for females. Usually this means developing an appreciation for others, a characteristic that is often guided, in behavior and thought, by a sense of community. An outcome of this characteristic is the generation of messages about life choices that are shaped and reinforced in areas such as the home, community, and workforce. Women, for example, have historically pursued careers involving the well-being of others, such as teaching, nursing, and social work. Women who have participated in *Images of Me* groups reflect this sense of community and caring for others: many were either "practioners in training" in the fields of education, nursing, and social work. With the Civil Rights Movement and the Women's Movement, African-American women began to expand their employment options and to assume nontraditional positions as physicians, professors, and psychologists. *Images of Me* women reflect this change.

One outcome of expanded career options has been increased exposure to the traditional White middle-class male value system. Thus, as women's career options have expanded, so have their physical, psychological, and emotional tensions. These tensions emanate from the pull of two worlds. While the world of the female gender values a relational approach to life, the workplace world of the traditional White male prizes individualism and competition. Hence, women often experience stress and strain managing relationships in an environment that tends to esteem individualism and competition. Women, for example, often feel alone as they aspire to equal opportunity and higher positions in the workforce and confused in their struggle to obtain assistance and identify coping strategies for dealing with discrimination.

To resolve this pull in values orientation, some women withdraw from the competitiveness of the work environment to seek greater involvement with home, family, and so on. All members of *Images of Me* have been or are currently employed. Though employment (professional or otherwise) is one criteria for group membership, an historic reality for African-American women is the need to work outside the home in order to survive. The need to work emerges from racial and gender realities inherent to the world of work in the United States. For example, racism and underrepresentation of African-Americans in specific areas of the workforce as well as sexism and the glass ceiling for women are obstacles to employment and reaching higher positions.

While workforce demands escalate stress and influence women's psychological integrity, other life stressors exist as well. A common problem reported by women clients relates to male–female differences, in particular difference in the communication of thoughts and feelings. Women often report that men do not freely share their personal feelings or that men fail to directly respond to women's feelings. That is, if a woman wants her significant other to share what he is feeling about a situation, he refuses to share feelings and instead shares thoughts, if he shares at all. Latifa angrily shares her sadness about male–female communications with members of an *Images of Me* group.

Latifa: I've been with my husband for seven years. He makes
   me so angry! He acts as if I have to tell him how to let me
   know that he cares for me. I figure by now he should know
   what I want and what I need. I shouldn't have to tell him. I
   shouldn't have to say things like, "Sam, when we argue, say
   to me, I feel scared," instead of your (Sam) saying to me, "I
   think you're making a big deal out of nothing" which is what
   I hear all the time. All I want is for him to share his feelings,
   no big deal!

Sue: I know what you mean. Men do have problems sharing
   their feelings. My husband never shares his [feelings]. When
   I cry or show that I'm angry, he tries to manipulate me. He'll
   say something like, "Why are you acting like that?" which
   seems as if he is trying to ignore what is going on right
   under his nose. It's like if he changes the focus, I'll be okay
   in his mind. He's looking for information about what I am
   doing and I just want him to see my feelings. All he has to do
   is say something like, "Baby, you seem upset. I love you." It's
   that simple!

Through the years, women's problems intensified and they
began to unite and organize movements to address their struggles. At the turn of the century, a movement, commonly
referred to as *Women's Suffrage* and generally fixed on White
women's voting rights and liberation, emerged to address the
struggles of sexism, particularly among the ranks of promi-
nent White women. Although the Suffrage Movement was necessary, equally necessary for women of color, particularly
African-American women, was the struggle against racism, a
holdover from the days of slavery. Both racism and sexism
were real and powerful experiences for women; however, the
similarities between racism and sexism (e.g., discrimination
and oppression) were not sufficient to unite women. In fact, the
issues of racism and sexism separated women.

To illustrate, Susan B. Anthony, a White woman and re-
nowned leader of the Women's Suffrage movement which
began in 1869, fired her stenographer for refusing to take dic-
tation from Ms. Anthony's Black friend, Ida B. Wells; but Ms.
Anthony refused to make her personal fight against racism a
public issue of the Women's Suffrage movement. Ms. Anthony
pushed aside the issue of racism for the sake of recruiting
Southern White women into the women's suffrage movement.
She did so to restrain the anti-Black hostility of her Southern

members who might withdraw from the organization if Black women were admitted. Thus, the separation of race and gender was born and thrives today with supporters of the women's liberation movement (Davis, 1981).

Race and the American Society

Daily we read about race and its role in American society. However, race is often confused with other issues such as ethnicity. Although race is a controversial construct and many in society question the meaning and/or existence of race, race tends to be a real-life experience for many African-Americans. Thus, to enhance communication we define *race* as a group of people who share a combination of genetically oriented physical traits, such as hair texture, skin pigmentation, and nose construction, that distinguish them from other groups of people. *Ethnicity* is a group classification whereby members are believed, by self and others, to share a common origin and unique social and cultural heritage such as language, religious customs, and traditions. Of significance is that these beliefs are passed from one generation to another generation.

It is important to be consistent in the definition of race as we discuss the racial dynamics in the American society. We acknowledge that race has two powerful and integral aspects, the basis of which are genetic and social. Race is biologically defined by certain attributes which human beings possess. These attributes consist of the invisible biological properties (genes) and the visible manifestation of these genes (physical appearance and characteristics). These physical characteristics are often assumed to be intrinsically related to nonphysical human attributes or abilities and so become social definitions of race. Racism and prejudice are two longstanding effects of the social definition of race and both influence behavior (Jones, 1991). What people believe and feel, what attitudes they hold about racial differences, and how people display their racist and/or prejudiced behaviors can contaminate a person's worldview and a person's interactions with racially diverse populations.

Latifa, a beautiful, young, dark-skinned (about the color of a chocolate bar) member of an *Images of Me* group, shares her experience of race in America as she and her husband moved to an apartment complex. Sue, a beautiful, light-skinned (about the color of light brown sand on the beach) group member, responds to Latifa's experience and shares her experience and perception of race in America. Note that skin complexion is a significant factor in this discussion because it has racial implications for African-Americans as well as for those who are not African-Americans.

Latifa: Sometimes I forget or maybe I just don't focus on who I am as a racial person. Then I'll get a reminder, like when I started my job with the bank soon after Mama died. Sam and I decided to move and a White female bank representative from the Human Resource Department helped us find a place to live. She was very nice and seemed excited to help. I asked her about an apartment complex that I had seen and was interested in. She was thrilled that I was interested in that particular complex and said she lived there. As she talked about the benefits of living there, she said with such excitement for herself and for me, "They have a tanning booth too!" Well, God gave me a natural tan, what did I need with a tanning booth? I believe she was trying to be helpful, but it was just another reminder of racial differences for me in that she was not sensitive to the possibility that something as simple as a tanning booth might not be of interest to me since I was born with a tan.

Sue: I think the lady was trying to be nice. A tanning booth sounds great to me.

Latifa: I'm always concerned about how my race influences my life. I know race is always there. I'm not paranoid but I'm cautious.

Sue: What's all the to-do with race? I have never had any problems with it. I get along with everyone. Race isn't an issue for me.

As Sue shares her thoughts, the group focuses on her because many do not believe that race is not an issue for her. Finally, Sue reveals an ongoing encounter that clearly exhibits racial implications.

Sue: Well, it's not unusual for my patients to call me nigger, one did so just last night.

Sue defuses the emotion associated with being called a nigger by acknowledging the mental state of her patients and her position of power.

Sue: They're sick and I know they have to come this way again. Then they'll know who's a nigger.

European-Americans often have difficulty perceiving themselves as members of a racial group: "We are all human beings so I don't worry about race." Rather than express race as a factor of life, many European-Americans simply refer to themselves and others as American or as a person—"I am an American." In part, European-Americans experience difficulty in self-perception and expression around race because of a lack of racial awareness. "I don't see color or other physical attributes, I see the person." Thus, many are insensitive to cultural and racial factors that are clearly a part of the lives of those who are not European-American. This insensitivity inhibits numerous European-Americans' ability to recognize and understand the experiences and worldviews of people of different races (e.g., African-Americans) who embrace their racial identity. Thus, interacting with people who embrace and share their racial realities as viable components of their life experiences often challenges members of the White race because of their monocultural worldveiw (Parham, 1993; Sue & Sue, 1990).

In addition, European-Americans experience a set of privileges extended to them as members of the majority race and the dominant culture (Ivey, Ivey, & Simek-Morgan, 1993; McIntosh, 1995). McIntosh (1995) refers to this privilege as "White privilege." She reveals that White privilege is profound and extensively reflected in the psychological and emotional life experiences and images of European-Americans. For example, a White American can say, "When I am told about our national heritage or about civilization, I am shown that people of my color made it what it is." An effect of White privilege which cannot be ignored is that European-Americans, as light-skinned Americans and members of the majority culture, tend to discriminate against those with darker skin (Ivey et al., 1993), such as African-Americans.

W.E.B. DuBois declared at the dawn of the twentieth century that the problem with the American society would be the color line and that color would influence how the White Western world would relate to other people of color (Parham, 1993). Historically, African-Americans have experienced racism and oppression in America. As a result, many generate numerous questions stemming from this color line and the White Western world. Familiar questions associated with racism and oppression generated among members of *Images of Me* include:

> "Why do I have to be judged by the color of my skin instead of who I am as a person?"

> "I'm sick and tired of people acting like they don't see me when I'm in meetings, why do they act like I'm not there?"

> "What makes a person say, 'When I look at you I don't see your color' and say it in the context of appreciating me as a person? It's as if my color is not important to who I am when it is very much a part of who I am and often what I experience. It's like, if we just don't see color then things will be all right. Is color the problem? I don't think so!"

To cope with realities of a racially guided environment, African-Americans have developed cognitive and affective mechanisms that assist in their individual and collective survival and adjustment. For centuries African-Americans have been challenged to survive and adjust to life's truths associated with basic needs such as proper nourishment, health care, safety, and love. A common cognitive survival technique evidenced in *Images of Me* groups, and one not unfamiliar to the African-American community, is realizing the racial realities associated with life's challenges and simultaneously affirming self as visible and viable. This realization and affirmation is intrinsic to words such as, "I know I did not get the job because I'm Black. I'm also led by God, assertive, and resilient."

Although the ability to identify positive survival mechanisms emerged from the challenges of being racially different, African-Americans have had, even through the 1990s, the dubious distinction of struggling to attain adequate education, pay, representation in traditional and nontraditional careers, housing, and health care. A skill that African-Americans have learned is how to live biculturally; that is, how to live in two worlds. One world reflects the cultural integrity of an African heritage. The other world reflects the cultural integrity of a White European worldview. Parham (1993) captures the psychological essence of this bicultural lifestyle in this statement: "I've got one mind for White folks to see, another for what I know is me" (p. 7). Clearly this psychological mindset influences the images African-Americans have of self and of other African-Americans. But for African-American females, the images of self and others are compounded by variables such as gender and gender identity.

The *Images of Me* Portrait of the African-American Female

Even though gender is a commonality among all women, racial and ethnic identity are not. Gender is shared among women. Yet, from birth a woman is also born a racial and ethnic being. Although women are frequenty portrayed as if one voice speaks for all, helping professionals must be careful to recognize the exquisite contextuality of human life and appreciate that women speak in different voices and consequently reflect diverse portraits. The female experience is a kaleidoscope of realities, life experiences, socioeconomic status, and racial and ethnic backgrounds (Arredondo, Psalti, & Cella, 1993; Hall, 1992), all of which influence worldview. The portrait of an African-American female reflects both racism and sexism (Arredondo et al., 1993; Brown, 1993; Evans & Herr, 1991; Jackson & Sears, 1992).

While African-American females create unique meanings for their individual worlds, these meanings share a universal quality with other African-American women. Dimensions such as socioeconomics, educational attainment, and occupational distribution are a few of the areas of concern and challenge reflected in the African-American female portrait. Each dimension prompts both individual and collective images and influences psychological, emotional, and spiritual maturation, development, and well-being.

Socioeconomics

One longstanding characteristic of the African-American female's portrait is discrimination. Discrimination has emotional and psychological consequences that can begin in early childhood and have longlasting pain through adulthood, and can affect childrearing strategies (Belle, 1982). For example, racial minority women are more likely than White women to share a number of socioeconomic risk factors for depression, including racial and ethnic discrimination, high stress jobs, unemployment, marital dissolution, and single parenthood (McGrath et al., 1990). A factor that influences the individual and collective images of African-American females and their portrait is a history of racism. As African-Americans they sustain social and economic challenges such as racism and financial depression. As females, they sustain social and economic challenges such as sexism and constraints in career planning.

African-American females have, for example, historically and in large numbers worked. They have worked primarily out of necessity and a similar trend is projected into the twenty-first century. Yet, despite a history of working, the opportunities for African-American females to enter and to advance in the labor force have been and continue to be sparse. African-American females have historically fallen behind White females in median income. In 1991, the median income of year-round, full-time African-American female workers was $18,720 compared to $20,790 for White female workers. In 1992, African-American women and White women were similar in their annual average labor force participation rates (58 percent); however, over the same period, the unemployment rate for African-American women (13 percent) was more than twice that of White women (6 percent) (U.S. Bureau of Census, 1990, 1992; U.S. Bureau of Labor Statistics, 1991). Questions that impact self-image emerge.

Three participants of the *Images of Me* group reflect the questioning voices of African-American females as they share thoughts and feelings about women and working.

Marie: I've worked all my life and so have my mother, grand-mother, and others. What's all the hype about working women or dual-career relationships?

Latifa: The problems and concerns of dual-career families didn't become an issue until White women started working. That makes me mad.

Sue: I'm sick and tired of training Whites, particularly White women, to do a job and then they get the promotion.

Educational Attainment and Earnings

African-American women's vocational roles began to expand after World War II. In the past five decades and particularly the 1960s and 1970s, the Civil Rights Movement and the Women's Movement have facilitated an increase in vocational opportunities. Many African-American women, against the odds and with strong family support, have earned advanced degrees in areas such as mathematics, research, higher education, and so on (Tucker, 1994). Vocational accomplishments of African-American women, although significant relative to their emergence from field laborer, sex object, and breeder during slavery, still remain questionable. Callie, a member of *Images of Me,* is a university faculty member and has fought many battles in pursuit of her status as a professor with a Ph.D. in psychology. Callie found that she was one of few African-Americans in a system that traditionally embraces women and racial minorities. Callie survived and weathered many challenges common to all graduate students as well as those related to her image of herself as an African-American female. For example, as an African-American female pursuing a terminal degree, she often found herself feeling isolated and alienated. The way in which Callie reached her goal is common to how many African-American women, be they members of *Images of Me* or not, voice attainment of their goals. She succeeded due to her interdependence with and support of her family and her strong faith in God.

Callie: Two major values in my life are a faith in God as my protector and the love and support of my family. It was through God that I knew I always had a friend when I felt lonely during the pursuit of my doctorate. I would listen to gospels to strengthen myself when I felt discouraged, invisible, and uncertain about what I should do to address my trials without "freaking out" on people. I spent a lot of money (and I had little to spend), calling home and talking with Mama and Daddy.

African-American females reflect a broad spectrum of educational attainment; however, they equivalently fall behind educated European-American females in earning power. Between 1980 and 1992, the earning power of high school African-American female graduates increased from about 50 percent to 68 percent. In 1992, the earning information for African-American and European-American females reflects an imbalance in earning power; Table 1.2 presents selected 1992 earning-power information. Note that 12 percent of all African-American females 25 years old or older earned a Bachelor's degree or higher. A common message heard among African-

TABLE 1.2 Earning Power of African-American and European-American Women

	High School Graduates / Full-Time Workers Median Income	College-Educated Average Earning
Black Females	16,440	$26,730
European-American Females	16,910	$27,440

Americans is, "...You have to work twice as good and twice as hard to get the same, more often less, than the White person gets." This message is frequently voiced by *Images of Me* group members.

Occupational Distribution

African-American females work in diverse settings and, in 1992, a number of common occupational distributions were evidenced. Table 1.3 presents four of the top occupations as revealed in research findings. However, the number of African-American women in nontraditional occupations, such as corporate America, is increasing. Tucker (1994) cites a *Wall Street Journal* report that, between 1982–1994, there was a 125 percent increase in African-American females in white-collar jobs and that African-American women outnumbered African-American men in most white-collar jobs, excluding clerical jobs.

TABLE 1.3 Top Occupations Among African-American Females

	Approximate Percentages
Technical, sales, and administrative support	40
Service industry	28
Operators, fabricators, and laborers	21
Managerial and professional specialities	20

Adolescence is the developmental link between childhood and adulthood. Factors that affect female adolescent development and influence womanhood include personal needs, values, and role models. Career and life planning is a complex task, particularly for young African-American females, in part because of their skewed employment perceptions, aspirations, expectations, and realities (Lee & Simmons, 1988; Simms & Malveaux, 1986). Although the number of African-American women in nontraditional and white-collar jobs is increasing, young African-American females often express high career and job aspirations but low expectations of reaching these goals. This discrepancy may be due to the realities of continued underrepresentation of African-American women in nontraditional and white-collar jobs.

African-American female adolescents (16–19 years) for the past five years have experienced a higher unemployment rate than their White female counterparts (Michelozzi, 1988; U.S. Bureau of Census, 1992). As these young women mature, their earning power remains stifled. Their reality is that, collectively, African-American women earn a smaller wage than European-American women. To match European-American women's straight-time wages or to exceed their overall wages, African-American women tend to work longer hours. Questions arise from these racial realities which influence young African-American women, their mothers, and other significant females in their lives: "How does a young African-American female become empowered to strive toward higher occupational aspirations in the face of oppressive conditions for African-American females?" As members of *Images of Me* struggle with their daughters' future, some ask, "How do I help my daughter cope effectively with the racism that will influence her career or job aspirations when often she sees me struggling to make it in the work world?" A major problem, unique to African-American women, is the dubious distinction of being a double minority in terms of both race and gender.

We have heard mothers in the *Images of Me* group, as well as numerous African-American mothers within our personal lives, share their thoughts and feelings about this double-minority distinction. A common message is:

My daughter is strong, independent, and somewhat naive about the realities of her African-American heritage. She presents herself well and seems to be on the road to professional advancement. But, at times, I question how helpful I am, have been, and/or can be to her when I'm angry about my own workplace struggles. How do I help her recognize racism and sexism without taking things so personally? How do I help her deal with realities like the "glass ceiling" for women and the bias and prejudice associated with being African-American? I don't want to project my anger on to her and indirectly teach her unhealthy ways to think, feel, and perceive. I want her to be emotionally, psychologically, and spiritually secure as she survives racism, sexism, or any other "ism" she may face.

In addition to the double-minority distinction, African-American females experience unique problems and needs associated with socioeconomics and employment status.

The Influence of Gender and Race on Identity

Identity is the image one has of self (Who am I?) and is influenced by both one's perception of self and one's perceptions of others (Harris, 1992). In this chapter, racial and gender identity are briefly presented as significant factors to visualize in profiling African-American women. We do not present an in-depth discussion of racial and gender identity development; Chapter 2 does this in more detail. We do, however, offer specific information about how race and gender influence identity development to assist in creating an accurate image of African-American females.

Gender identity is the image a woman has of herself as a female in a broad societal and cultural context. In formulating this identity, she ponders and responds to many critical questions such as: "Who am I as a woman? How does a woman behave, think, and feel? What cultural and societal prescriptions are given members of the female gender?" Answers to these and other questions about gender identity may or may not correspond to the general society and specific cultural roles, expectations, and perceptions of a woman prescribed her because she was born a member of a particular gender (female). For example, in the African-American culture women have historically worked outside of the home and have done so to survive, not necessarily for self-fulfillment. Yet, as participants in today's generally European-American society where women are struggling with issues, such as whether women work or stay home, some African-American women find themselves pulled between what women can and cannot do relative to working and staying home: "Do all African-American women work outside of the home? Do I work or stay home?"

Females, in general, African-American females, in particular, exhibit different attitudes about the degree to which they identify with societal and cultural definitions of womanhood. Some African-American women believe that as a member of the female gender, they are naturally nurturing, sensitive, and are expected to stay at home and care for the family. Others expect that women work outside of the home and share behaviors, roles, and responsibilities of the family with their significant others for the survival and happiness of the family. A common attitude among African-American females is that, "I work at home and on a job. I expect my husband to share the work at home while he holds a job. I expect us to share family responsibilities and I don't have to compete with him about work at home or work on the job."

Racial identity is the sense of identity an African-American has with the African-American community and is based on the perception of a shared heritage with African-Americans. Identity and subsequent perceptions of a shared racial heritage influence thoughts, feelings, and attitudes about distinguishable racial groups (Helms, 1994; Mitchell & Dell, 1992). Upbringing and experiences, cultural beliefs, and values of African-American females are significant to their individual and collective gender and racial identities.

Providing an answer to the question "Who am I?" is a developmental process. Gender and racial identity development are stage-like processes that facilitate a woman's potential to move from one stage of identity to another, while she is defining who she is as a racial being and as a woman (Helms, 1990, 1994; Ossana et al., 1992). A healthy womanist identity is predicated on how she defines herself (Ossana et al., 1992) and influences her perception of herself, other women, and possibly her connectedness (willingness to embrace similarities and differences among the female gender) to other women. An African-American female's racial identity is influenced by her reference group orientation and the quality and quantity of knowledge she has about African-Americans. Her affiliative identity with this reference group depends on her knowledge and understanding of the sociopolitical issues and history of

African-Americans and the extent to which she believes this knowledge and these people are personally relevant to her life. The union of her reference group orientation and affiliative identity brings into line her racial self and at this point she knows and states that "I am an African-American." The strength of her own identity enables her to respect the diversity of others and aspire to eradicate oppression. Ultimately, her identity as a woman and an African-American woman empowers her to state: "As an African-American woman, I won't permit racial and sexual oppression."

Each woman experiences and approaches race (racial issues) and gender (gender issues) differently. A crucial point to remember is that each woman has an experiential perception and some of these perceptions may be similar but some may be different. For example, two members of an *Images of Me* group, share the following experiences and perceptions. Marie is an outspoken, articulate, and well-dressed woman who works in a predominantly White environment and is challenged by White women on her job. Tanisha comes from a family where her sisters complain about working with White women, but she does not share their thoughts and feelings. Tanisha sees people as people, regardless of their racial characteristics; thus, she professes to get along with everyone.

Marie: It's a lot of work interacting with White women on my job. While I like them and have no real problems with them, it takes a lot of energy to explain how both my race and my gender are issues in my life.

Tanisha: I don't understand what all the to-do is about working with Whites. I see us all as people and have found that if I treat everyone the same, I don't experience what many African-Americans experience. What work? I get along with everybody. Just see *me*, not my color or my gender!

Factors that contribute to the differences in perceptions and attitudes held by Marie and Tanisha are their racial and womanist identities.

Helms' Racial and Womanist Framework for Identity Development

Helms (1990) offers a four-stage process of racial and womanist identity development (Pre-Encounter, Encounter, Immersion/

Emersion, and Internalization), each expressing cognitive, affective, and connotative experiences as one's personal racial/ gender identities become more conscious and fulfilling. The stages between development are marked by strong feelings for or against one's personal identity and the identities of others. The following sections describe the four stages of racial/gender identity and their application to African-American women.

Pre-Encounter Stage

African-American women in the *Pre-Encounter* stage of racial identity development devalue their Black identity as they attempt to gain resources, such as power and self-worth, by accepting and conforming to White social, cultural, and/or institutional views of race. The prevailing European-American worldview (e.g., competition and individualism) is embraced and a positive self-concept as an African-American or positive view of the African-American community is depreciated. The value of interactions with African-Americans is diminished while interactions with European-Americans are enhanced.

In the Pre-Encounter stage of womanist identity development, African-American women devalue their womanist identity as they attempt to gain resources, such as power and self-worth, by accepting and conforming to social, cultural, and/or institutional views about gender (women). Women in this stage have constricted views of women's roles and they behave in ways that devalue women and value men. Interactions with women diminish while interactions with men are enhanced.

If we recall our last visit to *Images of Me*, Tanisha shared her confusions about African-Americans experiencing discomfort with European-Americans. She was unable to understand why African-Americans did not just focus on themselves as people and disregard the emphasis on race. Tanisha's approach to life and getting along in life was to disregard difference (race and gender) and focus on the similarities evident in being a human being: "I don't focus on my Blackness, I focus on me as a person." Her statement may indicate that she is operating from the Pre-Encounter stage of racial identity development. If this assessment of her racial identity is accurate, Tanisha's confusion about the difficulty of interacting with European-Americans is understandable as she identifies with the White culture and embraces similar values, beliefs and attitudes.

Encounter Stage

Individuals operating from the *Encounter* stage are increasingly exposed to racial and gender diversity and beginning to question, challenge, and reject Pre-Encounter thinking. This questioning process may occur because of (1) a negative or a positive experience with European-American institutions or (2) heightened exposure to and contact with information about women and women's diversity that extends awareness of possibilities for female behaviors and offers new perspectives for womanhood.

African-American women in the Encounter stage of racial identity development may have faced a negative or a positive experience within a European-American institution that forced (in some cases) and enlightened (in other cases) their need to face their racial difference. For example, during group Sue shares this encounter that shocked her and triggered her anger with European-Americans:

Sue: I was a teenager attending a predominantly White high
    school. It was my freshman year and we were in gym. I over-
    heard one of my best friends talking with some other girls in
    the locker room. My friend and I had attended the same
    schools for eight years and I did not think our colors made a
    difference—we were tight, she was White. I heard the other
    girls tell her that unless she stopped hanging around with
    that nigger they would not let her be a part of what they
    were doing.

It was at this point that Sue became aware that her race made a difference in her life and in the life of her friend. Sue began to question her racial identity. As an African-American she questioned whether conformity to the dominant society as the primary means to succeed was in her best interest and began to perceive this type of thinking as perpetuating racism.

African-American women in the Encounter stage of womanist identity begin to question their identity as women as they find themselves increasingly exposed to and in contact with information about women and women's diversity. This information extends personal awareness of possibilities for female behaviors and offers new perspectives for womanhood. An African-American woman who is maturing in her womanist identity may ask, "Why do women have to stay home and take care of the children while men work?" In addition, she remembers that women staying home and taking care of the family while men work has not been her experience or her history as an African-American female. She questions whether conformity to the dominant society as the primary means to success is in her best interest and tends to view this type of thinking as perpetuating racism and sexism and poisoning her self-image as an African-American and a female. Her questioning often launches her into the immersion/emersion stage of identity development.

Immersion/Emersion Stage

African-American women in the *Immersion / Emersion* stage of racial identity development often become avid readers of and/ or advocates for African-American history and the elimination of racism in the United States. These women actively challenge racist values, beliefs, and behaviors. Hostility and anxiety are prevalent emotional realities around racial issues and situations. They appear driven to affiliate with African-Americans and become suspicious and confrontational with European-Americans.

In the *Immersion / Emersion* stage of womanist identity development, African-American women seem clearly aware of sexist attitudes, beliefs, and behaviors and intensely challenges such behaviors. Often these women feel hostile and experience anxiety when exposed to sexist approaches to life. It becomes important to seek women with similar perspectives about gender. They often are suspicious of and confrontational with men.

During an *Images of Me* group session, four women shared their thoughts and feelings about race and gender which may shed some light on their levels of identity development as African-Americans and females. One member, Shari, reflects a person in the Immersion/Emersion stage of racial identity development. Marie reflects a person who may be entering the Immersion/Emersion stage of womanist identity development.

Shari: Tanisha, you seem to forget who you are as an African-American! You keep to yourself at work. How in the hell can you tell if you're being treated differently if you keep your head in the sand and stay to yourself? You better get your head on straight, girl, and recognize who you are, BLACK and beautiful!

Cameal: I used to feel like you, Tanisha, but one day I realized that because of my Black skin people were treating me differently. Since that time, I decided I would have very little to do with White people; I feel affirmed with my sisters and brothers.

Marie: You know, I was talking to some women the other day about us, as women. In the course of the conversation, we got to talking about sexist attitudes around women and working. One woman had the nerve to say that if a woman was behaving as a woman should, she ought to stay at home and take care of the family while her man works to provide for the family's needs. I was pissed to say the least! How dare she imply that women who work are not real women! I got even more angry when I thought about the fact that Black women have historically had to work outside the home just to survive! It was all I could do to keep my cool! I can't stand women with such closed perceptions of the world and I stay as far away from them as possible! I get my power through associating with women who recognize the choices of and diversity among women. Don't let a man come at me with that kind of mess! I will put him in his place right on the scene!

Sue: Earlier in the group, I questioned what the "to-do" with race was all about and didn't see race as an issue for me. But when the group focused on me and helped me recognize my thoughts and feelings about my patients, I had to acknowledge that I have some issues around race. Actually, I've noticed that when I'm at work I have very little to do with the Whites in my area, particularly the White women. I found that when I socialize (or try to socialize) with them, they act like I'm not physically there. When I share that both race and gender issues are significant to our discussions, it's like White women don't understand and harp on gender—again I feel like I'm not visible. Sometimes it gets so bad that I've found myself asking myself, "Is this for real or am I just imagining that they act like I'm not here?" I recently met another African-American woman at work. She just started working there about three weeks ago. We're getting close. We talk about our experiences and she shares similar encounters that I have had. That helps me in that I know I don't have to take what's going on so personally. Gender is a key issue for the White women at work. Race and gender are both key issues for the two of us.

Internalization Stage

African-American women in the *Internalization* stage of racial and gender identity development exhibit a new and refined sense of self emanating from infusion and internalization of a newfound awareness of race and gender into social roles and personal identities. African-American women in the Internalization stage of racial identity development exhibit a redefined sense of Black consciousness and work hard to integrate and internalize new awarenesses that emerged during their Immersion/Emersion stage of development into their varied social roles and identity.

Although the redefinition process was useful and nurturing, this African-American must apply a new sense of Black identity beyond an immediate supportive Black referent group. Each woman must determine how her new consciousness affects the way she perceives and interacts with her new sense of being Black. She must do so to the degree that when in situations in which her Black perspective is not valued, she has the necessary sustenance to prevail. She may verbalize as a way to embrace her historical connection to religion and the role it played in survival: "As an African-American, I love the Lord and value Him as my savior. Even though God is not important to you and your life, I will continue to allow the Lord to guide my life. You do what works for you."

African-American women in the Internalization stage of womanist identity development reflect a new sense of consciousness about being a woman. Each woman aspires toward integration and internalization of their newfound sense of self that emerged from Immersion/Emersion experiences. This new image (psychological, emotional, spiritual, and physical) is significant to their definition of social roles and personal womanist identity. While growth during the Immersion/Emersion stage was useful, a new sense of being a woman/female transcends the support of their female referent group. Now the task is to determine how a newfound consciousness influences personal perceptions and interactions with being a woman/female to the point that she can prevail in the midst of real situations that do not value her as a women/female and as an African-American woman. You may hear a message such as "African-American females tend to work to survive, not for self-enhancement. That is my reality and I am proud of it. I appreciate that you as a White woman view women working to fulfill self."

Although race and gender are intrinsic realities woven throughout the life experiences of African-American females, a common struggle is understanding how race and gender merge to create the "double whammy" experience. Often this merging is so impervious that to attempt to blatantly separate what is actually occurring—racism alone, sexism alone, or racism and sexism—is clearly a dubious endeavor. Questions such as "Am I experiencing life this way because I am a woman?" or "Am I experiencing life this way because I am African-American?" often take a backseat to "Am I experiencing life this way because I am an African-American woman?" Of significance is that the "double whammy" of race and gender becomes more compounded when issues such as the following are evident:

- Racist oppression against people of both sexes
- Sexist oppression within the same race
- Sexist oppression in the workforce against women of various races

These issues are simply mentioned at this point and not discussed in detail as they have not been thematic among the numerous women who have participated in *Images of Me*. They are, however, valid issues that warrant consideration and research in another context.

Members of *Images of Me* represent a kaleidoscope of African-American women. Even though caution is advised in assuming that if you know one African-American woman, you know all African-American women, it is appropriate to acknowledge and to assume that because of race and gender African-American women share common realities (prejudice, racism, and sexism). Consequently, by-products of these realities and other "isms" related to being female and African-American (e.g., underemployment, underpayment on jobs) emerge and are often problematic to their personal, social, and/or psychological growth and development. Members of the group reflect various stages of racial identity development and gender identity development. As has been illustrated, some are unaware of their Black and/or womanist identity, others are in denial of their Black and/or womanist identity, and some are comfortable with who they are as African-Americans, as women, or as both African-Americans and women.

Summary

Historically, African-American females of all ages have experienced the influence of race and gender on the formation of personal images, images of other African-American females, and images of females in general. Racism, sexism, and their inherent oppressions have complicated perceptions of an accurate profile of African-American women. Generations of African-American women have questioned and continue to question their racial and womanist identity and images reflected because of their African and female characteristics. Two questions—"Am I crazy or is this what's going on?" and "Is this for real?"—have emerged in our many years of group work with African-American women. These questions exemplify the struggles inherent in developing an accurate profile for African-American women. This questioning process challenges the psychological, emotional, spiritual, and physical realities associated with gender and race in a society that struggles with racism and sexism. The profile of African-American women is further distorted when issues of feminism, race, and class emerge. Of significance is the influence of these issues on the mental health of African-American females and their personal and collective images.

Chapter 2 explores the concepts of feminism, race, and class, and their consequential relationship to the African-American female community.

References

Arredondo, P., Psalti, A., & Cella, K. (1993, April). The woman factor in multicultural counseling. *Counseling and Human Development, 25*(8), 1–8.

Asanté, M. K. (1980). *Afrocentricity: The theory of social change.* Buffalo, NY: Amulefi Publishing Company.

Asanté, M. K. (1992). Afrocentric systematic. *Black Issues in Higher Education, 9,* 16–17, 21–22.

Belle, D. (Ed.). (1982). *Lives in stress: Women and depression.* Beverly Hills: Sage.

Brown, J. F. (1993). Helping Black women build high self-esteem. *American Counselor, 2,* 9–11.

Brown, S., Sanders, J., & Shaw, M. (1995). Kujichagulia—Uncovering the secrets of the heart: Group work with African-American women on predominantly White campuses. *Journal for Specialists in Group Work, 20*(3), 151–158.

Cook, E. P. (Ed.). (1993). *Women, relationships, and power: Implications for counseling.* Alexandria, VA: The American Counseling Association.

Corey, G., & Corey, M. S. (1993). Becoming the woman or man you want to be. In *I never knew I had a choice* (pp. 103–133). Pacific Grove, CA: Brooks/Cole Publishing Company.

Davis, A. Y. (1981). *Women, race and class.* New York: Random House.

Doherty, P. A., & Cook, E. P. (1993). No woman is an island: Women and relationships. In E. P. Cook (Ed.), *Women, relationships, and power: Implications for counseling* (pp. 15–47). Alexandria, VA: The American Counseling Association.

Evans, K. M., & Herr, E. L. (1991). The influence of racism and sexism in the career development of African-American women. *Journal of Multicultural Counseling and Development, 19*(3), 130–135.

Hall, C. M. (1992). *Women and empowerment: Strategies for increasing autonomy.* Washington, DC: Hemisphere Publishing.

Harris, D. J. (1992). A cultural model for assessing the growth and development of the African-American female. *Journal of Multicultural Counseling and Development, 20*(4), 158–167.

Hayes, B. A. (1992). The impact of gender role socialization. In Lewis, J. A., Hayes, B. A. & Bradley, L. (Eds.), *Counseling women over the life span,* (pp. 55–76). Denver: Love Publishing Company.

Helms, J. E. (Ed.). (1990). *Black and White racial identity attitudes: Theory, research, and practice.* Westport, CT: Greenwood Press.

Helms, J. (1994). Racial identity in the school environment. In P. Pederson & J. Carey (Eds.), *Multicultural counseling in schools: A practical handbook* (pp. 19–37). Boston: Allyn and Bacon.

Ivey, A. E., Ivey, M. B., & Simek-Morgan, L. (1993). *Counseling and psychotherapy: A multicultural perspective.* Boston: Allyn and Bacon.

Jackson, A., & Sears, S. (1992). Implications of an Africentric worldview in reducing stress for African-American women. *Journal of Counseling and Development, 71,* 184–190.

Jones, J. (1991). The concept of race in social psychology: From color to culture. In R. J. Jones (Ed.), *Black psychology* (pp. 441–467). Westport, CT: Greenwood Press.

Karenga, M. (1995, August). Speech—Association of Black Psychologists Conference, Los Angeles.

Lee, C., & Simmons, S. (1988). A comprehensive life-planning model for Black adolescents. *School Counselor, 36,* 5–10.

Lewis, J. A., Hayes, B. A., & Bradley, L. J. (1992). *Counseling women over the life span.* Denver: Love Publishing Company.

McGrath, E., Keita, G. P., Strickland, B. R., & Ruso, N. F. (Eds.). (1990). *Women and depression: Risk factors and treatment issues.* Washington, DC: American Psychological Association.

McIntosh, P. (1995). White privilege and male privilege: A personal account of coming to see correspondences through work in Women's Studies. (pp. 76–87). In M. Anderson & P. Hail Collins, *Race, class and gender*. Belmont, CA: Wadsworth Publishing Company.

Meyers, L. J. (1991). Expanding the psychology of knowledge optimally: The importance of worldview revisited. In R. L. Jones (Ed.), *Black psychology* (pp. 15–28). Berkeley, CA: Cobb & Henry Publishers.

Michelozzi, B. N. (1988). *Coming alive fron nine to five: The career search handbook*. Mountain View, CA: Mayfield Publishing Company.

Mitchell, S. L., & Dell, D. M. (1992). The relationship between Black student's racial identity attitudes and participation on campus. *College Student Journal, 25*(2), 192–197.

Nobles, W. W. (1990a). *Afrocentric psychology: Toward its reclamation, reascension, and revitalization*. Oakland, CA: A Black Family Institute Publication.

Nobles, W. W. (1990b). *African centered educational praxis*. The Center for Applied Cultural Studies and Educational Achievement, CSU system & CSDE. Oakland, CA: The Institute for the Advanced Study of Black Family Life and Culture.

Ossana, S. M., Helms, J. E., & Leonard, M. M. (1992). Research: Do "womanist" identity attitudes influence college women's self-esteem and perceptions of environmental bias? *Journal of Counseling and Development, 70*, 402–408.

Parham, T. A. (1993). *Psychological storms: The African-American struggle for identity*. Chicago: African-American Images.

Robinson, T., & Howard-Hamilton, M. (1994). An Afrocentric paradigm: Foundation for a healthy self-image and healthy interpersonal relationships. *Journal of Mental Health Counseling, 16*(3), 327–339.

Simms, M. C., & Malveaux, J. M. (1986). *Slipping through the cracks: The status of Black women*. New Brunswick, NJ: Transaction Books.

Sue, D. W., & Sue, D. (1990). *Counseling the culturally different: Theory and practice*. New York: John Wiley and Sons.

Surrey, J. (1984/1991). The "self-in-relation": A theory of women's development. In J. V. Jordan, A. G. Kaplan, J. B. Miller, I. P. Stiver, & J. L. Surrey (Eds.), *Women's growth in connection: Writings from the Stone Center* (Work in Progress, No. 13) (pp. 51–66). New York: Guilford Press.

Tucker, S. H. (1994). Black women in corporate America. The inside story. *Black Enterprise*, 60–66.

U. S. Bureau of Census. (1990). Current Population Reports, Series P-20, No. 448, *The Black population in the United States*. Washington, DC: U.S. Government Printing Office.

U. S. Bureau of Census. (1992). Current Population Reports, Series P-20, No. 471, *The Black population in the United States*. Washington, DC: U. S. Government Printing Office.

U. S. Bureau of Labor Statistics. (1991, November). Employment and earnings, monthly, Bulletin 2307. *Monthly Labor Review* (from unpublished data).

2

An Exploration
of Feminism, Race,
and Class

Race, class, and gender, the "simultaneity of oppression"
research (Brewer, 1993) leads very naturally into a discussion
on the impact of the feminist movement. The feminist movement was the tool utilized by middle-class European women to
elevate equality for European middle-class women. The
"simultaneity of oppression" theory, as put forth by Brewer, is
examined more carefully and is central to our understanding
of African American women's labor and class formation. The
simultaneous forces of race, class, and gender are important to
the discussion of Black feminist theory (Brewer, 1993).

Overview

Many Black feminists stand firm on the necessity to eliminate
oppression of African-American women by "advocated" feminism (hooks, 1984). Continuing from Chapter 1's conclusion
that African-American women experience race and gender as
inseparable, this chapter examines the usefulness of the feminist movement as it pertains to African-American women and
class.

Issues of feminism (the political movement of the late 1960s
and early 1970s demanding social equality for women and rec-

ognition of the impact of sexism on social status) (hooks, 1981), race (the subgroup of people possessing a definite combination of physical characteristics, and genetic origin, the combination of which, to varying degrees, distinguishes one subgroup from another), and class (an economic category pertaining to the Women's Movement and plight of African-American women) began to appear in the literature by the early 1970s. The overall challenge is to examine in a group context, how the journey to freedom by African-American women interfaced with the feminist movement, a movement often "thought [of as] only for White or European-American women" (hooks, 1981, p. 9).

In this chapter, male–female relationship development is reviewed through the exploration of feminist psychotherapy to determine relevant commonalities among African-American and European-American women. The purpose of examining feminist psychotherapy is to highlight the benefits of using such an approach with women of color. The issues of sisterhood of women are explored in general and the inherent mistrust of African-American women for White women is discussed for the purpose of examining African-American women's level of psychological distress.

Finally, a framework for therapy, which utilizes Afrocentric psychotherapy and relevant elements from feminist psychotherapy for African-American women, is described. Cautions for each approach will be delineated and suggestions given for avoiding ineffective or untimely approaches.

The Feminist Movement

African-American women have finally pushed their way to the foreground, having clamored for recognition as a valued entity for centuries. Race presented a particular problem as it pertained to equality. From its inception, the Women's Movement attempted to perpetuate the devalued status of the African slave woman.

As discussed in Chapter 1, the issue of sex and race was confronted as early as 1852 by Sojourner Truth, a freed slave woman who stood before the second annual convention of the Women's Rights Movement in Akron, Ohio, and testified about her personal life, affirming that she could function in numerous roles: parent, spouse, endurer of physical abuse, and victor over persecution. Many African-American women can identify with her testimony; the African-American woman is seen as emerging triumphant and victorious. As far back as 1981, hooks noted:

> When feminists acknowledge in one breath that Black women are victimized and in the same breath emphasize their strength, they imply that though Black women are oppressed, they manage to circumvent the damaging impact of oppression by being strong—and that is simply not the case. Usually when people talk about the "strength" of Black women, they are referring to the way in which they perceive Black women coping with oppression. They ignore the reality that to be strong in the face of oppression is not the same as overcoming oppression, that endurance is not to be confused with transformation (p. 6).

Race and the Feminist Movement

When examining race and the feminist movement through a historical context, the explicit denial of White women regarding race becomes apparent. "Black women were placed in a double bind: to support women's suffrage would imply that they were allying themselves with White women, activists who had publicly revealed their racism, but to support only male suffrage was to endorse a patriarchal social order that would grant them no political voice" (hooks, 1981, p. 3). It was important to divide the issues of freedom into segments. For White women, strictly defined roles and limited access to the White male power structure were the forces they collectively worked at breaking down. As mentioned in Chapter 1, mixing the issue of race seemed to make the task insurmountable. To take a historical example, Susan B. Anthony (a White woman) refused to advocate for Ida B. Wells's (a Black woman) presence in a women's group for fear that it would alienate other White women and arouse racial hatred.

Racial hatred, bigotry, and oppression still abound in today's culture. The experience of slavery and the resulting historical transcendence of slavery cannot be shared with or understood by European-American women. The experiences of oppression, rigid role expectations, and relegation to lower, less financially rewarding areas of employment are the areas African-American women hold in common as forces with which to reckon.

European-American women enjoy access to power through their attachments to European-American men. Frye (1983) delineates the impact that this has had on race, privilege, racism and the inability to understand the connection: "Race and racism also have a great deal to do with the attachment to White men. We need to look at these connections more closely" (p. 125). An enlightening point that Frye makes is: "A White person must never claim not to be a racist, but only to be anti-racist" (p. 126). In *Theorizing Black Feminism: The Visionary Pragmatism of Black Women*, edited by James and Busia (1993), Black feminist theorists discuss the impact of the Clarence Thomas's nomination to the Supreme Court despite Anita Hill's testimony about the abuse she experienced from him. Johnetta Cole (1986) points to the reality that patriarchal oppression:

> Is not limited to women of one race or of one particular ethnic group, women in one class, women of one age group or sexual preference, women who live in one part of the country, women of any one religion, or women with certain physical disabilities or abilities. Oppression of women knows no such limitations. We, therefore, cannot conclude that the oppression of all women is identical (p. 272).

Some African-American women feel that European-American women have the attitude that, through the Feminist Movement, equal rights is only theirs to claim, the same attitude as that reflected by early European-American women members of the Feminist Movement (Boyd, 1990). Conversely, a belief that permeated the Civil Rights Movement and brought forth by Dr. Martin Luther King, Jr., held that none of us is free until all are free. It is this belief that drives the movement/thought of inclusion. On the basis of inclusion, African-American women bring to the Feminist Movement the needed qualities of the African worldview that is inclusive of all people.

According to Phillips (1990), the characteristics of an African worldview versus a European worldview are interdependence versus competition, collective survival versus rigid individualism, emotional vitality versus reserved sullenness, harmonious blending versus win/lose, the role of our ancestors and the elderly versus throw away the aged and the oral tradition. African-American women and European-American women can make the world a more equitable place when we all come together. The concept of interconnectedness and interdependence is the substance that drives inclusion and builds a working relationship. We will examine the concept of interdependence as it relates to building relationships within the format of group work with African-American women. Healing experienced within the group context embodies the Afrocentric concept of collective interdependence and is the salient factor that translates into wholeness for African-American consciousness. Group leaders encourage group members to embrace the characteristics of Phillips's African worldview.

An Afrocentric Approach to Group Work

Examples of Phillips's codified cultural worldview—interdependence, collective survival, emotional vitality, harmonious blending, and respect for elders and the oral tradition—follow. For examples of rigid individualism, sullenness, win/lose, please refer to the Glossary.

Interdependence versus Competition

Group work with African-American women is the optimal approach for healing. Interdependence works in the group's favor, for each woman gives and receives from the group. The value of relying on one another builds confidence within each member. The experience of breaking free from isolation escorts the group participant into building community and returning to an interdependent relationship with her sisters. Janiaba experiences it as getting back to her roots.

Janiaba was a slightly overweight woman whose face, although rather plain, seemed somewhat younger than a person of 56, perhaps because of her close-cropped, dark brown hair speckled with gray. She frequently wore black, gray, navy blue, or brown business suits. Her outfits were well-tailored, and she was quick to kick off her shoes when she entered the group room and sat down. Janiaba stated that she never wore shoes at home.

She gave the impression of constantly being active, moving from place to place as she carried out her job responsibilities. Her mannerisms, though quick, consisted of small gestures, and her voice was memorable because of its peculiarly penetrating quality, particularly when she laughed, which was not often. As she related her history, Janiaba provided detailed descriptions of situations. At times she lost track of the topics she had just initiated, carried away with complaints about co-workers and supervisors. There were moments when she caught herself and remarked, "It's just good to be in a group of Black women. I can just let it rip. I don't have to hold it in."

Janiaba brought in scrapbooks to share the events in her life. She started participating in the *Images of Me* group due to the mounting pressure she was facing in single life and her retirement. Not wanting to be alone in retirement, after a failed marriage of 25 years, she wanted to know how other African-Americans dealt with the issues she faced. She had spent her childhood in a large house in a small midwest town. Her maternal grandparents were Native American, her paternal grandparents were African-American, her three brothers were laborers, and her parents were educators. Janiaba shared her experiences and Latifa reached out to connect with her because her own struggles were mounting. They both worked in the same setting.

Janiaba: I have worked in all-White settings all my life. I graduated from high school and went into the corporate world by way of a bank teller job. No one was there to talk with to get the secret keys to success. One by one I watched the promotions of the girls. I was passed over many times but didn't know any better, so I just waited. The isolation was intensified each time a White girl was promoted.

After a year, during my second evaluation, I asked about my chances for a promotion. My boss, who was a White female, looked at me as if I had a third eye. She said, in essence, I thought you were happy with your job. You do it so well and cheerfully, I didn't think you wanted to change.

At that point, I got so angry my head started to hurt. In my later years, I realized I had high blood pressure, which probably began with the job I had at the time. I seemed to get one or two promotions after that point but something was different. It just didn't seem complete.

Five years after I began the job, they hired a Black manager in another branch. I waited to see how she conducted herself. I wanted to see if she shunned Black people. I went to her in secret and developed a mentoring relationship, which proved to be the best move in my entire career.

Latifa, a younger group member, took a risk during that session that carried surprises for her. Latifa was a 21-year-old single mother of a five-year-old boy. Her parents allowed her to live with them since she was single and trying to finish college part-time. Latifa's parents noticed her mood swings and suggested counseling. Her father was skeptical about suggesting counseling but went along with it because his daughter seemed unusually depressed. Latifa shared some thoughts with her mother that sounded like suicidal thoughts: "I'm tired of trying so hard and getting nowhere." "What's the use of living like this?" Although her parents were supporting her while she was in school, Latifa really wanted to be on her own.

Face tense, Latifa sat silently as she listened to the group. Her overall appearance suggested a person closer to 16 years old than 21. She wore little make up and her hair was long and straight. Her manner of dress left you with the impression that she had good taste, but had lost interest in coordinating her outfits. She had become unusually upset when she brought home a rejection letter from a department chair regarding a promotion, and thereafter withdrew, paying less attention to family conversation, and responding slowly to questions or requests. The only family activity she participated in was Saturday morning house cleaning; she took extraordinary pride in the neatness of her living area.

Latifa spent all of her spare time studying; since her interactions with her son had decreased noticeably, her parents became more involved in the care of their grandson. Latifa wanted more out of life but did not have the "connections" to obtain it. She wanted to know more about the banking world because she had just started a part-time banking job three months earlier. The following dialogue with Janiaba, who knew more about banking, is a good example of interdependence and of the ease with which Latifa reached out to Janiaba.

Latifa: Janiaba, can I ask you a question?
Janiaba: Of course (*firmly spoken*).
Latifa: I have been dying to ask you this ever since you told us you are in banking.
Janiaba: Fire away!
Latifa: How can I learn more about the banking business?
Janiaba: I wish I had had someone to ask that question of when I began. I'm honored you are asking me. There are a lot of

secrets in this business. For the sake of time, I'll just say
that you have to keep your ears and eyes open at all times.
Let's get together after group tonight to talk about strategies.

Latifa: I'm only too glad to!

Collective Survival versus Rigid Individualism

The interdependence experienced by Janiaba was outside the
group setting while the experience for Latifa occurred right in
the session. Darlene was a 40-year-old mother of two children
and was then married to an engineer. The couple literally built
their family wealth through sound investments and conserva-
tive spending early in their marriage. They were able to send
their children to private schools. However, when their oldest
child became pregnant during her first year of college and
decided to take a break from school until her child was old
enough to go to day care, Darlene was outraged with her
daughter's decision and asked the group for their help in
understanding Darlene's reaction.

Darlene's belief system depended on learning from others.
Rather than trying to figure the conflict out on her own, she
reached out to the group members and one of the other
younger group attendees gave her the feedback she was looking for. The younger group member, Harriette, told Darlene
that she herself had to make the very same decision and faced
the same reaction from her parents; she shared this story.

Harriette: I know my parents worked hard to get me through
   school and into college. I was a good kid. I make one mistake
   and now my parents act like my whole world will end. They
   act like theirs ended too. It's just one mistake, just one! I am
   willing to take the responsibility for it. I don't blame them
   or even myself. My boyfriend and I had been dating for two
   years and just became sexually involved. We want to get
   married. We both have good jobs, [and though] they aren't
   great jobs, they do pay the rent and bills. . . . I want my
   parents to let me make my own mistakes and have their love
   as I correct them.

   Don't get angry with your daughter, just be there for her
   as best as you can. Don't reject her. You are angry at her
   because she did not fulfill your dream. It's okay. She will fin-

ish school just like I plan on finishing. It will just take a little longer, that's all.

Collective survival abounds throughout the essence of the groups. The acknowledgment of the responsibility of the women for our future is discussed by another group member.

Josi: We have a lot of responsibility to help our children survive this Crack shit. I let Tyrone live with his grandparents during the week and with me on the weekends because he was getting into too much trouble. I don't get home from work until 5:30 P.M. Tyrone has been home since 2:30 P.M. I know he means well but it was just too much time alone for a teen. His grandparents never liked me because their son, Tyrone's father, began using drugs when we were married and I think they blame me.

I know they love Tyrone, so I asked them to help me keep him alive. . . .I said it just like that because that's what it comes down to. Since his Dad is nowhere to be found, I pay them the amount the courts would have him pay in child support. That way everybody is happy. I don't think I would have a son if it weren't for them.

Vy then shared the near loss of her son, Craig, who was returning home from a friend's house.

Vy: My 16-year-old son said he was walking down the street, minding his own business, and a slow-moving car came down the block. He was aware of the tactic used in "drive-bys" so he began running. The boys jumped out of the car and tried to catch him. Thank God, he's a good athlete because he jumped a fence and hid by trash cans. The boys could not find him and left.

Come to find out, the house whose trash can he hid behind was owned by a friend of ours. After an hour, he felt safe enough to go to the door and call me. I don't think he would have made it home for fear of being killed. My friend said he cried without stopping. She just held him. I thanked her endlessly because if it weren't for her, who knows if my son would have made it home.

A willingness to care for another's child as if he or she is our own is the basis for the survival of many.

Emotional Vitality versus Sullenness

Emotional vitality is the release from the stresses of the day, week, whatever, and comes out when stories are told. The following are some of those mannerisms:

- *Loudness*—vocally speaking louder than is necessary to be heard.
- *Excitability*—expressions of joy, anger, gratitude, and so on are overstated.
- *Praise of God*—with words of expression such as "Thank you, Lord" at the end of a phrase or at the beginning of the phrase (Ex: "Thank you, Lord, for waking me up this morning in my right mind" and "You know, Sistah, there are many days I wonder how I got over but thank the Lord I did").

Janiaba demonstrated emotional vitality as she responded to the question posed by Latifa. The other members chimed in with their excited expressions. When one group member listened to Janiaba's story, she responded with an affirmative, "Uh-huh, you go girl." Other members said encouraging statements such as "I wouldn't let them get away with that stuff" and "Get you an attorney, see if they like that!" Many of these comments were made at the same time Janiaba and Latifa were talking, and did not appear to disturb the ongoing conversation. The group members acknowledged that staying in control, according to "White society's" terms can be awkward.

Freedom of expression is what group members found most comforting as they related to one another in the group. Many times, they entered the group and said things such as the following:

"Sista, you know it's crazy out there," said one, speaking of the society outside the group. Fortunately, it was safe for them to express themselves in whatever manner they chose within the group itself.

"Oooooh, look at that," speaking of how wrong it was for someone to have to unnecessarily go through something or have to deal with an unjust situation.

"Child, listen," spoken before she says what she will accept from society or another person; for example, "Child, listen. You don't have to let that boss woman treat you that way. I'd go get a lawyer and let them feel the heat real quick."

Group sessions often began with multiple conversations, and many greetings and comments of happiness for being back in the group. The comments continued to convey a sense of safety and freedom. There were discussions that openly talked about the need to acquire a "sullenness" in one's behavior and communication patterns. "The world of work is very critical of our way of expression," as one group member put it. Many sessions were spent discussing the reality of a developed and acquired manner of communication that would increase the chance of acceptance. Many members spoke of it:

> "We have to make sure our 'T's' are enunciated and every syllable spoken with great accuracy."
>
> "Monday mornings are the quietest time of my week. While my job requires dialog with multiple staff members, I find I have to make a conscious effort to mentally shift. If I have to speak at length with anyone, I always have to take a deep breath before beginning. What a chore!"
>
> "It's kind of funny.... I have this conversation with myself, reminding me to speak in my 'other language.' I don't think of it as 'standard English,' it's just what White folk understand."
>
> "Sometimes I just don't care and speak in whatever way I choose and let them ask me to explain. I find that they (Whites) are envious of our way of relating to one another."
>
> "The young White kids are always imitating our speech patterns. It really looks funny and sounds funny to see them attempt to be something they are not. I wonder if it looks funny when we attempt to imitate something we aren't."

There were members who, not aware that they made adjustments in the workplace, began to recognize the shifts they made unknowingly. They shared their thoughts:

> Now that you mention it, I too make some kind of change when I am at work. There is a me I never let them see. It's the more lively, vibrant side of me. They (Whites) seem to be so

unexpressive. I just mimic that behavior because it's a way of getting along.

Funny you should talk about getting loud. I remember a supervisor tapping me on the shoulder and saying I didn't need to speak so loudly. I didn't take it as an offense because my supervisor is Black. The co-worker I had directed my comments to had wrongly accused me of leaving a project unfinished. She was a White woman, new on the job, and she caught me off guard on a bad day. Before I knew it, I was in her face, telling her what she could do with her inaccurate observation. I stopped after the supervisor became involved. I just didn't realize how it was being interpreted.

I tend to be on the quiet side. My family is like that too. So my expressiveness is not necessarily in volume or intensity but more in the way of body language. I didn't realize I was so animated until one of the group members asked me how I was doing, that I looked very upset. Just coming from work, having been told I had additional responsibilities and no additional pay made me angry but I didn't know it showed.

Emotional vitality is a natural emotion, while sullenness is a manufactured one and foreign to us as a people.

Harmonious Blending versus Win/Lose

Harmony is the attempt to strive for peace within the family, community, and so on. Striking a point of agreement moves the relationship toward congruence. The Nguzo Saba's principle of Umoja, discussed in Chapter 5, emphasizes the importance of striving for and maintaining unity. When we talked about unity, we seemed to come together with our various understandings. Most talked about the importance of the family blending in harmony while others shared their efforts in the community. Becoming aware of internal, intrapersonal functioning is one level explained by a group member:

Zena: We really have to look at this mass destruction among our people. Where is it coming from? I believe we need to look really deep. We have a responsibility in this madness. Only we can change the trend.

I've done a lot of reading since joining this group and I see over and over the theme that only we can make a difference in the lives of our people. . . . Yes, there are many societal oppressions that affect us. I will not deny that, but the core of our illness is our beginning. What I mean by "core" is what we believe about ourselves, what is placed in our hearts as truth.

We can change what has been placed in our minds and hearts as mean and hateful concepts. We can truly switch them to affirming concepts. I believe that is where unity begins.

We have a responsibility to reach out to each other in the attitude of cooperativeness, not the "win/lose" way of this society. When we work toward a "win/win" solution, we are able to "do the right thing."

I really want to strive toward understanding my people and endeavor toward healing. It feels right to do that. Even when I am met with hostility, I understand it now. The hostility comes from people acting out of feeling bad about themselves. It has very little to do with me. I look inside of me and check how my spirit is doing. If I find I've been injured by my encounter with a negative person then I get busy with repairing it. The repair comes initially by acknowledging the presence of God in my life. I expand the thinking to owning that God is the center of my very existence. I am made in His/Her image. I just meditate on that for a few minutes. I emerge healed of any attack or insult.

Another group member takes the understanding of unity to an interpersonal level in which she described an interaction between her and her sister:

Sonia: It's been a very interesting admission I've had to make to myself. . . My sister does not like me. She is not comfortable around me. There had to be something to the seemingly endless tension between us.

My sister is eight years older than me. I have a brother, two years older than me, which makes her six years older than him. She puts us both in the same category, "young and selfish." Granted, she had to care for us when our parents weren't around during our growing years and we used to try to team up against her. But I didn't take it too seriously when she ended up with the upper hand, no matter how well laid out our plans were. You know what it's like to have a substitute teacher? You pull out all the stops and try every trick in the book to see if you could get away with it. But you didn't quite think of the pending doom...the return of the regular teacher with a full report on the events during her absence... then you pay for it big time. It never failed...our parents always returned and we were dead meat.

That was then, but this is now. She always seems distant. Lots has happened in the intervening years in her life and mine. During our adult years we've not lived in the same state so our families did not get to know each other like we got to know our cousins, but somehow a connection was maintained by my many trips to her house. It seemed more rational for me and my family to go there than the reverse because she and my brother lived a half hour apart.

The older I got, the more distant we grew. My efforts to develop a friendship fell flat. I was constantly being accused of one thing or another—anything from not liking her children to "siding" with my brother against her.

Since our father's death many years ago, our mother chose to live with her. That made sense since they appeared to have that kind of relationship. Plus, at the time, Mom wanted to be around her first grandkids whom she was extremely fond of.

My sister and I would get into these big blowouts over minor things. The final time, I decided no more—no more false accusations, no more putting me down, no more personal slams about my brother and me conspiring. I acknowledged that she didn't like me and I was willing to accept that now. I told her that I loved her and have always idolized her as a big sister and I was sad that that didn't come across. I drew the line. I will not allow her to yell at me and falsely accuse me of things which, strangely enough, had to do with her parenting or decisions she made about her life. I let her know how I would respond, which was to acknowledge the negative conversation and say good-bye if we're on the phone or walk away if we're in each other's presence. The bottom line is that as an adult I can control, to some degree, the amount of disrespect that comes my way.

When I took a step away from all that negative energy, I learned many, many things. It took me about a year to mourn the loss of my dream—a close sisterly tie. The most painful part is seeing her be there for others and admitting it will never be there for me. Then, if that wasn't painful enough, I realized my sister actually felt bad about herself. It wasn't me at all—she really hates herself!!

At this point, we basically avoid each other. I initiate all contact. I feel the responsibility since we have an elderly mother to collectively care for and families that love each other. I work out of maintaining unity in the family. Communication is possible if it's kept short and to-the-point. The topic normally concerns caring for our mother and accomplishments our children have achieved. If she had it her way, we would never talk; somewhere deep inside me, I still need to hear her voice. It hurts me to know she is in so much pain. I try to reach out in small ways so she doesn't reject it. It's not mutual so I don't push it. I guess I have the hope that she will heal inside from the hurts. I stay mindful that her harsh tone isn't meant for me, it's just a reflection of how she feels about herself. Being able to talk about a few things is better than talking about nothing.

Finally, a group member talks about her efforts in the African-American community:

Maura: Our children need us to prepare a way for them, to advocate for them, and to protect them. The school system in my community wanted to cut programs and divert funds to this vague entity no one knew about. At least none of the parents had a clue. Well, when we, a handful of parents, caught wind of this, we pulled out our old "60s" tactics. The Board of Education meeting is public so, you know, we got busy. We sent around fliers announcing the time, place, and agenda. We got together the weekend before to plan our strategy. Two hundred parents showed up at the meeting to plan our "attack." I couldn't believe it! Two hundred! We were cookin' now. We developed a phone tree—the school puts out a directory, how handy; a letter of protest and collected signatures—these are elected officials; we made hundreds of posters, one at a time; finally, we rallied our children together—they came up with a chant/rap song. We were ready!

The school board meeting started on time. Over a thousand parents showed up. We marched; the kids taught us the chant and don't you know, those school officials did not touch that money!! You talk about victory—we were ecstatic.

We resolved to keep that intensity going and make them honor their roles with the responsibility we entrusted them with. It truly showed me, and I'm sure others, that when we unite, we are a powerful group. Our children have no one but us to count on to provide a way for them. They can't do it without us.

The stakes are very high. Our children are our future. They feel powerless. That's why they are self-destructing. We've got to get behind them, in front of them, beside them, and get them what they need educationally so that they can become the geniuses God intends them to be.

On a lighter note, harmonious blending is demonstrated by Binta's synchronization of her life story with Tanisha's life story:

Tanisha: I work long hours and am not able to have time for myself and friends. My children are grown and have homes of their own, but they act like they can't cook or go to the grocery store.
Binta: Oooh, girl! I get tired of being thought of as the only kitchen in town.
Tanisha: When they walk into my house, whether I let them in or they are bold enough to just walk in, the first place they head for is the kitchen and open my refrigerator.
Binta: Then they have the nerve to ask what's good.

Other group members are laughing as the two continue sharing the same experience of nurturing mothers.

Tanisha: I point them toward the cat food and can opener.
Binta: I'm going to start charging them, see how they like that.
Tanisha: I wouldn't know what I'd do without them. They make me feel joy and peace and I praise God for their hungry mouths.
Binta: Me too!

Although on the one hand these women find it irritating to be expected to meet the every need of the family and struggle with picking and choosing which needs to meet, on the other, they are thankful for the working together of the family unit and the strengthening of the bonds by their own acts rather than competitive "one-upping" to see who is "best" in the role of "nurturing mother." It is more of a joining in of a mutually enjoyable role.

Respecting the Wisdom of Elders and the Oral Tradition

The role of ancestors is delineated by collecting the wisdom of our foreparents. Group members freely relate the customs handed down for generations—anything from pearls of wisdom to health concerns—in short, the extension of an oral tradition by word of mouth. Recounts are shared that remind the group members that our wisdom is a collective one. Our existence did not begin in this lifetime, but thousands of years ago.

The value in the African-American community lies in the ancestors and the elders who are the keepers of the wisdom that has been passed down through the ages. Our responsibility is to preserve it by learning the wisdom of our elders and ancestors and passing it on to our children.

It is important to acknowledge the distinct differences that exist between our culture and those of the dominant culture. One group member put it well when she compared her life to that of a White co-worker:

Toni: A co-worker and I went to lunch together the other day. We got to talking about our mothers. I told her that I am making preparations for my mother to move in with me this fall. She has gotten too old to care for that big house we grew up in and has felt lonely over the past year. My Dad passed away five years ago. I couldn't believe her comment: "You couldn't pay me enough to let my mother live with me. Why don't you let her get a smaller place or move into senior citizens' apartments? There is not a house big enough for the two of us. She is too picky and insists on having things her way, at all costs."

I knew we weren't functioning out of the same value system. They (Whites) seem to be very intolerant of the elderly. That is a strange concept to me. While we will need to develop a relationship that honors who is who around the house, I can't imagine her not living with me. I guess if she wanted to, she could live in a senior citizens' apartment, but she hasn't mentioned it at all. She brings so much wisdom to our family and our children really listen to her. What a treasure!

Another group member told of the remedy for the common cold:

Shari: We had the cure for the common cold all along. All they
(White people) needed to do was ask us. My grandmother is
part African, Cherokee, and some kind of White. She had a
cure for everything, naturally. Her cures were from nature.
When we got a cold, she would make this thing to put on
your chest and sometimes your back called a "mustard plas-
ter." It was a mixture of different herbs and made into a
paste. She spread it on a piece of cloth and put another cloth
on top of it, had you lie down, and placed it on your chest
while it was still hot. Of course, this was after the dose of
caster oil. You would sleep all night with it on your chest.
By morning you were back in the swing of things. I never
missed a day of school, thanks to Grandma.

Janiba related the words of wisdom given to her at her wedding reception:

Janiba: I was feeling relieved that the service was over and we
were at the reception. While I stood around talking with my
cousin, three of my aunts came over. I couldn't imagine what
they had to say, but they excused my cousin and surrounded
me. "Janiba," they began. "You will get your own checking
account and not let anyone know about it. You will arrange a
trip once a year just for yourself. You will not let anyone
know where you are except your mother and we will help
you invest your money."
    Then as quickly as they came, they left. Needless to say, I
took their advice and have never regretted it. I think that was
the secret to a happy marriage because I'm going on 25 years
and never regretted it one second.

Ancient wisdom from Africa is one area the group leaders
have incorporated into the group. As African-Americans, our
appreciation for Africa has only just begun to develop. Previously, Africa was seen as shameful to be connected to; the
changing of our consciousness allows the yearning of wisdom
to reveal itself. The reading of proverbs from Africa is a common practice in the group. The group leaders are usually the
first to bring ancestral wisdom, which is quickly embraced by
the members into the group. Sayings—such as "It takes a vil-
lage to raise a child" and "Anger is like the blade of a sword. If
you hold onto it too long, it is bound to do harm"—are excellent
examples. Iyanla Van Zant's collection of inspirational writings

encourages us to examine our faults. Group members often share meaningful selections from Van Zant's 1993 writings.

It is through collective survival, emotional vitality, harmonious blending, and respect for our ancestors' collective wisdom that we experience healing. Connecting with one another, we gain an understanding that African-American women are valued participants in society as a whole. As African-American women speak to their experience of vitality and strength through the belief that unity is key to survival, they will no doubt move onward and upward. The element to be examined next is the role of the African-American male, what he contributes to the factors that the African-American female brings to the group.

Gender Commonalities

It has been challenging to explore the concept of male–female issues as they pertain to group work with African-American women. Elements from feminist psychology can be seen when an awareness transition occurs. The legacy of victories and success stories often told by African-American women can be illustrated throughout Marie's life.

Marie: I hold down a full-time job that requires overtime. I leave there to go home to a son who relies on me to help him do homework. I step from one world to another and meet demands after demands.

Later she realized:

Marie: If I am able to do all these things for others and still remain sane, then I can afford to use these self-contained resources for my own peace of mind. I am a strong Black woman. I can make my life more manageable. I will begin to turn this around. I will not allow my White boss to dump on me as if I am her slave....

Marie continues her self-proclaimed litany of turning her oppressive life around.

African-American women face the issue of effectively relating to African-American males. They feel a kinship due to their common history, yet are challenged with the expectation of many African-American men to follow the traditional European-American female role of self-denial. In the days of slavery, the African-American male adopted the position of the White master when it came to the expectations of the African-American women. She was considered less than equal and had strict role expectations. That is not to say that the African male did not resist cruel treatment of the African women but held to the belief that there is "women's work" that he would not do under any circumstances. We can bring that way of thinking into the 1960s with the Civil Rights Movement. Many women were placed in less powerful positions and viewed as subservants. African-American women in the Civil Rights Movement were not viewed as equal to their African-American male counterparts. It will have to suffice to say that the current evidence of the oppression of African-American women is their position on the welfare rolls and the White oppressive system that keeps them there. Vy shared the following story in one of our *Images of Me* group meetings:

Vy: I have come so far from where my family started. My mom
and her sisters are on welfare. My two sisters are on welfare.
I have chosen to go to school and have managed to provide
for my three children with assistance from welfare (Medicaid
card) and government grants. Working has really helped me
develop pride and self-belief that I can make it. I refuse to be
like women in my family—trapped by the system. But I just
learned that my medical benefits will run out next month
and I have one more quarter to finish school before gradua-
tion. (*Through tears, Vy continues.*) I have to quit my job and
go back on welfare to make sure my kids have coverage.

The system has temporarily, it is hoped, halted a movement toward independence.

The common battle for equal treatment is fought by and for both African-American and European-American women against men and society. The difference is that race and class are thrown in as additional variables. It is like fighting a battle on two fronts: African-American women risk the loss of a comrade in the battle on racism when they take up the cause of women's equality, and European-American women fight the battle on a single front while "sleeping with the enemy." hooks (1984), in *Feminist Theory: From Margin to Center*, maintains that the contemporary feminist movement in the United States called attention to the exploitation and oppression of women globally. This major contribution to feminist struggle highlighted sexist injustice and the ideology and practice of male domination. Racism and class structure are perceived as stemming from sexism (hooks, 1984). White women were tired and bored, having only home, family, and leisure time to occupy them; they wanted to be employed outside the home in meaningful and fulfilling careers. The African-American woman historically has been employed both in and outside of the home. hooks (1984) defines *oppression* as the "absence of choices" (p. 5) and explains that many women do not experience an absolute lack of choice. They may know, for example, that they have been discriminated against on the basis of sex, but they may not equate this with oppression. She adds that the absence of extreme restrictions leads many women to ignore the areas in which they are exploited or discriminated against, and it may even lead them to imagine that no women are oppressed. hooks (1984) identifies this distorted view as "competitive, atomistic, liberal individualism" (p. 8), an idea that undermines the radicalism of the feminist struggle.

Group work with African-American women borrows from feminist orientations in psychotherapy. The unique conditions of African-American women and the synthesis of feminist psychology is the focus of McNair's (1992) work. She illustrated the most necessary and unique approach formed by the synthesis of two models of therapy for African-American women (p. 11). McNair believes that the synthesis directly shows the intersection of racial and gender oppression in the lives of most African-American women (p. 12).

The concept of empowerment for women is borrowed from feminist psychology and assists in facilitating positive personal growth even as African centeredness is maintained. The psychological health of African-American women requires the authentic approach in order to secure personal growth. Afrocentric psychology represents a self-affirmation, reawakening, and rebirth of personal beliefs and behaviors. Feminist psychology focuses on other societal forces that shape behavior (McNair, 1992). It recognizes the ways in which women have learned to be helpless and feel powerless in a sexist society. McNair explains it this way: The feminist approach explores and identifies cultural and societal causes of psychological problems, while Afrocentricism remains true to its concept, spirituality, and kinship.

Empowerment is a term used often in feminist psychology. *Kujichagulia*, a form of empowerment for African-American females discussed in Chapter 8, means drawing on the African-American community for strength and support. African-American women by racial and ethnic heritage tend to be community-minded. Two characteristics, gender and race, providing nurturance for the good of the community, have been handed down from our African ancestors. We migrate toward each other naturally, and draw on one another's strengths intuitively. In a group, we emphasize strong bonds and celestial connections that link us spiritually, and revisit the ancestral wisdom that lies deep within our genetic makeup passed down to us by our ever-present Creator.

Sisterhood is a natural concept for African-American women: It is not unusual for the concept to be discussed in a group setting. Deep within the concept of sisterhood for African-American women lies the conscious and sometimes unconscious issues for all women. A level of confusion and mistrust springs up when inclusion involves only European-American women. The group tosses around the issue, as can be seen in Tanisha's observations:

Tanisha: I'm not sure what my sisters (biological sisters) complain about so much when they talk about encountering White women. They discuss hurtful experiences and the anger that spurs in them due to the encounters. I can't understand why they continue to put themselves in such situations or even allow themselves to let the anger build to a point where they are livid. I would think that if it was that hurtful to be around a person that you would merely not be around them, even if you had to remove yourself emotionally and/or psychologically.

Then Janiba begins to delineate her experience of the encounter:

Janiba: Tanisha, there are numerous experiences of denigration that simply catch you off guard. I don't deliberately involve myself with other White women but there's no avoiding it when I find myself in my educational process taking classes when I am the only Black female. There's very little chance that I would be able to avoid that situation short of simply not taking the class. It seems as though they have no awareness of anything other than their own White world. And they make no attempt to get to know anything other than that reality when you explicitly tell them that there's more to it than living in the comforts of privilege. They resist and deny their responsibility in contributing to the plight of Black women. There's simply a gap, that's more like a crater between my understanding of life and their understanding of life. I would just prefer to be around women who understand me when I'll use a certain expression or demonstrate a certain movement that basically defies explanation but I know culturally my Black sisters know when I flip my hand in the air and suck air through my teeth while stating "forget it" means that I'm taking a temporary break from having to deal with a complicated issue at hand. It would take too much to describe what I meant to a White women, particularly if she's in denial about the encounters of White society on Black society.

The women in the group who have had positive experiences with White women will begin their explanations as this member did:

Shari: It's not so much that I hate White women but there are some who are so ignorant that it makes it look bad on other White women. But I have this friend, Gloria, who seems to know that when I hurt, there's something deep and wide about that hurt. She knows that when I come into work and maybe my hello isn't as chipper as in other days, that maybe the burdens of being a single mother have overwhelmed me last evening. And then there's been times when she's walked into my office, closed my door behind her, and sat down and said I need to share this with you because I think you're the only person around here who could understand my pain. And she begins to talk to me as if our worlds have been intricately twined together for centuries. The pain she experiences when her daughter has gone out drinking too much and how she is fearful of her future. The hurt wrestling with deep emotional nurturing parental feelings for a moment take a mutual turn. When we emerge from our talk, life for me seems more manageable and Gloria's burdens seem a little more bearable for her. We hug each other, we'll wipe each others' tears and go on with our day, knowing that if we need to do this again, or even the glances we share throughout the day or the week, the connection is there, the connection as women.

The discovery of sisterhood is possible, especially since the issues of feminism and racism are intricately interwoven throughout the fabric of solidarity.

At the heart of the struggle is the thinking of Dr. Martin Luther King, Jr., the African-American pioneer of the Civil Rights Movement, who stated it well in his 1967 Christmas sermon:

> It really boils down to this: that all life is interrelated. We are all caught in an inescapable network of mutuality, tied into a single garment of destiny. Whatever affects one directly, affects all indirectly. We are made to live together because of the interrelated structure of reality (p. 69).

African-American women's struggles and thoughts about sisterhood can be understood through the concept of racial identity. Challenges from many aspects and angles confront the African-American female in her racial development. Like her, as we develop, we make the choices of whether we will allow ourselves to be treated like a reference group.

Assimilation and acculturation are two factors with which African-American women continuously struggle at balancing on a conscious or unconscious level. The internal struggle of resistance is constant. African-American women strive to define themselves, and resist being defined by persons who do not have their best interests in mind. The strength of that resistance is evidenced in Alice Walker's 1992 book, *Possessing the Secret of Joy*, in which she shares the secret of joyful resistance. Women of African descent inherited the strength of self-determination. The key to healthy self-determination lies in defining oneself, a goal focused on by members of the *Images of Me* group.

Group leaders encourage members to bring in spiritual readings to share and illustrate an element of their journey. Maxine shared a poem, "Mother to Son," by Langston Hughes (1949). Maxine had experienced many tribulations prior to her first group experience. Chapter 1 explained how African-Americans have developed mechanisms, such as inspirational readings, that assist in their individual and collective survival and adjustment.

Sylvia read the Maya Angelou (1978) poem "Still I Rise" for the group. The theme of self-determination can be found throughout the group's experiences, capturing the importance of resisting outward definitions and embracing the internal messages of greatness and wholeness.

African-American women, on the whole, have developed healthy personalities that leave them available to build community. Issues regarding racial identity are viewed from the perspective of the Nigrescence or racial identity development model and perspective. We picked the Nigrescence perspective instead of the African-American client-as-problems (CAP), outlined by European writers, because the former sees/portrays African-Americans as adapting personalities in response to racial discrimination (Parham, 1989). (Please refer to the Glossary for more information.) It incorporates the strength of the African-American community and personality. The focus of the *Images of Me* group is on identity issues as they relate to self-definition versus White-defined identity. While there are no European participants in the group, *Images of Me* participants often look at their development or metamorphosis of ethnic identity through the eyes of European society.

Marie explains how her participation in *Images of Me* revealed an important factor:

Marie: I didn't realize that buying *Glamour* and other magazines promoting White beauty had such an affect on me. I looked at those pictures and wanted to look like them. I compared how I felt as I looked at *Essence*. I didn't realize my level of envy until I put *Glamour* down and picked up *Essence*. Wow... I cried and then wondered what image I was passing on to my daughter!

Marie, through the levels of racial identity that became clear, was able to resolve her struggle of understanding self. Refer to Chapter 1 for an explanation of the stages of racial identity according to Helms (1990).

Marie comes to the *Images of Me* group at the transition from Pre-Encounter (Stage One) to the Encounter (Stage Two) phase of identity development and shares another experience:

Marie:
I live in a community that is all White. My parents broke up when I was very young, which left my mom as the sole pro-

vider. Her factory job required that she work third shift. For fear of our safety, she moved to the Whitest community she could find. My five sisters and I made a pact. We pledged to be as good as possible so we can help Mom out. I hated the idea, but had no choice. I never got into trouble. I did all my school work. I didn't make friends because I might risk playing too hard. I just stayed home and cooperated at all cost. We had our little sibling squabbles, nothing to call attention to.

I remember subtle put-downs about Black people. My father was the target of most of the criticism. Much of this confused me because, even though he was scarcely around, his presence made me feel happy. I don't remember my parents' fights but my older sisters do. My sisters made themselves very scarce when he was around. The put-downs expanded from him being a drunk and poor father to all Black men being worthless and, finally, all Black people being untrustworthy. My sisters and I never had Black friends as children due to the all-White environment we lived in. We all went to small White colleges, very few Blacks. I went to an all-White Christian girls' boarding school for high school and the same type college. Things seemed to flow along very smoothly. I relied on my Christianity as a connection to the students. Our lives were very similar. I joined in everything going on at my school. I felt lonesome but I just attributed the feeling to missing my family.

To this day, I cannot recall doing anything mischievous or off-centered. I dated only one guy and never dated again. In my house men were lower than were rats. I don't date today and I'm 34 years old. I live in this all-White community and until lately, I loved it.

The change came when a "well-meaning" neighbor requested to gain access to legal information about property lines. We work on the township association together so I couldn't figure out why she wanted that information. I just had to ask, ya know?

A Black family was moving in the home behind her and she wanted to put up a fence. I asked if the fence would go all the way around her place. She snapped, "Of course, I've had enough of the n _ _ _ _ _ s _ _ _.

She must have forgotten who she was talking to. When she tried to suck those words back in, she made numerous apologies. Of course, I accepted them. She never put the fence up but moved out the next month, without even one good-bye. I thought this was a single incident, but many more happened.

The school has had to bus children to the school in our community. Parents were meeting without inviting or informing me. Come to find out, I was the only member of our community not present. The issue of racial hatred showed its ugly face. Everything looked different from that moment forward.

These incidents led Marie into the Encounter stage (Cross, 1971, 1978) in which an individual experiences a significant event. Marie grew up in the comforts of what Cross (1978) describes as the Pre-Encounter stage in which the person is apt to view his or her world from a White perspective. While distressed by the experience, Marie, after a period of time, reclaimed her roots by embracing the culture of African-Americans and viewing that culture as positive. Marie then entered Stage Three, Immersion.

Marie began participating in all the African-American activities. She wanted to sell her home, but decided against that idea for the time being. The group helped her process her rage and anger.

Marie: I found myself shopping around for a Black, I mean, an African-American church, buying African clothes, and reading books by African-Americans. I changed my doctors, my dentist, and so on to African-Americans. I decorated my home with African-American and African art. While it was fun, I was very much aware of my rage. I chose this group because it was all African-American women.

Group Leader: Let's look at the anger, Marie.

Marie: I feel it very intensely!

With African drum music playing in the background, the facilitator invited Marie to move with the music.

Group Leader: As you feel the intensity of the music and drums, let your body move.

Marie hesitated at first, but began moving. The group leader stood next to Marie, assisting with the movements, then began to move herself. Other group members joined in by humming, clapping, and stamping their feet.

Group Leader: Marie, what are you aware of right now?
Marie: A lot of pain.
Group Leader: Where?
Marie: My heart... my head... I feel like I can't breathe....
Group Leader: Take a nice long breath... and another...
    another.... Let's breathe together....

The group joined in by breathing deeply. Marie began to cry. The music was turned up louder. Still there was moving and dancing.

Marie: This feels good to let this go.
Group Leader: What are you feeling?
Marie: Lightness.

The group was instructed to stand and hold hands. They began to sway back and forth. While still humming, Marie began to cry harder.

Group Leader: What are you feeling now?
Marie: So much anger...
Group Leader: What would you like to do?
Marie: Hit something.

Pillows were placed on the floor. Marie knelt down and pounded them with her fist. She cried and screamed.

Group Leader: Who are you screaming at?
Marie: My mother... my father... God! I have a messed up life.
    They told me wrong....
Group Leader: What did they need to tell you?
Marie: Quit controlling me!!!
Group Leader: Let's put you in the driver's seat.

The music was changed to a soft jazz instrumental and the group members were instructed to have a seat and hum softly. Marie picked herself up and moved to the center of the room. Affirmation exercises were performed which concluded with a *libation* (a renewal ceremony that calls upon the strength and wisdom of ancestors). The session ended with prayers offered by various group members.

At the end of the 10-week group session, Marie began Stage Four, Internalization. Marie's identity was brought out through personal thoughts, feelings, and behaviors rooted in the values and fabric of Black/African culture itself (Parham, 1989). However, identity development comes from the interaction between internal (individual) and external (environmental) factors (Parham, 1989).

The positive self-image emerged through the skillful assistance of the group leaders. The use of the Nigrescence model provides the framework for positive psychological change. The model also posits that any cognitive, affective, or behavioral activity that promotes continued growth and development is, at some level, self-actualizing (Parham, 1989, p. 331). Rogers (1961) describes self-actualization as the inherent tendency of the organism to expand and develop itself. Incorporating concepts from feminist psychology strengthens the emergence of identity development and the "actualizing tendency," or expansion of self, for African-American females (McNair, 1992).

The following is an outline of issues used by *Images of Me* group leaders with group members. This framework for group therapy assists in the development of a healthy self.

Framework for Group Therapy

1. The therapist should be aware of her or his own values regarding race and gender issues, especially as they influence one's assessment and evaluation of client's behavior (McNair, 1992, p. 16).
2. Theories of behavior based on biological differences between the races and genders should be viewed as inappropriate for work with African-American women; rather, a synthesis of Afrocentric and feminist models is more appropriate (McNair, 1992, p. 16).
3. A focus on the social, political and economic factors that have contributed to the African-American woman's psychological status is imperative. Such an orientation assumes that psychological distress is an undeniable consequence of racism and sexism; further, no "blame" for psychological difficulty is placed on the client (Brewer, 1993; McNair, 1992, p. 16; Parham, 1989).
4. The therapist needs to actively consider that the personality characteristics or behavioral styles of African-American women, as reinforced by cultural experiences, may be strengths rather than weaknesses. For example, the characterization of African-American women as "domineering"

may more accurately be stated as "assertive" and "responsible" (McNair, 1992, p. 16).

5. When appropriate and feasible, community supports and resources should be utilized or recommended. Historically, such resources have been viewed in the African-American community as accessible, culturally compatible, and less threatening than traditional mental health services. In addition, the use of such supports reinforce the Afrocentric notion of community-oriented solutions over individually based ones (McNair, 1992, p. 16).

6. The goals of therapy should include the social and political factors that originally contributed to the client's distress, to facilitate coming to a communal solution rather than an individual one. Attention to strengthening the client's sense of self through empowerment is consistent with her approach to goal-setting (McNair, 1992, p. 16).

7. Identity development, to enhance self-esteem, needs to be based on sound principles built on African self-concept, as in the Nigrescence models (Parham, 1989, p. 332).

8. The members become aware of how racial identity attitudes influence the dynamics (i.e., relationship) of the therapeutic process itself (Parham, 1989).

9. The goal of therapy should stress the necessity of achieving congruence between the real and the perceived or ideal self to help a person become a fully functioning and well-adjusted individual (Nobles, 1986; Rogers, 1961).

The preceding areas are suggestions to keep in mind when working with African-American women. Readers may find additional guidelines to augment group work with this population. In any case, racial identity and equality, based on gender, are the main themes of group work with African-American women. Parham (1989) suggested also keeping the following in mind:

Critical Points to Consider

1. Recognizing the perceived racial identity of the group leaders
2. Not knowing the racial identity stage of the group member
3. Timing correctly the movement of the client into the next racial identity stage
4. The actual racial group membership of the leader

First and foremost, the relationship between therapist and client must be closely monitored and handled with care, for their relationship is a vital link in the therapeutic process (Highlen & Hill, 1984). Cohesiveness in group therapy is the analogue of the "relationship" in individual therapy (Yalom, 1985, p. 50). Yalom noted that the best research evidence available overwhelmingly supports the conclusion that successful therapy is mediated by a relationship that includes certain essential elements: trust, warmth, empathic understanding, and acceptance. This relationship among the members must also be continually measured.

A strong working alliance with the client sets the groundwork for racial identity development. Parham (1989) illustrated how racial identity attitudes affect the therapist's ability to utilize social factors that may cause conflict. The therapist must know her own level of racial identity (Pre-Encounter, Encounter, Immersion/Emmersion, or Internalization) and at which stage the group member currently stands.

An example of this can be found in the work Marie did in the previous example. The group facilitator was in the Internalization stage, as Marie came to the group, moving from the Pre-Encounter to the Encounter stage. It was imperative that the group leader be aware of Marie's racial identity stage, and recognize that Marie was at a different stage. Further, sufficient time needed to be allowed to promote her fluid movement into and through the stages via therapeutic techniques. Timing proves essential to productive and empowering transition into the next stage of racial identity.

Summary

An Afrocentric approach to group work with African-American women can be augmented by concepts from feminist psychology. A key factor to keep in mind is the group leader's level of racial identity. The group participant can move through the stages of positive racial development with the support of other group members.

Women, in general, have a common obstacle to confront: the oppression imposed by the White male power structure in society. Inclusive of the issues of race, class, and gender, the "simultaneity of oppression" as Brewer (1993) put it, women can "advocate" feminism (hooks, 1984) to fight against oppression. Care needs to be taken when African-American women decide to confront the "male privilege" in African-American males. The skill must be developed in such a way that she is equipped with the ability to confront, challenge, and resolve the equality issues without alienating African-American men. For if one of us (male or female) is still in chains, then we all are in chains.

The benefits to be gained from group work utilizing an Afrocentric worldview are the focus of Chapter 3. The ways of working within the paradigm of mental health for minorities and providing effective group counseling are explored, and readers can review and/or learn what the literature has to offer as tools for successful group work from an African-centered approach.

References

Angelou, M. (1978). *And still I rise. A book of poems by Maya Angelou.* New York: Random House.

Boyd, J. (1990). Ethnic and cultural diversity in feminist therapy: Keys to power. In E. White (Ed.), *The Black women's health book*, (pp. 226–234). Seattle: Seal Press.

Brewer, R. M. (1993). Theorizing race, class, and gender. In S. M. James & A. P. A. Busia *Theorizing Black feminism: The visionary pragmatism of Black women* (pp. 13–30). New York: Routledge.

Cole, J. B. (Ed.). (1986). *All American women: Lines that divide, ties that bind.* New York: Free Press.

Cross, W. E. (1978). The Cross and Thomas models of psychological Nigrescence. *Journal of Black Psychology, 5*(1), 13–19.

Cross, W. E. (1971). The negro to Black conversion experience: Towards a psychology of Black liberation. *Black World, 20*(9), 13–27.

Frye, M. (1983). *The politics of reality: Essays in feminist theory.* Freedom, CA: The Crossing Press.

Helms, J. (1990). *Black and White racial identity.* Westport, CT: Praeger.

Highlen, P. S., & Hill, C. E. (1984). Factors affecting client change in individual counseling: Current status of theoretical speculations. In S. D. Brown & R. W. Lent (Eds.), *The handbook of counseling psychology* (pp. 334–396). New York: John Wiley.

hooks, b. (1981). *Ain't I a woman: Black women and feminism.* Boston: South End Press.

hooks, b. (1984). *Feminist theory: From margin to center.* Boston: South End Press.

Hughes, L. (1949). *The poetry of the negro, 1746–1949.* New York: Doubleday.

James, S. M., & Busia, A. P. A. (1993). *Theorizing Black feminism: The visionary pragmatism of Black women.* New York: Routledge.

King, Martin Luther, Jr. (1967). *The trumpet of conscience.* New York: Harper & Row.

McNair, L. D. (1992). African-American women in therapy: An Afrocentric feminist synthesis. *Women in Therapy, 12*(1/2), 5–17.

Nobles, W. (1986). *African psychology: Towards its reclamation, reascension and revitalization.* Oakland, CA: Black Family Institute.

Parham, T. A. (1989). Nigrescence: The transformation of Black consciousness across the lifecycle. In R. L. Jones (Ed.), *Black adulthood, development and aging* (pp. 151–166). Berkeley: Cobb & Henry.

Phillips, F. (1990). NTU psychotherapy: An Afrocentric approach. *The Journal of Black Psychology, 17*(1), 53–74.

Rogers, C. (1961). *On becoming a person.* Boston: Houghton Mifflin.

Van Zant, I. (1993). *Acts of faith: Daily meditations for people of color.* New York: Simon & Schuster.

Walker, A. (1992). *Possessing the secret of joy.* New York: Harcourt Brace Jovanovich.

Yalom, I. D. (1985). *Theory and practice of group psychotherapy* (3rd ed.). New York: Basic Books, Inc.

3

The Efficacy of
Afrocentric Group Work

The consistent underutilization of psychological and mental health services by African-Americans has prompted counselors, psychologists, and mental health workers to take their services beyond the boundaries of their offices and into the communities they serve. For instance, at one of the writers' institutions, counselors and psychologists offered psychological services to an African-American undergraduate class and taught them basic principles of psychology and personal adjustment skills. Essentially, these skills were deemed necessary to facilitate survival on a large white southeastern university campus. In one class activity, all students were required to join a small personal adjustment group led by interns from the university's Counseling Center. The interns conducted small group counseling experiences once per week and reported to senior staff for supervision.

One such intern, a European-American male, met his supervisory team and reported that he had met his group twice and had been surprised, amazed, and disappointed because his group members would not talk. He reported that they were either reluctant to speak or spoke without the psychological sophistication expected of college students. All the negative stereotypes about African-American people were manifested to this young European-American male intern. He reasoned that the participants must be nonverbal, come from broken homes, have poor self-concepts, have poor work habits, have low career expectations, are poor tests takers, lack an internal frame of reference, are angry and resistant, and/or manifested all the basic stereotypes and biases that often exist in multicultural counseling settings.

Unfortunately, this young European-American male intern terminated this group before the members could become engaged in working through the issues and goals for which the class and the group was intended. This young leader was not aware enough of the historical experiences of African-Americans or comfortable enough to establish rapport with them. He was oblivious to the fact that the lack of self-disclosure by these African-American students might have been a basic survival mechanism similar to those practiced by their parents and ancestors to protect themselves in the oppressive world in which they lived. Ridley (1984) suggested that Blacks' reluctance to engage in self-disclosure might be due to their distrust of counselors who might take what they say and use it against them. Others have suggested that self-disclosure by African-Americans could lead to erroneous diagnoses. For example, many writers have pointed out how African-American people who distrust the system they perceive as racist and unfair are often diagnosed as paranoid. Grier and Cobbs (1968), in their book *Black Rage*, viewed this response not as paranoia, but as a healthy response to racism.

Clearly this young European-American male intern made many of the same errors that many well-trained psychologists have made in trying to explain Black behavior or understand styles of African-American people by using traditional theories developed by and for European individuals (Nobles, 1991; Sue & Sue, 1990; White, Parham, & Parham, 1980).

White et al. (1980) suggested that when traditional theories are applied to meet the counseling needs of Black people, incorrect conclusions are drawn. Specifically, many European-American therapists see African-American clients or group members as weak, inferior, and psychologically unsophisticated. Although many European-American therapists have not bought into the notion that African-American clients are genetically inferior, they still might not be aware of the strength that these clients bring to the group. White et al. (1980) suggested further that if counselors were knowledgeable about the Black experience, they would see the intellectual stimulation provided by Black newspapers, popular Black magazines (*Ebony*,

Jet, Essence, and others), rapping, and so forth. They would have a better appreciation for Black speech patterns as a valid and legitimate forms of communication rather than as a manifestation of ignorance and shame. Such knowledge and insight could have made a major difference in the overall group effectiveness of the young European-American intern.

Many African-American group members bring levels of mental toughness and survival skills to the group from which other members can benefit. To survive in their communities, many African-American individuals have had to demonstrate psychological strengths and creativity. They have learned early in life that there is pain, suffering, and misery, and that it is a struggle to survive. Yet many have refused to succumb to these difficult life conditions. One African-American female client told us how challenging it was to go to and from school. She reported that bullies attempted to take her lunch money, put her down because she made good grades, attempted to encourage her to use and sell drugs, and tried to persuade her to have sex. She recalled the day-to-day maneuvers she used to avoid harassment and fighting. In essence, she gained respect by showing no fear and by being assertive or confrontive at appropriate times. The point here is that these life survival skills are valuable and should be viewed as vehicles for character building and personal growth.

In light of Sue and Sue's (1990) allegation that the counseling profession has failed to meet the counseling and mental health needs of ethnic minorities, it should not be a surprise that the young European-American intern failed miserably. Specifically, he stated that of all ethnic minorities who are reported as having attended counseling, 50 percent drop out before completing the counseling process as compared to a 30 percent drop-out rate by White clients. He proposes several reasons for high failure rate, including (1) inappropriate counseling goals, (2) imposition of White counseling theories and techniques on ethnic minority clients, (3) imposition of White values on ethnic minority clients, and (4) stereotyping, patronizing, and having low expectations of ethnic minority clients.

Overall, group counseling for ethnic minorities, in general, and for African-Americans, in particular, has failed due to the hidden agenda and belief that African-Americans and other ethnic minority clients would get along better if they would abandon their perspectives and values and incorporate the values, lifestyles, and worldviews of middle-class European-Americans.

The paucity of literature coupled with the tremendous need to provide effective psychological group work services for African-American women drove our effort in writing this book. We believed that the principles of African philosophy applied to African-American women's groups would yield greater results than the predominant Eurocentric psychology. The remainder of this chapter discusses a historical perspective of African-American women in group work, Afrocentric philosophy and group work, barriers to efficacy for group counseling, facilitating efficacy in group counseling, and the efficacy of women's groups using African philosophy.

A Historical Perspective of Group Work

There is a serious need to reverse the cycle of failure of ethnic minorities who receive mental health services. There is an even a greater need to provide effective group counseling services for African-American women who have been reported to have the greatest need for psychological and mental health services among all other groups but who receive appropriate and effective counseling least often. In a review of the historical development in group work, Shapiro (1978) outlined and discussed the various periods of group work and the major contributors, but none included groups for African-American women. Realistically, one should not expect to find group models for African-American women during the pioneer and developmental periods because psychology was so deeply entrenched in White male ideology and Eurocentric philosophy that inclusion of African-American women would not fit. However, it is disappointing to see that so little effort toward group counseling services existed for African-American women during the more recent period. Aubrey and Lewis (1983) outlined an extensive list of social issues and the potential audience for group work. The closest category to African-American women was "single parents," resulting from the disintegration of the family structure. It has only been during the past decade that formal group counseling for African-Americans has been reported in social science literature; among those contributors are Boyd-Franklin (1991), Gainor (1992), Mays (1985), and Trotman and Gallagher (1987).

The Afrocentric Philosophy and Group Work

We are discussing African philosophy here because we believe that African-American women in groups would achieve more from an African-centered approach to group work than from a European-centered group approach. Psychological needs of African-Americans have not been met through group work because their needs have been based on beliefs and ethos of European-Americans. Because there is a set of beliefs and ethos of African people, it stands to reason that Black psychological principles should be applied when working with African-American individuals (Nobles, 1991). It is also important to incorporate Afrocentric principles into groups because African-American people still maintain many African values even though their ancestors came here more than 375 years ago.

Nobles (1991) believes that slavery encouraged the retention of the African philosophy because the slaves were isolated and separated from the American system. During slavery and many years after, many African-Americans remained segregated in their own communities in Southern towns or in Northern cities and held onto many of their values and traditions. Nobles (1991) also states that a large number of Blacks were exposed to the White world or Western style of behavior in the 1950s with the invention of television and other media. African traditions persisted because African-Americans were viewed as inferior and generally were not accepted by mainstream America.

The group provides a natural form of helping since African people are so group-centered. Nobles (1973) contends that the African worldview is that the individual exists so that the group can survive and that individualism can be appreciated through the prosperity of the group. Placing the individual above the group would be considered undesirable behavior. The importance of the group in African philosophy is further emphasized by Mibiti (1970) who stated that individuals owe their lives to members of not only their immediate families, but also to deceased ancestors and those not yet born. Individuals do not exist unless they are communal—Africans operate on the premise that the community (tribe) made, created, and produced the individual. Rites of passage are designed to instill a sense of corporate responsibility and collective destiny. Therefore, when one hurts, everybody hurts; when one member celebrates, all celebrate. When couples marry, they are not alone but are part of the larger community. Children from marriages belong to the collective body.

According to Mibiti (1970), the African self-concept is "I am because we are; and because we are, therefore, I am." This philosophy is diametrically opposed to White Western values and is the missing link in therapeutic qualities needed to improve mental health for African-American people. When these are applied in the *Images of Me* group, African-American women experience a great deal of success.

Problems African-American Women May Encounter

A group for African-American women that incorporates African principles should be quite valuable in meeting many of their psychological needs. Many important life issues of Black women can be explored and worked through. Boyd-Franklin (1991) states that support groups provide opportunities for Black women to experience psychological growth because such groups make use of these women's strengths and create a supportive atmosphere where they can work through a great deal of their pain and can experience growth and change.

While African-American women are making progress in every field of human endeavor, many of them experience isolation, loneliness, hopelessness and sometimes despair. These conditions exist even though they are well educated and hold professional positions. By virtue of their educational level and professional status, many women are geographically isolated from their families of origin who otherwise could be a natural source of support. In addition, some of the women who work for large White corporations and institutions often occupy outgroup status on their jobs and suffer even more loneliness. This isolation is especially difficult for Black women from extended families who are accustomed to continuous interaction and support from extended family members, including grandparents, aunts, uncles, cousins, and friends. Clearly, there is a need for a homogenous group for Black women in which they can share their experiences, doubts, and fears in a nonthreatening and a supportive environment.

Boyd-Franklin (1991) suggests that such groups can provide opportunities to build support networks that are essential for their survival. The importance of unity among African-

American women is well illustrated by Terry McMillan (1992) in her book and movie, *Waiting to Exhale*. Although some negative comments have been made about the these works, they do show how valuable friendship and support can be for African-Americans. Mays (1985) discussed problems Black women encounter that could be explored through African-American groups. The more African-American women enter higher level professional groups, the more stress they will encounter and the greater the need for group therapy for stress reduction. In addition, two studies showed that divorced Black women encounter greater levels of stress than non-divorced Black women. Self-help groups provide support (Gottlieb, 1982) and develop a sense of community and group membership, which can lead to an increased sense of well-being (Katz, 1985).

Barriers to Efficacy for Group Counseling

It is vitally important that African-American women in group work have a positive experience and receive the help they need. This point is especially important because many women are having their first group therapy experience. Therefore, to increase the chance for a successful group experience, group leaders need to become aware of some of the key barriers to efficacy for group counseling with African-American women. The three barriers to be addressed in this section are: disregarding boundary management principles, application of Eurocentric group approaches, and manifesting bias in group counseling.

Disregarding Boundary Management Principles
The overall purpose of boundary management in group work is to set limits and to establish guidelines to increase the probability of having a successful group experience (Singer, Astrachan, Gould, & Klein, 1975). Groups without boundaries are like highways without speed limits or busy city streets without traffic lights, signs, or signals. A dangerous chaotic condition would persist with a high potential for people to become out of control or even physically hurt. Singer et al. (1975) suggested the following possible negative results when boundary management principles are ignored:

1.   Leader and member expectations may differ.
2.   Inappropriate tasks may cause casualties.

3. The desired outcome may be difficult to achieve.
4. Members might suffer psychological damage.
5. Confidentiality might be violated.
6. Tension within the leader not knowing what is *in* or *out* could occur.
7. Leaders may extend themselves beyond their expertise.

In their haste to get groups started, many leaders ignore boundary management issues, especially with regard to the selection of group members and in communicating the purpose of the group being offered. One of this book's writers is aware of a counseling case where one member was so disappointed with her group experience that she attempted suicide. This client, who had deep emotional problems, had signed up for a group intended to help college students adjust to college life. Closer attention to the principles of management in group selection would have been useful and might have saved her from an attempted suicide. African-American women, many of whom are not accustomed to psychological work in groups, do not succeed in groups because they are often not screened well and given a clear orientation about the process and expectations of the therapy to be done.

Many novice group leaders have unsuccessful group experiences because they accept all comers in an attempt to fill their group quota. Frequently such groups include members that Yalom (1985) has labeled undesirable. Often the qualities that make candidates undesirable for groups are those that prevent them and others from profiting from the group experience. According to Yalom (1985), those qualities include the following:

1. Mentally retarded or brain damaged—difficulty with insight and expression necessary for group
2. Paranoid—divisive
3. Extremely narcissistic—tend to monopolize
4. Hypochondriac—committed to denial/substitution
5. Suicidal—will keep group in crisis
6. Addicted to drugs/alcohol—invested in not changing lifestyle
7. Acutely psychotic—insufficient reality contact
8. Sociopathic—disrupt and control the group to meet own ends
9. Undergoing disruptive life crisis—may need to grieve more than construct new lifestyle at this point. (*Note:* If this type

of person has finished grieving over a loss, they can provide valuable input into a group.)
10. Successful recent experience with brief individual therapy—tend to resist group modality
11. Person overwhelmed by groups—tend not to interact
12. Strong fundamentalist/zealous religious person—uses belief in service of denial

We strongly suggest that this list be viewed through the lens of one with knowledge and understanding of the African-American experience. For example, in selecting a member who seems paranoid, try to determine if the paranoia is functional or clinical (Ridley, 1984). Functional paranoia is more a reaction to an environmental condition than clinical paranoia which tends to be a more internalized, deep-seated psychological condition.

Group work is complex and requires the best management a leader can provide to ensure success. Disregard for group boundaries has no place in the work of group leaders who work with African-American women in their struggle to survive and to achieve higher qualities of life. Such a positive outcome can be assured if groups are well planned with clear boundaries or set limits, using the purpose of the group as a guiding force.

Application of Eurocentric Group Approaches

Many therapists believe that "one size fits all," that individual or group therapy for European-Americans is equally effective with African-Americans, regardless of cultural/racial differences. Eurocentric therapy places the individual and his or her needs and concerns above everything or everybody else. Katz (1985) provides an outline of the white culture components, which are very similar to the components of counseling. The following list was adapted or paraphrased from a table in Katz's article:

1. Rugged individualism—Values independence, autonomy, individual responsibility and places the individual in control of his or her environment.
2. Competition—Winning is the most important goal in life—win at any cost.
3. Action orientation—Must take action to control life circumstances.

4. Communication—Standard English is the only acceptable language and is equated with the individual's intelligence.
5. Time—Must be adhered to rigidly.
6. History—Is based on European experiences in the U.S.
7. Protestant work ethic—Work hard to achieve goals.
8. Future orientation—Based on one's life or future events, delayed gratification is accepted and excepted.
9. Scientific method—Emphasis on rational and linear thinking. Quantitative results are more valuable than qualitative.
10. Status and power—Based on ownership of goods and property; positions, titles, and credentials are important.
11. Family structure—Male is head of household—focus is on a nuclear family based on the patriarchial system.
12. Aesthetics—Music and art are based on European cultures.
13. Religion—Based on Christianity only.

These values are deeply entrenched in the American culture and have a major influence on counseling theory and practice. Yet, while many group counseling leaders may acknowledge cultural differences in working with African-American women, they continue to apply Eurocentric approaches and techniques. This practice is a powerful barrier to African-American women's success in groups because these Eurocentric values are deeply embedded in the theories, practices, and worldviews of many therapists. Katz (1985) shows how components of counseling parallel the components of European culture. The following list is a brief outline of the cultural components of counseling:

1. The individual is the primary focus of therapy.
2. The individual client should take charge of her or his own life.
3. Clients are expected to exercise verbal skills, self-disclosure, and make eye contact with the therapist.
4. The goal of therapy is insight, awareness, and personal growth.
5. Client changes as a result of hard work.
6. Focus in counseling is primarily psychological versus the physiological.
7. There is a strict adherence to time with regard to scheduled appointments.

8. The nuclear family is preferred.
9. Counselors prefer clients who are young, attractive, verbal, intelligent, and successful.

Many therapists are not aware of the impact that their presence as European-Americans may have on African-American group members. According to McIntosh (1989), they are blind to White privileges they enjoy. Neither are they cognizant of the fact that they are beneficiaries and benefactors of racism in America and how such naiveté serves as a barrier to cross-racial communication and interaction (Helms, 1984). Unfortunately, counselors continue to explain African-American behavior or to understand African-American lifestyle using traditional theories developed by European and European-American psychologists. Given these factors, it should not be surprising that the counseling needs of ethnic minorities and African-American women have failed so miserably.

Manifesting Bias in Group Counseling

A second barrier to group counseling with African-American women is bias. Pedersen (1987) stated that many social scientists and psychologists look to psychological theory based on assumptions specific to European and American cultures. Because these assumptions are so implicit, they are rarely challenged even by broad-minded psychologists. Pedersen suggested that these unexplored assumptions often result in institutionalized racism, sexism, ageism, and various forms of cultural bias. Pedersen (1987) outlined the following 10 assumptions of cultural bias in counseling, most of which negatively affect the efficacy of counseling with African-Americans.

Normal behavior is defined the same by all cultures

1. *Assumptions regarding normal behavior*–Normal is limited to those standards of behavior practiced and accepted by middle-class European-Americans in general and by European-American men in particular. For example, the standard or norm for beauty in the Western culture is a White female who is thin with blonde hair and blue eyes. Other norms established by European-Americans place a tremendous burden on African-Americans whose standards are quite different. For

example, the communication patterns for some African-Americans consist of many people talking at the same time, joking, putting one another down, and talking loudly. These patterns, compared to communication patterns of some European-American families, may appear chaotic and dysfunctional to the European-American family therapist.

Individualism is pre-eminent

2. *Emphasis on individualism*–From the Western perspective, success in therapy depends on the development of the individual measured by factors such as autonomy, self-discovery, self-awareness, and self-actualization. It has already been stated that success in therapy from the African-American experience incorporates the development of the individual in concert with his or her unit, family, or community, based on a spirit of cooperation. Contrary to the Western perspective in therapy, African-Americans seek harmony with the family as a therapeutic goal in therapy.

Academic disciplines best serve the goals of therapy

3. *Fragmentation of academic disciplines*–In many cases, Eurocentric psychologists assume that clients can only be helped through social sciences including psychology, sociology, anthropology, theology, or medicine. Little or no value is placed on other disciplines where behavior might be understood or explained. Such cultural encapsulated boundaries place serious limitations on assistance from other sources clients could receive (Wrenn, 1962). For example, African-American women may receive help from their ministers, certain family members, relatives, beauticians, and several other natural caregivers other than counselors, psychologists, and mental health workers.

Abstract, theoretical communication best serves the ends of therapy

4. *Dependence on abstract thinking*–Counselors and psychologists from the Western perspectives use abstract words and phrases to the extent that many ethnic minority clients cannot comprehend them within the context of their life experiences. One of the writers' clients reported that she discontinued therapy with her European-American therapist because he did not sound "real" to her. Rather, his communication with her seemed more like he was reading from a psychology or sociology textbook. Certain words beyond the context or experience of the African-American individual have little or no meaning to them and are sometimes an impediment to rapport and to the development of the counseling relationship

Independence

5. *Overemphasis on independence*–Simply stated, many Western psychologists believe that one individual should not depend on another. Yet, in African-American communities and families, dependency is necessary for survival. Many stories are told about African-American families where the oldest member takes a job and sacrifices his or her education goals to help a younger sibling attend college. When this sibling finishes college and gets a job, her responsibility is to help a younger one. This process continues until the entire family is educated. Clearly, the assumption of dependency is not endorsed by Western, White, middle-class individuals but often does apply to many African-Americans. In our African-American women's group, the dependence of participants on one another is one of the strengths of the group.

Devaluation of clients' support system

6. *Neglect of clients' support systems*–Counselors often overlook the natural support system (family peer group, ministers, and so on) many ethnic minority clients use. This is unfortunate in light of the fact many counselors are unfamiliar with formal or professional helping agencies. Telling secrets to any stranger is unthinkable in many cultures. Pedersen (1987) suggests that clients' natural support systems should be mobilized rather than abandoned. Many African-Americans themselves learn this valuable lesson when they move their elderly parents from their homes, churches, and communities to live in larger city dwellings with them. The lack of support for the Black elderly is so devastating that they often lose their will to live. Extensive use is made of the natural support systems of our African-American participants.

Support for linear thinking

7. *Dependence on linear thinking*–Again, linear thinking and cause-and-effect relationships fit the Western model of counseling but often are confusing for other cultural groups who are nonlinear in their thinking. Many ethnic minority groups accept their effectiveness on faith or on some qualitative measure rather than by an objective measure that can only be proven through the empirical process. Recently, a program for African-American males was quite successful in improving grades in school and helping the boys feel better about themselves. The program lost its funding, however, because the effectiveness of the treatment program could not be proven through some standard or empirical method.

The individual must change to fit the system

8. *Focus on changing the individual, not the system*–"Is the goal of counseling to change the individual or the system?"; this is an age-old question in the counseling profession. There is a built-in assumption that the client should change to fit in. Therein lies the problem for many African-American clients who would prefer to drop out rather than buy into a system they perceive to be unfair and unjust. Some broad-minded social scientists have advocated that counselors should serve as change agents to change the system that impinges on their clients. When counselors become partners on behalf of their clients, they tend to do better. Draguns (1976) suggested that there be a balance between the client and the system, in which both the system and the client change for the growth and development of the client. Many African-American women believe they have spent most of their lives changing to fit what others need of them. Fortunately, many of these African-American women are beginning to stand their ground rather than give in to every societal expectation. In particular, we are referring to African-American women not buying into traditional sex role stereotypes.

Client history has negligible importance

9. *Neglect of history*–Many counselors believe that listening to the client's history is a practice of intellectualization and is a waste of their time. Such Eurocentric counselors are "here-and-now" focused and prefer to discuss only present events. Even though present client circumstances relate to the past, many counselors become bored and refuse to hear the stories. Historical traditions and events are an integral part of African culture and must be respected and understood. In African philosophy, past events hold special significance for African people. What has already happened and what is happening now are both important (Mibiti, 1970). A common statement by many African-Americans is: "If you don't know where you have been, you can't know where you are going." Discussing past events is the centerpiece for therapy. Group leaders for African-American women need to understand this phenomena because these women have stories to tell that must be heard. Many counselors become uncomfortable with historical information especially when African-Americans give accounts of racist practices and events during their early lives, often preferring not to hear these guilt- and shame-engendering stories.

Cultural perspective is not important

10. *Danger of cultural encapsulation*–According to Pedersen (1987), one of the greatest barriers to efficacy for group counseling with African-American women is the culturally encapsulated therapist who refuses to examine or challenge assumptions. More specifically, such individuals do not acknowledge their bias; therefore, they never take any responsibility for changing them.

Group leaders for African-American women are advised to examine personal biases and become aware of any negative biases they hold and use with regard to their feelings and behaviors toward ethnic minority individuals. Awareness is believed to be the first step toward change.

Facilitating Efficacy in Group Counseling

Efficacy is the capacity or power to achieve a desired result or outcome. In the previous section, we discussed some barriers to group efficacy with African-American women. This section identifies and discusses some of the forces that facilitate success for African-American women who participate in Afrocentric counseling or therapy groups. Specifically, the following paragraphs discuss: the role of Afrocentric group leaders, Afrocentric therapeutic forces, and the application of traditional counseling theories.

The Role of Afrocentric Group Leaders

The key to effective group outcome with African-American women using an Afrocentic approach is the group leaders. They have the tremendous task of managing the events and of balancing the emotions of the group. Because the basic African philosophy is essential, the leaders themselves must adhere to an African-centered belief system. Gainor (1992) believes the Black female leader needs to be aware of her own internalized oppression, especially as it manifests itself in her role as a group leader. She must seek a balance in her identity as a Black person. Overidentifying with members may lead them to have a lack of responsibility for their own lives. If she under-identifies, a leader might create a nontherapeutic atmosphere by appearing insensitive or noncaring (Trotman, 1984).

Gainor (1992) also believes that Black women who lead groups for Black women should ensure that they find the time and space to work through their own issues of internalized oppression in order to be able to deal with countertransfer-ential issues more effectively. She also suggests that these women leaders seek personal counseling or consultation to address their own issues. In addition, Gainor (1992) suggests that these leaders continue their professional growth by becoming more knowledgeable and insightful about internal-ized oppression. Chapter 9 discusses an approach to help women leaders achieve the key to effective group outcome with African-American women using an Afrocentric approach in more detail. We address the specific issues and realities for "sisters" promoting the mental health of "sisters" and the necessity of support for group leaders while they simulta-neously promote the mental health of African-American females. When worked through by members and leaders, the efficacy of groups for African-American women is much more powerful and productive. Group therapy is especially impor-tant for African-American women due to their out-group sta-tus based on dual low ethnic and gender status, building of a sense of community through identity, and certain stress reduc-tion interventions that may reduce stress and increase their ability to deal with emotional conflicts.

Of great importance for self-improvement among African-American women in the *Images of Me* group is their belief that the group facilitators will understand their problems or know their frame of reference. Given the circumstances in which African-American women find themselves, it is difficult to imagine who could direct an African-American women's group better than African-American women themselves; however, it is reasonable to assume that leaders from other racial/cultural groups could be effective with training. Exposure to the African-American experiences would enhance the potential effectiveness of therapists who are neither female or African-American. One or two workshops, a convention program, a course and reading materials on diversity are insufficient for effective Afrocentric group leadership. To develop empathy toward African-American women, leaders need to become involved with them on a personal level over a long period of time.

Afrocentric Therapeutic Forces

The healing qualities, or those factors that help group members grow and change, are called therapeutic forces. Yalom (1985) outlined several therapeutic forces in group therapy that seem to coincide with the characteristics of an African-centered philosophy. Based on this premise, the application of these therapeutic forces should yield positive results in group therapy for African-American women. The therapeutic forces we tend to employ consistently in an *Images of Me* group follow:

1. *Instillation of hope*–The key to efficacy is the belief that group work will help the participants reach their goal. The leader can facilitate the instillation of hope by providing encouragement, support, appropriate feedback, and knowledge about successful groups in the past. The leader can also help to instill hope by being optimistic about the value of the group experience. Hope is crucial for African-American women, many of whom have experienced so little success.

2. *The notion of universality*–Through universality, group members discover they are not the only ones with a problem (Yalom, 1985). One can observe this therapeutic force at work when African-American women come together in unity, discovering that they are not alone in their misery. Such experiences have the potential of lightening the load among African-American sisters. The counselor's or leader's role is to link these experiences and universal life events. Universality is facilitated more effectively when the leaders are African-Americans who are very familiar with the life experiences of other African-American women. The great number of common factors among African-American women

are uncanny. Fortunately, these commonalties can serve as a source of help.

3. *Altruism*–Altruism is the need to help other people. Altruism is reflective of Afrocentric thought because the individual group member receives her meaning and purpose by helping other group members. It is representative of the sense of collective responsibility when the individual feels responsible for her community, her tribe, and her family. Group members can be informed that one way to grow and change is through altruism, helping others. These writers believe that all group members have something special to offer others. Our role as leaders is to help members identify their gifts and to use them in a therapeutic manner.

4. *Existential factors*–Realizing that even though life is tough at times, it must be faced. Group members can benefit from sharing their life circumstances and by sharing ways they have been able to cope with those tough life conditions. When members become aware that they are a part of a larger family who love and care about them, they are much better able to go through the various storms of life.

5. *Group cohesion*–According to Yalom (1985), group cohesion is one of the most powerful therapeutic forces operating within a therapy group. When group members come together and share their most intimate world with others and are accepted by them, regardless of how severe their problems are, healing often takes place. The other key ingredient in group cohesion is the ability to trust and help other group members. Giving and receiving help often brings about a powerful sense of belonging unequal to other experiences members encounter. Several research studies have shown that group cohesion has contributed to most positive outcomes for group members resulting in feelings of security, acceptance, and a strong sense of belonging.

Group cohesion is achieved through facilitating intermember acceptance, recognizing similarities of group members and leaders (all African-American women with similar problems), and by encouraging specific contributions from each member. As group leaders, we really work hard to achieve group cohesion among our African-American women's group because with it we can bring about the therapeutic changes these women deserve.

The Application of Traditional Theories

Although we have attempted to show that traditional Eurocentric approaches are not always suitable for understanding and explaining the behavior of African-Americans, certain of these approaches do tend to coincide with African-American experiences. Group counseling approaches in general are appropriate for African people because they coincide more with African orientation. The nondirective, "do-it-yourself " approach is often seen as threatening and less appropriate. Many counselors believe that certain traditional counseling approaches might be helpful for African-American women. Specifically, some suggest that a cognitive-behavioral approach might be useful for meeting African-American women's therapeutic needs because there is a focus on changing behavior and cognition. Many traditional approaches do not work, often because they are so passive, indirect, and abstract. For example, in client-centered therapy, the responsibility for growth and change rests on the shoulder of the client who is given little or no structure or direction. In addition, theories like transactional analysis consist of such a wide range of abstract words that participants become lost or lose sight of their reasons for being in therapy.

Existential Approaches

Some social scientists have suggested that existential approaches are valuable for ethnic minority clients. It is reasonable to believe that the five qualities or factors representing existentialism advanced by Yalom (1985) would be appropriate for African-American women's groups. These existential factors include: (1) recognizing that life is at times unfair and unjust; (2) recognizing that ultimately there is no escape from some of life's pain and from death; (3) recognizing that no matter how close one gets to other people, he or she must still face life alone; (4) facing the basic issues of life and death, and thus living their lives more honestly and being less caught up in trivialities; and (5) learning that one must take ultimate responsibility for the way he or she lives life, no matter how much guidance and support he or she gets from others.

In the existential approach, clients are directed to deal with the realities of life as they are rather than how the individual would like life to be. This model seems appropriate for African-Americans because their lives are filled with many painful realities, suffering and pain. Yalom (1985) states that existential therapy is not a set of techniques but an attitude toward life. This approach suggests that the individual's basic struggle is for survival in the world in which he or she lives. Existential therapy helps group members deal with the realities of life.

Cognitive-Behavioral Therapy

Another traditional group therapy approach to use with African-American women is the cognitive-behavioral approach, which focuses on the role of thinking in influencing our sense of well-being and in controlling our mental health. Many social scientists believe there is a link between emotions and behaviors and cognitive processes; therefore, how people think about themselves can largely determine how they feel, behave, and perceive the world.

Cognitive-behavioral group approaches overlaid with Afrocentric philosophy would be an excellent place for African-American women to think through many of their conflicting and troubling issues in an understanding and supportive environment. Thinking through issues can often reduce the size of certain gigantic issues to more manageable levels. If cognitive-behavioral therapies are conducted by sensitive Afrocentric group leaders, positive results may occur. Yet this approach is not a "cure-all" and should be used with caution; that is, the leader needs to be careful not to focus so much on the cognitive that he or she neglects the emotional examination of clients. Readers are advised to remember that African philosophy emphasizes wholeness and not departmentalization.

The Efficacy of Women's Groups Using African Philosophy

It has been suggested throughout this chapter that African-American women participating in African-centered groups led by Afrocentric group leaders would receive tremendous therapeutic benefits. This section points out some of the benefits of participating in such groups. We are convinced that a well-developed group conducted by or coordinated by an African-American with a positive racial identity will result in regeneration, self-renewal, and meaningful communication. Such a group process would provide internal cleansing, meaningful reflection, and, in general, serve as a corrective guide. Boyd-Franklin (1991) reasoned that many important life issues for African-American women can be explored and worked through in groups. She states further that support groups offer opportunities for African-American women to experience psychological growth and change. These groups make use of strength within these women and provide an atmosphere or condition where these participants can explore and work through a great deal of the pain they often encounter.

Gainor (1992) suggested that African-American women's groups provide members the opportunities to explore their personal beings as African-American persons in general and African-American women in particular. With other African-American women, there is a sense of sisterhood and belonging, as well as an opportunity for personal growth. Trotman and Gallagher (1987) also suggested that members within groups that are comprised solely of African-American women are able to address issues of self-confidence, multiple role conflict, powerlessness, and personal and career goals within an environment of their most important support and peer group. Gainor (1992) also pointed out that internalized oppression and incorporation or acceptance of mistreatment, prejudice, and racism can be a major distraction in meeting the goals of African-American women in groups. Manifestations of internalized oppression may include some of the following:

1. Finding fault, criticizing, and invalidating one another so that the group might become divided.
2. Attacking, criticizing, or having unrealistic expectations of leaders.
3. Developing defensive patterns of fear of other African-Americans by being embarrassed or hurt by them.
4. Accepting a narrow view of what it means to be African-American; that is, criticizing other African-Americans for talking a certain way, because they like classical music, or because they can't play basketball.
5. Tolerating and internalizing other forms of oppression such as classism, sexism, anti-Semitism, and homophobia.

These layers of oppression must be removed if successful group experiences are to occur.

Itzen (1985) believes that working to eliminate internalized oppression helps groups of oppressed people function in a more productive manner. African-American women work through their fear of other African-American women and move toward developing group cohesiveness.

McNair (1992) outlined several issues African-American women face that could be worked through in group, including the following:

1. Stereotyping as being strong and domineering as opposed to being feminine and intelligent. This condition may result from African-Americans' role during and after slavery when women worked alongside the men.
2. A second issue is that an African-American woman is viewed as the Black matriarch, the "boss" who heads the family household. Because these women are expected to be strong and aggressive, they may have difficulty acknowledging their pain and may be reluctant to receive help from psychological services.
3. African values or extended families in which members help one another may be viewed as pathological. Many successful African-American women help their parents, grandparents, nieces, nephews, and other family members. Many of these women have been known to provide financial assistance to family members going through difficult times.
4. Successful, well-educated African-American females also feel pressure finding suitable males. These women struggle over questions about relationships. Should they date men from other racial/ethnic groups, select men below their educational and career status, or settle for living their lives as single females?

Again, the group can help in dealing with these issues.

Adherence to the Principles of Boundary Management Is the Key to Group Efficacy

We are confident that the group process principles set forth in this chapter will yield positive results in meeting many of the mental health needs of African-American women; however, group leaders can be even more assured of success if they follow the basic principles of boundary management advanced by

Singer et al. (1975). Simply stated, the main purpose of boundary management is to set critical limits conducive to accomplishment of a group's task. The key boundaries to be managed in an African-American women's group are leader qualities, member suitability, and the appropriateness of the group's task.

Leader Qualities

We have already suggested that the ideal group leaders for African-American women would be other African-Americans. The specific qualities of these women leaders were outlined by Cross (1991) in the advanced stages of the Nigrescence Model. The brief descriptions of stages 4 and 5 that have been adapted from Cross's model.

Stage 4: Internalization

- The individual achieves inner peace and a more realistic analysis of the oppressive racist system.
- Proactive Black pride, self-love, and a sense of connection to the African-American community is achieved.
- Perception of one's self as an African-American is what gives purpose to life.
- The individual sees herself/himself as a builder of bridges between Blacks and Whites.

Stage 5: Internalization–Commitment

- Translates personal sense of Blackness into a plan of action.
- Rethinks what it means to be African-American from a more mature stage of development.

Additional qualities are those commonly known as facilitative conditions including trust, caring, warmth, acceptance, and unconditional positive regard. Research has shown that when these conditions exist, people change and grow in a positive and healthful direction.

Member Suitability

The second boundary is member suitability for the group. When this is given high priority, probability of success rises. Yalom (1985) listed the following six categories or general considerations for success in group:

1. The client has had successful group experiences in the past, which could include experience with peers, family, school, and so on.
2. The client is willing and able to make a commitment to change in specific ways with the help of the group.
3. The client has positive expectations for the group experience.
4. The client is less devoted to social inhibition, therefore can serve as a catalyst for the group.
5. The client is recommended by the previous therapist (beware of the therapist who refers someone to a group instead of terminating a client).
6. The client is work-oriented.

When exploring these categories for selecting group members, leaders need to examine each suitability consideration for appropriateness for the African-American experiences. In other words, this selection process should be done with the life circumstance of African-American women in mind; for example, many will never have had any previous group therapy experience. Therefore, the group leader would have to find another way to determine how those participants would function in a group. For example, we have used role-plays during the pretherapy training period to determine appropriateness for group participation. This book's authors also determine suitability through casual conversation and interaction. When members are found to be unsuitable for an *Images of Me* group, we put forth special efforts to find other appropriate modes of treatment.

Task Appropriateness
The task boundary monitors the appropriateness of group activities with the purpose of the group. A key management task is seeking a balance between the amount of cognitive and emotional material to examine or explore. If one follows the African philosophy, she would be comfortable in allowing the emotional and cognitive material to flow in a natural manner rather than attempting to control it too strictly. Another task management challenge is to provide culturally relevant activities to which these African women can relate; activities reflective of African-American values, customs, and traditions are the most appropriate. Some of these activities are described in later chapters.

Actualizing Efficacy through the *Images of Me* Group

In this chapter we have discussed the efficacy of Afrocentric group work with African-American women. We are well qualified to discuss the application of African principles in group work because we have operationalized these principles and practices in a group we have conducted for more than 10 years. The group about which we are speaking, titled *Images of Me,* is a group for African-American females. The group, which originated on a predominantly white university campus, was organized to meet the counseling, mental health, and psychological needs of African-American female students. In particular, these women presented a wide range of problems and issues, including isolation, anger, depression, confusion around gender and racial identity, as well as racism and sexism.

Although the *Images of Me* group originated on a university campus, it has since been offered off campus for African-American women in a variety of community agency settings and in private practice. The leaders of *Images of Me* groups are diverse African-American mental health professionals such as psychologists, licensed clinical counselors, and social workers. We have often used previous members as co-leaders, especially those who have exhibited exceptional skills in leadership, assertion, empathy, openness to learning, and knowledge of racial and gender issues.

Selection of Members

An important variable to the success of the *Images of Me* group is the selection of appropriate group members. In general, we select African-American women who have the ability to communicate with others in a caring and supportive manner. It has been our experience that most women who volunteer for our group are suitable. Many of them are isolated, alienated, angry, confused, and are often conflicted with racial and gender identity issues. The high level of patience and caring by the leaders allows for acceptance of members with severe problems that ordinarily would not be viewed as suitable for some of the more traditional counseling or therapy groups. However, we tend to screen out women in crisis and those whose problems are so severe that they cannot interact with others. When we determine that a member's presence in the group would be a barrier to the growth and progress of the group, we deselect her and assist in finding more suitable modes of treatment. For example, women in severe crisis, resulting from divorce or a death in the family, tend to do better in individual therapy. However, we make these selection decisions on a case-by-case basis.

Procedures for Advertising the Group

A variety of methods and procedures for advertising the *Images of Me* group is used. Perhaps the most consistent procedure is "word of mouth" in which women who have participated in previous groups recommend the group to their friends. A second procedure for advertising the *Images of Me* group is through church announcements because many African-American women do attend church. A third method is to make announcements about the group to African-American women organizations such as sororities, civic organizations, and social clubs. Fourth, we use many of the traditional advertising media such as radio announcements, newspaper articles, brochures, flyers, and so forth.

Getting the Group Started

An *Images of Me* group can be initiated in most communities where African-American women live. We offer the following guidelines for those who would like to initiate a group in their community:

1. Identify two African-American female mental health professionals with training in group process, racial and gender identity development, and an appreciation and knowledge of and skills in using an Afrocentric approach to mental health.

2. Identify a location for the group that is within the community where members live; examples include the church, a professional office building located near the community, and a school/ university setting that offers a warm and nurturing, culturally appropriate environment. The environment could be enhanced by selecting proper music, videos, literature, helping interventions that reflect the African-American female and send the message, "You are welcomed and appreciated here."

3. Use a wide variety of procedures for recruiting members including "word of mouth" and other strategies to connect with African-American women where they usually are involved—churches, sororities, social, and civic organizations.

4. After members have been recruited, prepare them for the group experience by (1) explaining the group process,

(2) clarifying expectations, (3) establishing group rules, and (4) developing a group contract.

5. Design a closed group by setting a limit of 10 women who will attend all sessions from the beginning to the end.

6. Be reminded that the task of the first meeting is to establish the structure of the group, to help the women feel safe and secure, and to have them feel a sense of belonging. Introduce the issue of confidentiality by informing and educating group members about the significance of "What is said and done in the group, stays in the group." The honor system is strongly encouraged and often couched within the concept of family and sisterhood. Prayer generally is a part of ending sessions and helps to cement the need to be a family and to keep our work within the group. Outside cliques are discouraged and we discuss the influence of such cliques. We encourage the group to function as sisters and to do so collectively.

7. Begin each group meeting with some degree of preparation so members will know what is expected of them. End each group with some degree of assessment or evaluation to give members the opportunity to examine the extent to which their goals have been achieved.

8. Group leaders are encouraged to discuss or summarize each group meeting with other leaders for both planning and evaluative purposes.

9. Group leaders are encouraged to model the skills they want members to learn, especially those centered around communication and interaction. In addition, leaders need to be symbols of hope because many group members have very little hope at the time they join a group.

10. Group leaders also need to be skilled in leader functions such as caring and emotional stimulation. Many of the women in an *Images of Me* group need to be nurtured and given valid reasons to enjoy and to be excited about life. African-American female leaders are the most appropriate ones to actualize these qualities in group work.

Preparing Members for the *Images of Me* Group

Because ethnic minorities are not as habituated to using psychological and mental health services as members of European ancestry, they could benefit more from preparation for these services. In particular, we believe that African-American women can gain more from group counseling or therapy when they are prepared for it. It has been our experience and belief in our work with the *Images of Me* group that the better the members understand what group counseling or therapy is, the more they will gain from it once the group is started. We have observed that there are several reasons to prepare African-American women for group; the following are some of them:

1. *To reduce anxiety*– Many African-American women are afraid of any kind of psychological services simply because these activities have not been an integral part of their cultural values.

2. *To help members understand the group process*–African-American women need to know how the group works if they expect to gain the most from it. We explain how participation in group will help to reduce their pain or solve their problems.

3. *To clarify expectations*–When group members know what to expect from the group experience, their anxiety is reduced and they come prepared to work with much more confidence.

4. *To demystify the therapy process*–Historically there is something mysterious about psychological services. Such ideas and thoughts are usually erroneous and serve as barriers to the therapeutic process. We let these women know that they have a certain amount of control over what happens to them in group therapy.

5. *To enhance group effectiveness*–Again, African-American women who are prepared for group therapy come ready to work rather than spending the first few sessions in fear that some unknown thing may occur.

6. *To reduce fear by giving information about the group*– Essentially, we explain in plain language how the group works, what rules we expect to follow, what barriers we expect to encounter, and what roles members and leaders may play.

Several methods have been used to prepare members for group including the cognitive approach, the vicarious approach, and the experiential approach. In our preparation procedures, we use a combination of all three because we provide some information (cognitive approach), we do a certain amount of modeling about what happens in group (vicarious approach), and we actually get members involved directly in their therapy (experiential approach). Experience shows that a combination of methods is better than any one of the three methods alone. The cognitive approach is quite useful for teaching group members about (1) expected behavior, (2) explaining the therapy process, (3) developing a contract, and (4) explaining group rules. The vicarious approach helps when we have members who seem to learn best through role-plays or role rehearsals. In particular, we use role-plays (vicarious) to show effective ways to confront, to give feedback, and to illustrate how group members can self-disclose their feelings. We believe that it is essential for African-American women to learn how to express their true feelings and to feel comfortable doing it.

In an *Images of Me* group, pregroup preparation serves several important functions. First, we are able to build rapport, a first step toward forming therapeutic alliances. In this process we try to reduce anxiety, explain the therapy process, and establish some of the group norms. The second function is to do an assessment of the members' ability to communicate with others. For example, we might ask a future member how others would feel in certain situations or what suggestions or advice they might offer to another member with a problem. A final function of pregroup preparation is to clarify therapeutic goals and to identify a specific agenda for achieving the goals. Before the group begins, we find it extremely useful to help members become crystal clear concerning the problem or issue they choose to address; clarity about the goal for being in therapy is half the battle.

In the process of pregroup preparation, we cover at least two content areas of information. The first area of information is about group therapy. Not wanting to overwhelm new members with too much information, we discuss the value of self-disclosure as an avenue toward personal growth and toward improved interpersonal relations. We explain that, in general, people who express their feelings not only enjoy better mental health, but also experience better physical health. Members are told that they will be giving and receiving feedback, and that such feedback will be given in the present time or as it happens. Past events may be discussed as long as they can be linked to immediate issues and concerns.

The second content area covered in pregroup preparation is group process and development. Here we explain the group process through stages and discuss roughly what to expect at each stage. For example, we provide the following summary about group stages:

1. *Initial*–Acceptance, belonging, and security are key issues.
2. *Transition*–Competition, power struggles, and resistance are key issues.
3. *Working*–Cohesion, cooperation, unity, and problem solving are essential characteristics.
4. *Termination*–Closure, completing unfinished business, summarizing, and making follow-up plans are major tasks.

We usually end the pregroup session with some information concerning the value of the *Images of Me* group. Here we initiate the instillation of hope by discussing the benefits of the group. We tell stories of African-American women who were able to learn, grow, and change by committing themselves to the work of the group and by having high expectations that they could get better.

Summary

African-American women working with other African-American women to help meet their psychological needs, using African-centered philosophies, offer hope for improving the life circumstances of thousands of women. Efficacy will not be achieved unless group leaders identify the barriers and seek to overcome them. Group leaders and members alike can be a powerful source of destruction or efficacy, depending on how their positions are used. We believe that it is important for leaders to achieve ego statuses or attitudes that approach advanced levels of racial identity development. They should feel good about themselves as Americans with African ancestry. They must be knowledgeable about the African worldview and well connected with their African-American communities. While these leaders have a strong African-American identity, they are knowledgeable about those Eurocentric models or therapeutic concepts that tend to meet the counseling and mental health needs of African-American women. African-American women have lost too many battles to lose again. We need to assume that they will win the battles through culturally relevant boundary management of psychological work in groups. Management of these essential boundaries can be actualized with the supportive care of African-American women.

Given that many African-American women have limited experiences with psychological groups and for other mental health services, we strongly advocate pregroup training or preparation. The purpose of such preparation is to put these women at ease and to provide them with a sense of control over what will happen in the group. We have learned that members gain more from the group experience when they know what to expect.

The next chapter focuses on purpose, which offers even clearer guidelines toward the achievement of efficacy among African-American women. Purpose cannot be overemphasized because it is the centerpiece of the group.

References

Aubrey, R. F., & Lewis, J. (1983). Social issues and the counseling profession. *Counseling and Human Development, 15*(10).

Boyd-Franklin, N. (1991). Recurrent themes in the treatment of African-American women in group therapy. *Women in Therapy, 11*(2), 25–40.

Cross, W. (1991). *Shades of Black*. Philadelphia: Temple University Press.

Draguns, J. G. (1976). Counseling across cultures: Common themes and distinct approaches. In P. B. Pedersen, J. G. Draguns, W. L. Lonner, & J. E. Trimble (Eds.) *Counseling across cultures* (pp. 3–21). Honalulu: University Press of Hawaii.

Gainor, K. A. (1992). Internalized oppression as a barrier to effective group work with Black women. *Journal of Specialists in Group Work, 17*, 235–242.

Gottlieb, B. H. (1982). Mutual-help groups: Member's views of their benefits and of roles for professionals. *Prevention in Human Services, 1*(3), 55–67.

Grier, W., & Cobbs, P. (1968). *Black rage*. New York: Bantam Books.

Helms, J. E. (1984). Toward a theoretical explanation of the effects of race on counseling: A black/white interactional model. *The Counseling Psychologist, 12*, 153–163.

Itzen, C. (1985). Margaret Thatcher is my sister. Counseling on divisions between women. *Women's Studies Internalizational, 8*, 73–80.

Katz, A. H. (1985). The components of White culture: Values and beliefs. *The Counseling Psychologist*, (p. 618). Beverly Hills: Sage Publications, Inc.

Mays, V. M. (1985). Black women and stress: Utilization of self-help groups for stress reduction. *Women in Therapy, 4*(4), 67–79.

McIntosh, P. (1989). White privilege: Unpacking the invisible knapsack. *Peace and Freedom, 49*(2), 31–36.

McMillan, T. (1992). *Waiting to exhale*. New York: Pocket Books.

McNair, L. D. (1992). African-American women in therapy: An Afrocentric feminist synthesis. *Women in Therapy, 12*(3), 5–17.

Mibiti, J. S. (1970). *African religions and philosophies.* Garden City, NY: Anchor Books/Doubleday.

Nobles, W. W. (1973). Psychological research and the Black self-concept: A critical review. *Journal of Social Issues, 29,* 11–31.

Nobles, W. W. (1991). African philosophy: Foundations of Black psychology. In R. L. Jones, *Black psychology* (3rd ed.) (pp. 47–63). Berkeley: Cobb & Henry Publishers.

Pedersen, P. (1987). Ten frequent assumptions of cultural bias in counseling. *Journal of Multicultural Counseling and Development, 15,* 16–24.

Ridley, C. R. (1984). Clinical treatment of nondisclosing Black client. *American Psychologist, 39*(11), 1234–1244.

Shapiro, J. L. (1978). *Methods of group psychotherapy and encounter: A tradition of innovation.* Itasca, IL: Peacock Publishers.

Singer, D., Astrachan, B. M., Gould, L. J., & Klien, E. B. (1975). Boundary management in psychological work with groups. *Journal of Applied Behavioral Sciences, 11*(2), 137–176.

Sue, D. W., & Sue, D. (1990). *Counseling the culturally different: Theory and practice* (2nd ed.). New York: John Wiley and Sons.

Trotman, F. K. (1984). Psychotherapy with Black women and the dual effect of racism and sexism. In C. M. Brody (Ed.), *Women therapists working with women* (pp. 96–108). New York: Springer.

Trotman, F. K., & Gallagher, A. H. (1987). Group therapy with Black women. In C. M. Brody (Ed.), *Women's therapy groups* (pp. 118–131). New York: Springer.

White, J. L., Parham, W. D., & Parham, T. A. (1980). Black psychology: The Afro-American tradition as a unifying force for traditional psychology. In R. L. Jones (Ed.), *Black psychology* (2nd ed.). New York: Harper & Row.

Wrenn, G. G. (1962). The culturally encapsulated counselor. *Harvard Educational Review, 32,* 444–449.

Yalom, I. D. (1985). *Theory and practice of group psychotherapy* (3rd ed.). New York: Basic Books, Inc.

4

Am I Crazy or Is This What's Happening?—Nia

Nia (nee-ah) means purpose; that is, to make our collective vocation the building and developing of our community to restore our people to their traditional greatness. Developed in 1988, it is the fifth principle (see Preface and Chapter 1) of *the Nguzo Saba* by Dr. Maulana Karenga (Hoyt-Goldsmith, 1993). As the principle of purpose gives our lives direction, "we focus on actions and the consequences of our actions" (Hoyt-Goldsmith, 1993, p. 20). Group members' constant quest for meaning and purpose is framed in the Afrocentric tradition of Nia.

The women in our groups examine the joy of having purpose and sharing their purpose with others. Purpose seems to build a bridge that enhances connections to others. Marie describes her yearning as the "expectation to serve others in a meaningful way." When we examine the Nguzo Saba principle of purpose, we believe in the setting of goals with the intention of accomplishing them.

In honor of purpose, "we think about our actions and the consequences of our actions" (Hoyt-Goldsmith, 1993, p. 20). The women of our groups have many things in common, one of which is the belief that God is at the center of our existence. When one thinks and behaves in a God-centered manner, one begins on a different plane than the person who does not have any consciousness of God. Our actions are essentially watched and evaluated by the Being we allow to ultimately guide our actions. We struggle with the task we must carry out to benefit our people. As a group, we evaluate the task or behaviors of the group members as they pertain to purpose or usefulness. We discuss the importance of task usefulness to the empowerment of our people as a whole.

Group members struggle to reorient their thinking and, in some instances, to reach for a way of thinking that is mindful of purpose. For one group member, Marie, purpose becomes an effort to work toward a common good by serving people who, due to societal ills, become disadvantaged. Those social ills include lack of employment or underemployment, welfare—"a system that seems to keep you helpless," according to Marie—and inadequate knowledge of how to effectively change their circumstances. Marie talks about seeing herself as Harriet Tubman, showing people the way and empowering them to move toward their goals in spite of adversity; she shares her purpose with the group:

Marie: I see myself as a person with many gifts and talents. My parents had the means to protect me from many of society's harsh realities. I went to college, completed and got out to get a job that will help people. My thinking is to put a stop to the harmful things that happen to people. The stuff that keeps them from showing their God-given talents... [*pause*]... idealistic, huh? I believe it with all my heart, just like Harriet Tubman. There is nothing that I'll let stand in my way. Sister Tubman had it too. She had it real bad. She risked her life. She wasn't afraid of anything. No one, absolutely no one stood in her way. That's me. Each time I read more about her, the stronger I feel it. Nothing, nothing, nothing will stop me.

My mom once told me, "Girl, you have some drive." Well, let me tell you how I see taking as many with me as possible. I have administrative responsibilities. That means I make policy. Do you know how important it is to be in a position of making policy? Let me tell you, that and being in the budget department are where we can make sure our people are well-served. We know what they need, not those self-serving, narrow-minded White people who seem to only want to keep low-income people in the "one down" position. I know that sounds harsh. I don't dwell on their lack of understanding, I just move on as best I can.

Vy looks at Marie and comments:

Vy: You really see yourself getting things done that help people. How did you get there? My thinking gets so-o-o-o-o-o bogged down that I can't see what's going on.

Marie: Well, Linda (group co-leader) helped me understand the drive I had internally. It's like this. If I see a child being sad and unhappy, I'll ask that child what's wrong. Maybe she lost her pencil or nobody is playing with her. Well, I can help her find the pencil or teach her how to look for things that will help her be more effective in her search. You know how kids look for things. They don't look under or behind stuff. So I'll show her how. Then I'll teach her how to identify a special place to put her pencil so she can put it there when she is done next time. We'll see if she can buy two or three pencils to keep as spares if she misplaces the pencil again.

I really like problem solving. Linda called it energy and drive. We looked at how the energy and drive can be directed. As a young child, I was labeled "hyper" by my teachers which made me feel bad. I would get in trouble for being so energetic. I felt horrible and got into so much trouble. Linda said to think of it as helping people prepare for living better, more fulfilling lives. It's like I could hang a usefulness to this feeling I have and then I could learn to direct it toward the good of my people. When we talk about Nia, you know, the Kwanzaa word that means purpose, it makes me feel good about being a high-energy person so I let it work for the betterment of my people. So the little girl and the pencil example is what my theme is in life. It can be taken to many levels. This group has helped me define my direction and redefine how I can be useful. I've also been encouraged to learn about my African history and ancestry to find examples that urge me on. Harriet Tubman is one of my favorites.

Dr. Karenga (1966) stated "The first step forward is a step backward to Africa and our roots. We use the past as a foundation on which to construct our future" (Hoyt-Goldsmith, 1993, p. 7). When African-Americans are searching for a place and meaning, it is important that they receive guidance concerning the most empowering and affirming places to begin one's search. To begin with a philosophy that views the African way of being as positive and healthy permits African-Americans to lay a firm groundwork for success, and places them on the road toward embracing their true identity. The women in *Images of*

Me groups collectively explore the individual and a collective purpose in building and developing our community.

Vy shares with the group how helpful it was for her to hear Marie explain what she does with her energy and drive:

Vy: That is good to know, Marie. You really helped me in a big way. I think I make things complicated and confusing. The pencil and the little girl example was great. I remember hearing a person say once "keep it simple." I try to make too much of the situation and lose focus, something that I work on here in this group. The end product is confusion. But if I stay focused on Nia, the purpose, I don't get baffled. Learning to change my thinking from serving self to serving the betterment of my community. There is a balance. I know I can't give, give, give without nourishing me. Giving too much will only weaken me and make me ineffective and even sick sometimes. Being a part of this group taught me to draw on history and to reorient my thinking. As I reorient my thinking, I study African-American history and African history. Doing that helps me feel proud and good. Wow! Did they ever do a lot, and some with very little resources. I know I have much more going for me than those in slavery, so I just use whatever I have. Sometimes all I have is myself. I am learning that the "picture" is much larger than just here in this town. As African-Americans, we have the responsibility of lifting up the whole world! Not single-handedly, but many-handedly. I love being in this group. It shows me that, as a people, we can go a long way. Our community can get better. Even if it is one person at a time.

We work with the "natural curative power" of an African-centered process of group work (Harris, 1992).

Collective survival and interdependence group work for African-American women works because we rely on one another and a group form provides the environment for enacting collective survival and interdependence. The group examines interactions in a variety of ways, as can be seen through Shari's and other group members' accounts.

The group has been meeting for three weeks. Shari struggles with examining her motives and searching for purpose in her relationship with her partner. The problem is fresh in her mind and she discusses an experience she had the morning before the group; later Mary adds commentary. Shari begins by personally examining her motives, and a possible PMS experience, and by recounting her inevitable difficulty in reducing the anger.

Shari: I attended a planning meeting with teachers and administrators. My role as advisor to the Black students is to work toward their involvement in the program of the school.
The agenda was set and I was not on it to present the goals and objectives of the student group I represented. First, I thought they merely made a mistake. It was one person in particular, Joan, who had dismissed my request in the past. It's going through my mind that Joan is up to her old ways. I resisted blaming her and found myself wondering if this all-White Christian group was showing how prejudiced they were by ignoring my request. I started to get really angry, but I didn't want to believe that, so I decided to wait and see. I'm keeping an account of these events to see if it will occur again.
Mary: Shari, sounds to me like you're keeping "score."
Shari: [*Shari looked surprised and attempted to deny it but caught herself. She chuckled and smiled.*] Yeah, I guess so.

The group launched into the subject of anger: Anger lies just beneath the surface for many African-American women attending the group and it manifests itself in many forms. Shari worked hard at denying her anger, but there is a good possibility that she remained unaware of its intensity until the group probed deeper. The form of anger Shari exhibited is not unusual; for years she has had to compromise her wants and needs for security, a security that appeared false, and has received much more in the way of negative energy than she bargained for. It seems that Shari has also received many negative vibes in her marriage. Sadly she realized there was no purpose in her marriage. We tried to return to the issue of her place of employment, but quickly reverted to the more pressing issue of Shari's marriage. Sadness flowed through her expressions:

Shari: Work for me is an escape but lately it's been no joy. It is nice to come to group. I have a lot on my mind... [*pause*] ... yeah, I'm keeping score with my boss and anyone else who bothers me. I think the source of my troubles is my home life. Nothing seems to go right. I feel myself going down and down. It is a long and sad story. Other homes and marriages seem so much better than mine. [*Shari inserted her experience of "carrying" her husband.*]

I'm tired of looking at this man in my house doing nothing! Every time I look at him, I get mad. He does nothing for our son, nothing around the house, pays very few bills, and demands that things go his way. He's crazy! Why do I put up with this mess? Last night as I was getting ready for bed, I noticed his washcloth. It had crabs on it. I called it to his attention but he denied having an affair. We haven't had sex for a year and, believe me, it won't happen again, ever.

Tearfully Shari talked about her anger and how she waits and wonders what to do, as did Mary. The group focused on Shari's "no win" situation.

Mary: Why do you stay?
Shari: I've been married before. I left and divorced because he was unfaithful. While living on my own with my children, someone broke into my home. I don't mean just got a door open and came in, but busted the whole door frame out from the wall. When I came home, everything was a mess. I was too scared to stay there, so a friend, now my husband, offered to let me stay with him. My youngest son was soon to go off to college, so I just stayed with Gerald. I caught myself pitching in by cooking and cleaning. We both worked full-time and shared the expenses for the house. Well, one thing led to another and we decided to get married. I didn't love Gerald then, I don't love him now. But I got pregnant and had Benjamin. I believe a child should have a relationship with his father and so now, 10 years later, here I am. I want to do what's right. I paid for my divorce last year. My attorney won't send the money back because she says I will file again, but I don't know what God wants me to do in this situation. I created all of this and now a child is involved. Gerald is a crazy man and I'm stuck. I feel pulled in all directions.

Exercises to Help Demonstrate Experiences

The exercises that follow were developed from spur-of-the-moment creativity by group leaders. In *Images of Me* groups, we attempt to behaviorally demonstrate the words and stories described by a group member.

The Push–Pull

The group leader invited Shari to participate in an exercise physically demonstrating what Shari had described. Shari willingly agreed. The leader instructed three volunteers from the group to stand on Shari's left and three volunteers to stand on her right. Shari was asked to extend her arms at shoulder height out to her sides. People on each side clasped her arms and began to gently pull and push, sometimes in opposite directions and sometimes in the same one. Group members began to verbally make demands. Voices either represented persons from Shari's place of employment, her family members, or her circle of friends and acquaintances.

The chatter modulated from loud to soft, never stopping completely. Through most of the exercise, Shari smiled, remarking how confused she felt. Actually she felt very tense. Shari's smile eventually changed to a mixture of worry and anger, and she attempted to answer the numerous requests and demands the voices made; however, the requests came too rapidly, one overlapping the other. The group leader instructed her to speed up her answers, using those with one-word. Shari's frustration level quickly became evident and she began to cry, unable to speak for several minutes. Group members discontinued the pulling and pushing at that point. While the group members held Shari, a motion intended to convey warmth and support, she expressed her confused and overwhelmed feelings. Processing the experience became a group effort. Supportive phrases, such as the following, were used:

> "You look very uncomfortable, Shari. Is there anything I can do for you?"
>
> "I think you are about to make a decision about your life, I can feel it."
>
> "Whatever you decide to do, we are with you, no matter what."
>
> "You can do anything you put your mind to."
>
> "Remember, there is a bigger picture."
>
> "Fear is only a feeling. You can overcome it and do the right thing."

Later, a former group member shared her summation of the group experience. She made a point of taking the time to keep a journal throughout it, a recommendation the group facilitators explained to each member. While keeping a journal is an option, we find that the women who do so get more out of the group experience than those who keep only a sporadic one or none at all. The group member reports:

Latoya: I have so many things to be thankful for since attending the group. The feeling of being alone with my problems disappeared. I feel less burdened. Many comments made by the group members touched me right where I needed it to. I do not want a lot out of life, just peace.

The most important lesson, or maybe just a reminder, is that by putting God at the center of my life, everything else falls into place. I have figured out how to keep a God-centered life. I pray or have devotions two to three times a day. I have learned to see the good in people and that I must meet my own needs, not expect others to do so. That puts the responsibility on me fully.

I had to admit to being a self-righteous person, always looking and noticing the faults of others. Seeing their shortcomings was easy for me. I spent so much time doing that and no time looking at me and my issues. I used to get angry at the people in my life for being so imperfect. I realized I just wanted them to take care of me, and I took note of each and every time they didn't. Well, don't you think that is time consuming? Believe me, it is! All I had to do was spend 10 percent of that energy on solutions to my problems.

Confronted with that reality as a result of attending group therapy meant it is time to take responsibility. Yes, today and from now on. I don't have a man in my life. I realize I'm not healthy enough yet, but I'm fixing me. I'd like to have a man but only when it's the right time. When I heal, I won't be so harsh and critical of anyone, especially a man. I mean to stick to this plan with God's help.

The group processed the push–pull exercise and moved into the next phase.

Shake, Shake, Shake Loose
The group leader moved to an exercise called "Shake, Shake, Shake Loose." Movement in treatment with African-American

clients has proved rousing, any kind of movement, whether standing up and stretching hands as high above the head as possible, or pounding a pillow. Our ancestry is filled with movement and music and church has often been the central place where we expressed movement in our connection to God. Parties, African dances, plays, and other areas in our lives also allow for movement.

Movement is incorporated into the "Shake, Shake, Shake Loose" exercise; it is mildly intense in the beginning, but increases in intensity as time goes on. The hope and intent is to shake the binding energy and life issues loose: It is the way to get nervous energy out while examining the origin of the tension. The African drum music in the background is very moving and evokes deep feelings that can only be expressed through physical movement. Words cannot describe the depth of the intensity.

The exercise is intended to assist the group participant in moving toward the next issue, to clear her mind and the physical tension, all of which will open her up to consider as many options as possible. The group facilitator keeps the focus on the issue, "the purpose"—Nia. Having a strong sense of purpose helps us reorganize our thinking from the destructive path leading to the annihilation of our people to the constructive one, pointing to the preservation of tradition and culture.

As African drum music played in the background, Shari was requested to shake the *hands* loose. She shook her arms gently at first. Then the movement intensified, making it appear as if she had killer bees trying to eat her alive. Shari stated that the shaking felt so good that she didn't want to stop. Allowed as much time as she needed, Shari finished shaking and focused on the next step. She asked, "What's the purpose? Why must I stay in such a meaningless relationship?" Anger, coupled with confusion, overshadowed her feelings of the moment. She ended with the statement that she would take time to examine what purpose her present situation served.

Processing the exercise was lengthy, for the healing took place on a number of levels by many group participants. Shari continued to quietly process her new sense of reality while others shared the growth experience. One participant summarized her internal work very effectively:

Donita: As soon as Shari started, I knew she was living my story—a life of great demands. Demands are harder to live

out when you lack motivation. Watching Shari shake made
me feel jumpy. I had a hard time sitting still so I just stood
up. The other group facilitator noticed me standing and
came to stand next to me. I did not want to interrupt Shari,
but I knew I had to do something, so I just stood.

I felt it. Like clothes falling off of you after having lost 50
pounds. They just drop off. Then suddenly I knew I had let
go of something I did not have to take care of. The longer I
focused on what needed to change in my life, the better I felt.
I focused and prayed. There were no quick decisions but
gradual shifts. The problem became divided into sections,
then one section held more of my attention than the others.
So I got busy on that section. The first section dealt with the
ache in my heart. I took my time to feel the hurt, like Linda
said. Sherlon, the other co-facilitator, told me to breathe
slowly. What a combination! I took my time and the healing
feeling grew. Wanting to rush it was tempting, but this time
I wanted to be thorough, learning as much from this experience as possible.

Yet another group member testified that she knew she had
missed an opportunity; she explained:

Tamara: First, this guy I met was too good to be true. He was
good looking, well-dressed, divorced eight years ago, and
unattached. He had a few little quirks but I chose to overlook them and stick with it for awhile. The little things
became big ones. I was encouraged by Linda to put off the
sex until I knew more about him, especially since I had
already noticed a few things I did not like about him.
Well... [pause]... I guess I didn't heed the advice because
I hadn't had sex in months, so I was more than ready.

I had put him off long enough and he said I was being
difficult. You know... [pause]... I knew better deep down
inside. Maybe I brought this all on myself but I just couldn't
put it off. He was equally interested. I knew I had avoided
facing the deeper issues. Avoiding intimacy was what I had
to admit to myself. He treated me like an object. Somehow in
the back of my mind I was at fault. Decidedly I planned to
leave the group and do individual work. Feeling ashamed
and like a piece of s_ _ _, I was going to beat myself up. The
group wouldn't hear of it, so we got busy looking at the
situation.

Yes, no doubt about it, I wanted to see things only a certain way. He had some good points but mostly negative ones when it comes to my understanding of a relationship. It was obvious that he did not want to let me get to know him. When I would ask questions, he called me critical. The questions were simple ones, such as "Do you like women who have a strong will?" or "What happens when I want to do something I feel is important and you could care less, would you go with me anyway?" He would respond to me by putting the answer off by saying "Let's wait until that happens," "You just want to start an argument," or "Can't we just drop it?" I don't think my questions were premature or out of place, but I let him influence me. We did not touch those kind of questions. We talked about other things that were interesting, such as current events. The discussions about current events and even sports fooled me.

I learned that I did not have to take the full blame for this relationship flop because hindsight and processing this with the group showed me he had no intention of going any further than sports and current events. He simply was not interested, period, or didn't know how to relate on an emotional level. For either reason, he was not the person for me. The reality is that I continue to pick the same kind of man. My divorce of 21 years ago was for the same reason. We had nothing in common.

Being more selective does not mean taking myself out of the social life, but being more honest sooner. What made it worse is I had sex with him anyway. That's when I really got down on myself. It's true. I see myself with a mate but I'll say one thing, if I don't stop making unnecessary mistakes, I will be worn out. When the right one comes by, I'll truly miss him. The readings I have included in my devotional study guided me toward understanding that I play a role in every relationship I participate in. I have said yes when I wanted to say no. Going into a situation full of doubt usually means it's the wrong one to begin with. I had to let go of what could never belong to me. The change is gradual but change with purpose, no less.

The group began to focus on the energy Shari began to demonstrate. Another exercise emerged, the "Energy Flow Exercise"—the name hints at what occurred.

Energy Flow

Shari was led through a breathing exercise that facilitated relaxation through the use of imagery. Positive energy is replaced by negative energy as soft jazz is played in the background.

Group Leader: Shari, you and I will walk slowly through an exercise. You will learn how to use your breath to cleanse your mind and body of negative energy. Cleansing your mind and body of negative energy makes room for positive energy, which leads to more productive and purposeful actions or behaviors.

As you get yourself comfortable in the chair, uncross your legs and rest your glasses on the table next to you. Take your shoes off if you wish to. The other group members are welcome to join in the exercise. If you choose not to join in, please do not disturb others around you.

Shari, at some point you may feel more comfortable closing your eyes. You will not need to be concerned about falling asleep. You will find yourself at a conscious level at all times, sometimes aware of many things going on around you and other times you will only be focused on the internal processes occurring in your body. If you are ready, we can begin...

The chair you are resting on will support you completely. You may be aware of the chair supporting you and at other times you will not focus on it at all. Trust that the chair will be there. Allow your attention to turn to your breathing. Notice how deep or how shallow your breathing is at this moment.

The first step is to learn the complete way to breathe. Picture a baby... notice how the baby breathes.... Now, picture your first baby and how you noticed everything about her, right down to the length of her fingernails ... examine her breathing... closely watch her stomach move in and out.... Now, slowly match the movement... in and out, slowly.

In and out,... okay... that's how it's done.... (*Watch for the proper breathing indicated by the movement of her stomach fully expanding.*)

Now, continue to breathe deeply and slowly, slowly... slowly and deeply... [*pause*] It looks like you are fully relaxed and attending to my words... good.

Let's take a journey.... You won't need anything but yourself and your imagination.... This journey will take us back in time.... It is important to remember that I am here at all times... if you want to end this exercise, all you need to do is open your eyes and look at me. Okay? (*After getting an affirmation by a head nod, we proceeded.*)

Using your imagination, picture a light that begins at your toes and touches each and every cell... slowly.... With your imagination, this light will collect all tension and stress. Allow it to move slowly, all over your toes and feet... all stress and tension attaches itself to the light.

Moving up through your ankles, collecting all stress and tension... up through your calves and knees, collecting as it moves and touches each cell. Continue to breathe slowly and deeply.... Notice how your breathing aids the light to move....

Your lungs fill and empty, helping the light expel the stress and tension it has collected. As you breathe air in, you are bringing in oxygen necessary for aiding the cells to function. Now, as you exhale, you also expel the waste products of stress and tension....

The light continues to move through your thighs and buttocks, leaving calmness and smoothness in each muscle it touches.... Now the light is in your stomach area, moving slowly up to your chest and back, slowly, breathe....

Always remember to breathe deeply and notice how soothing the calm it creates... letting go of stress and tension... moving down each arm... breathe... and back up to your shoulders....

Notice how your shoulders relax as the light collects the stress and tension... breathe.... Allow the light to move to your neck. Your neck does a marvelous job of holding your head at any angle you choose.

You've given yourself a moment to rest as you lay your head on the headrest. Take your time as the light does a particularly marvelous job of collecting the stress and tension... breathe....

Traveling to your chin and jaw, let the light smooth out the muscles that cause your jaw to tighten when you get angry or tense. See how wonderful it feels to let your jaw relax.... The light can move up into your face, collecting all stress and tension.... Moving into your head, sweeping the stress and tension away.

With your breath, you can exhale the remaining tension and negative energy out of your nose and mouth. Take three nice deep breaths ... inhale ... exhale ... slowly.... Good ... inhale ... exhale ... slowly.... Good ... inhale.... and exhale....

Deep breathing signals the brain to release certain chemicals to induce relaxation. Now that you've relaxed your whole body, allow your mind to travel to a favorite vacation spot ... you will do some work here and take mini-vacations as you rest from the work....

You have an issue in your life that seems to be blocking you from making a healthy decision.... Let's take a walk back through history, keeping in mind that decision making is a skill handed down to use from our parents ... recall a moment your parents exercised their decision-making behavior.... Your parents, like any other parents, made good decisions and bad decisions. You have learned the good ones and the bad ones. You can unlearn the bad-decision habit if you will take a moment to reflect on the process.... Bad decisions or choices are made out of fear for safety, or out of ignorance or haste.

Many African-Americans come with a history they attempt to minimize or forget. We come from a continent that had vast riches and wisdom.... The attempt to rob us resulted in a condition called slavery ... our foreparents, who were descendants of slaves, functioned out of fear at times. There were also moments of great risk-taking which brought us out of slavery. You have the capacity to function out of either world since you, as did your ancestors, have the ability to exercise choice.... They risked their lives to save it ... you can do the same....

One element that proved to be essential for our ancestors was their connection to God/Spirit/Creator ... and their connection to each other.... Their survival depended on these two elements.

God's strength and greatness is given to us in the form of energy.... We can build on that spirit/energy daily. You will find the same strength that our ancestors used to "move mountains"—that horrible condition called slavery. You can move your mountains, too....

Take a moment to picture yourself moving your mountain, walking past fear, since it is only a feeling ... a feeling you have walked past before.... Picture yourself at a time when you were afraid and figured out a way anyhow.

So you do have the skill... it was handed down to us from people who did not know where their next morsel of bread would come from; nonetheless, they knew they would not take another "crumb" from their "owner's" hand.... They moved past the fear into risky business... you have the skill.... Take a moment to visually take your risk....

Make notes on the task you need to complete as you visualize the taking of the risk.... Since you can visualize the completion of the risk, you are ready to move to a different level with your risk-taking behavior as it pertains to fear.

You will also be able to convert your experience into other areas, but for now you have worked hard enough. ... Allow yourself to focus on the special, wonderful vacation spot chosen as your favorite spot.

Imagine all the sounds that accompany your vacation spot. Imagine all the smells and other sensory experiences... it must be special if you picked it.

Great vacations with lasting memories take time and planning. You have a task at hand... you are well prepared to deal with the task and complete it with success.... [*pause*]

Now that you have spent this time working toward healing, you can count on great results.... I bid you God's speed as you work through this issue in your life.

You can come back to this room where the group resides as slowly as you need to.... You can stretch and open your eyes when you are ready.

Shari came back to the group; she was stunned by the experience and asked to be left alone to be with her thoughts. We were glad to accommodate her request.

After Shari completed the 10-week group, she testified about the experience:

Shari: Suddenly things became clear to me. I made a list of tasks and began doing them, one by one. Some tasks were small and others were large. I will probably not leave my husband at this point, but the relationship has to change. I will attempt to strike an agreement regarding the responsibilities around the house. Nothing more.

I am not sure why I don't want to leave without a plan, but I will leave soon. I know that from the very depths of my soul. This relationship is a bad one and it is affecting my mental well-being. He is a very sick man, in much denial, and his denial is stunting my growth. Rather, I am allowing his denial to negatively influence me. I do realize I have a plan in the making; I just want to get my bills in order, not paid off necessarily, but organized.

I am a fair and honest person and will work toward a dissolution rather than a divorce. We don't need to give away money we don't have. Ya know, as I think about this, I don't think he wants to be in this relationship. He just lacks the guts to get out. I am prepared to move past fear and take the risk.

Anger and the search for purpose continued as topics. The group respected Shari's request to switch focus from her struggle to that of another group member. The subject shifted to Vy's "Catch-22" in which she found herself trying to survive an educational system without compromising her values the whole way; she explains:

Vy: I'd completed rounds with the medical staff. My internship was well underway, so I felt comfortable talking about my personal opinion concerning a patient. I was quickly reprimanded by the instructor who said that as doctors we were not to moralize; we were simply to treat the patients for their illness. My comments cost me the "A" in the class. My father, who is a dentist, told me I'm not there to be a social worker. He said I should just get them well. I can do that, but some of the situations get my attention and I will spend a half hour with a client on a slow day and tend to their other needs. I'm furious about being told how to be a doctor. But I just bear it and do the work.

Cameal: Bear what?

Not waiting for an answer, Cameal talked about working within a system and "boiling" the whole time, her anger and frustration simmering right on the surface. Cameal was tired of playing by someone else's rules: The rules she was raised by did not seem to exist in her situation. Cameal was raised to believe in honesty, consideration, lots of hard work, and imposition of the same rules for all. Well, she was in for a very rude awakening. Cameal described her experience, one that is not uncommon, but is startling when it continues to catch people off guard.

One group member testified at her closing session as the group ended:

Joi: I stopped being surprised at the things White people do. The ones with a little bit of power flaunt it and step on anyone in their way. For the most part, I have grown to expect it. That cuts down on the surprise element that has left me stunned, losing precious moments of responding.

I have accepted that racism exists on every level of society and it's the well-meaning so-called Christians who do the most damage. They keep quiet about wrongs and deny they have any responsibility in "righting" them. The best part about my new reality is that I feel I have 20–20 vision almost overnight. I also don't get as angry. Not getting intensely angry has lowered my blood pressure and healed my ulcer. My mind shifts to corrective action when I experience discrimination rather than intense rage.

I still get angry and that is okay with me because I have answers now. If I don't have the answers, I know where to find them. I may find the answers from my Bible studies, other individuals, or our legal system. There are plenty of answers. Can you tell how happy I am with the simple fact that there are answers to be had? I know everyone does not operate with the same morals I was raised with, but I know that God has a plan. That plan is that every person will be viewed as whole and complete, worthy of being loved.

I have learned that their ignorance is hurting them too. Some of them know it and some of them are unaware of their source of sadness and emptiness. God put us here to demonstrate our likeness in him first and to love one another. We are all created in His likeness. I believe we are all good and we all have the capacity to be God-like. The reality exists that many of us are very far from being anything close to resembling God's characteristics. Some of us are stupid enough to think that one person is superior over another, just based on color.

There are people who act on their stupid beliefs. Well, I've got something for them if they come at me with that stuff. I will fight, resist, go legal, or whatever it takes to let them see they are wrong. With God as the center of my life, and I pray daily, the stress won't get the better of me. I will handle as much as I can and I will take breaks and time-outs; then go back at it with passion. This group changed my life. Mostly, the group helped me make use of my anger. And I am grateful.

Cameal, on the other hand, is right in the midst of discovering the evil of "double standards." While Vy is painfully attempting to assess her position, her confusion is amplified by the presence of an African-American authority figure, who, though like her, is apparently "straddling the fence." Attempting to understand where to place her trust, Vy is stuck wondering what to do, how to "be." The two recount their problems:

Cameal: I work it their way, following the rules, meeting deadlines, complying with policy, and yet when it comes to evaluation, I am cheated out of a raise because what I do is not recognized. I haven't tooted my horn loud enough or I haven't "stroked their feathers" at key times. Sure, they want you to do it their way, but what the hell is their way? The rules are constantly changing.

Vy: My supervising doctor wanted me to maintain a morally neutral position. At what length do we have to go to figure out what they mean? My supervisor says one thing and does another. I am constantly guessing and as soon as I think I have it, the rule changes. Now I've got to go through my files for the entire year and pull out my accomplishments. The strange issue for me is that I have a new supervisor. She is African-American and I knew her from another setting. I don't know if she is operating under the director's (White rules) or her own set. This is very confusing. I have not felt that she was in my corner for her short, six-month employment. It's as though she sells me short whenever I need her support. She always falls onto the director's point of view or position. What standards do I strive for? I feel crazy most of the time. If there are times I don't feel crazy, I think something is wrong. My mom tells me if you know the rules, you're a step ahead, but I don't find that to be true. Sometimes I know the rules but other times not having access to the information, "rules," I am left frustrated and angry.

Like our ancestors, we work toward contributing something meaningful and purposeful. Vy is drawn to the caring and compassionate part of her job. She wants to live out her inner desire to be more than just a professional to an object! She is caught between the required reputation or precedent set by the profession of medicine and her natural desire to be personal. Her chosen profession was that chance to live a purposeful life. While the group experience was not as fully beneficial to Vy as to other participants, she found some of the aspects helpful.

Vy came to the group as a step toward getting to know the community she recently moved to directly out of medical school. Her attention was challenged by the demands of the transition. She stated that maybe the group wasn't the best choice because of the demands of the new medical practice. While she attended the majority of the group meetings, her energy was very low. Exhausted, Vy was known to doze during the sessions. Anger was her focal point. Compounded by the challenges of starting a new practice and matriculating through a White, male-dominated profession, Vy was on edge much of the time. At times she voiced frustration and directed her anger toward the group leader. In attempts to process the anger, Vy became protective of herself and withdrew.

At her closing session, she shared the difficulty in dealing directly with her issues: "At times I felt the other members needed more immediate attention. Their problems seemed more serious." The group leader urged Vy to be more revealing of her issue, but hesitation prevented her from fully processing her anger. Vy shared that she learned how destructive anger can be if left unchecked. She also realized she had made a habit of expecting others to live up to her expectations. There was little room for debate or negotiation. Decidedly, Vy agreed to examine her issue around anger on her own. Treatment ended with many loose ends, but one certainty remained—defining the most effective way to live out a purposeful career.

Many blocks exist, not only the systematic denial of the intelligence of African-American women by society, as a whole, and the many ramifications that accompany it, but also the existence of unchecked anger. Sometimes clients who leave therapy before harnessing the power of anger and redirecting it toward optimal use experience unnecessary and preventable blocks in effectiveness. There are many routes resolving of anger can take—continuing in a group with the focus on processing angry reactions by utilizing the therapy technique of immediacy, designing a psychodrama to dramatize the experience of anger, or enacting the Gestalt technique of the empty chair to talk to the person with whom the member is angry.

Individual treatment is another effective route. In any event, the issue will tend to resurface until it is resolved. It is hoped that Vy will be persistent.

Marie's Story

Turning our attention to Marie, we will walk through her experience of developing or establishing Nia. Marie is a 35-year-old, tall, thin, articulate, well-dressed, attractive professional woman. She came to therapy with exact goals, initially requesting individual sessions. She sat stifly, upright in her chair, staring straight ahead with her hands clasped together on her lap. Her complexion was clear and her features a relaxed mixture of the African, Native American, and Caucasian races; her hair was carefully styled. When she was addressed, Marie made direct eye contact and held it constant throughout the conversation. In the therapist's office, she settled herself carefully in her chair and tried to smile pleasantly, but looked somewhat ill at ease. When asked what her complaint was, she began to tear slightly. She quickly caught her tear by wiping it away with her hand and apologized for crying.

Marie explained that over the past year she had experienced multiple symptoms of what she guessed was nerves. She said that many things contributed to her feeling sad (the tears began again) and she often felt anxious without quite knowing why. She also suffered periodic headaches. Reportedly, Marie sought the advice of her family physician and was told that her symptoms were due to stress. She perspired excessively, a symptom that bothered her considerably because she was hypersensitive to the stereotype that African-Americans have a strong body odor. She also suffered from insomnia; she could not fall asleep even though she went to bed early and tired. She would lie awake, tossing, then get up, read, and clean house, often not sleeping until long after midnight. She tried sleeping pills to no avail, but she had been advised by her physician that overuse of these tranquilizers could lead to an addiction. Her appetite also had been sporadic—at times she would not feel like eating at all and could not join her family in regular meals; at other times, she would feel voraciously hungry and be at the refrigerator at odd hours. Surprisingly, her weight changed little. She explained that everyone in her family was thin, so she never worried about weight. Sometimes she felt rather dizzy with spots before her eyes but, although she felt faint, she never lost consciousness. Since she seemed to suffer these symptoms more frequently during her menstrual periods, she thought that she might be going through menopause. Although her menses were regular, they had always been a painful source of tension. Although her gynecologist had kept careful track of her complaints, he found no organic cause for her symptoms, and also suggested counseling.

Marie was made even more uneasy by the second suggestion to seek counseling—first by her family physician and then by her gynecologist—because she had always regarded psychologists as those who dealt with people who had severe problems they were unable to correct themselves. She was worried that she would be labeled with a "weak mind." However, she tried to dismiss this as a "silly idea" because she knew several of her friends, who did not appear severely disturbed, were seeing psychologists. In addition, she had read various articles in women's magazines about psychological guidance. Marie asked openly if the practice of psychology was largely concerned with "mental illness" or if she could receive some kind of "guidance" here.

She also explained that, despite her reluctance to be classified as "mentally ill," her symptoms so disturbed her and interfered with her life that she felt it was necessary to do something about them. She was afraid to leave these concerns unchecked for fear of "exploding from the pressure." Marie also felt that she would be quite embarrassed if she began to cry or "have the jitters" in public. She had dropped her book reading club and stopped attending the women's circle at church. By avoiding these and many other social events, she could hide her tearfulness. She was employed full-time as an administrator in a government agency and continued to work even though she was concerned about crying in public. She had to make an extra effort to get to work every day and often felt so exhausted that she had to push herself to do her work and was always glad when the day ended.

Asked how her family regarded her symptoms, Marie began to cry again. She stated that she felt guilty that she might be neglecting her husband and son and that it was also a strain to keep up with the chores at home even though everyone did their part. She quickly added that her family had had no complaints and seemed very understanding. She described the complaints from her children as "normal kid stuff." "We really have pretty nice children, full of excitement about life and doing okay in school," she said. With regard to her spouse, Marie was equally clear, saying that she did not believe he was aware of her crying but knew of her complaints about work. She did not want to bother him with any added details about her tendency to cry so easily.

During the first few interviews, Marie denied that she had any idea why she was so sad—"Maybe there is something deeper but I don't know what that could be. I guess that's why I'm here." Having children and a spouse who was pleased with his employment, she saw no need to worry about them. Their combined incomes gave them a modestly comfortable standard of living and a sizable savings account. They owned their own home in a "mixed" neighborhood, owned two well-running cars, and had just completed some remodeling projects on the house. They had a small circle of friends with whom they socialized.

In Marie's initial search for some reasons for her anxiety, she remarked that she "guessed" that she felt a lot of stress on her job. She had worked in the same office for nine years, with her duties and position changing over the years. Promotions occurred based on merit. Pleased with the progression of events, she explained that she had reached the top of the employment possibilities. She had begun as a clerical supervisor, then moved into a clinical position after completing her degree. Two years later, she moved into a supervisory position, and a year later, was promoted into administration. She felt the moves were too close together, but enjoyed each position. She had experienced various stressors on the job in the last nine years, but none that had had such an affect on her as now. Her main stresses on the job came from institutional changes and conflict with her immediate supervisor, who happened to be Caucasian. Marie felt the strong conviction to help her organization deal with diversity issues. There were a multitude of them, from the appropriate services and programs for clients, to minority representation among the various levels of employment. The higher in the organization, the "Whiter" the management became. At times she felt she carried the entire responsibility for ensuring that equality occurred at all levels. She felt anxious, lest she be internally criticized for not meeting her responsibilities.

Over the past year, her supervisor had seemed friendly but uneasy. Marie described her as an older woman, second-generation immigrant from Germany, who was descended from victims of Germany's persecution of the Jews. She liked this woman who, in some ways, sought to be friendly to her, yet she also felt uneasy whenever this supervisor engaged her in conversation beyond the needs of the job. Marie felt that her supervisor was not very competent, making many little mistakes which Marie ended up correcting, lest the mistakes reflect on her. Marie attempted, in various ways, to point out the errors, but her supervisor would become irritated and deny any wrongdoing, putting the blame for mistakes back on Marie. Marie was most uncomfortable whenever her supervisor was friendly or intimate with other people in the office, particularly with Marie's supervisees—"She doesn't seem to follow the line of communication." Marie thought that perhaps part of the frustration with her job was due to the fact that her immediate supervisors and the directors had changed frequently. For the past six months, several positions in the organization had remained unfilled due to a hiring freeze. Questioned, she denied that she had ever been interested in a promotion beyond her present rating, and besides, she was not considered by the administration to be the "right material" for a director position.

Marie felt prejudice and discrimination at her job. She could not put her finger on how it affected her. She described another African-American woman, Alice, as loud and aggressive. "Alice brings the negative reactions on herself due to her argumentative tone," which sharply contrasted with Marie's almost mild manner of responding in interactions. As we continued to talk about discrimination, Marie grew more agitated. The offer to attend a group of African-Americans with similar concerns was met with guarded hesitation, but after further discussion, she agreed that a group would be an interesting place to process the anxiety. Having identified discrimination as part of her experience, she began to feel a little less anxious.

Past History

Marie was born and reared in Richmond, Virginia. She is the oldest of four children, two boys and two girls. Her father worked on the railroad and her mother was a maid for three families. She described her father in glowing terms as a kind man, devoted to his family, religiously devout, and a good provider. She had fewer words for her mother whom she described as very busy taking care of other people and often tired. Like her father, her mother was home very little. The children were largely responsible for themselves. Many extended family members lived in close proximity so there was always an older cousin or aunt to supervise until she was old enough to take on the responsibility. Marie admitted that in the South "no Black feels like a human being" and for that reason, she could never bring herself to leave her present location to live in the South again.

Marie watched her parents work long days and gain little. The sole purpose for the long work hours was to send all four children to college. Obedience was demanded of them, even when the parents were not present. There seemed to be the normal sibling conflicts such as chore list arguments, and so on. All Marie's siblings took school very seriously with the exception of her brother, Al. Al was an average student who loved working on cars. After a period of time, Marie's parents accepted that Al would not go on to college. Instead, he opened his own auto repair shop while the others obtained college degrees. During her childhood Marie felt her parents were harsh and demanding when it came to responsibilities at home. She welcomed the chance to go to college. Academically Marie excelled and obtained a scholarship to attend a school in a state 400 miles away. The family was afraid to let her venture off so far, but decided to accommodate it since the child next to Marie was just a year younger and would be attending school within the year.

It was during her last year at college that she met her spouse. She found him to be a handsome and honest man who incidentally swept her off her feet. She loved to dance and found that she enjoyed the college parties to which she had never gone before. Her family liked her boyfriend initially, but her mother later learned that he came from a "broken home" and his father was an alcoholic. Marie's parents became concerned and critical, and they did not want Marie to marry him. After a whirlwind courtship, they were married anyway in an elaborate church wedding to which the whole community was invited. Immediately after the wedding Marie discovered that her spouse had no intention of living in his hometown because he did not get along with his family.

They moved three times within the first year and a half of their marriage. They settled in a small Northeastern city where their children were born. His job required him to move to the Midwest, to a city they have been in since 1985. They settled in there and now consider it home. The family attends church regularly and is active in the community. She made many trips home to visit her parents until their deaths and her siblings live in different cities. They get together about once every other year.

Treatment

Marie's symptoms began to subside once she began in the *Images of Me* group. She remained, however, at odds with her supervisor. Gradually she began to express issues of inappropriateness and irresponsibility to her more directly. Early in the group process she shared her confusion and personal questioning.

Marie: Am I crazy or is this what's going on? I am angry, confused, but determined not to give in to any negative consequences that might emerge from my thinking. When I am in meetings, for example, I find that I am often being discounted or, at the very least, ignored. It feels like I am invisible, that I am talking and sharing my thoughts and ideas and those in my presence simply do not hear or even see me. I try again to make my point but it takes a lot of energy to continue. I know I am strong and intelligent and often, when I continue to make myself heard, I do so in a professional way, but then I am perceived as aggressive or something negative. Then I find myself asking myself again, "Am I crazy or is this what's going on?"

Other group members identified with Marie.

Binta: Yeah, I know what you mean. I share my thoughts with my boss who is a White woman. She acts like she doesn't even hear what I say.
Callie: I find that I am perceived as too direct and aggressive. I say what I think and am prepared to professionally defend my stance. When I take on an issue, I do my homework and invest a lot of time and energy to be sure that I know what I am talking about, that I am not reacting, and that I have a plan. This is often perceived as an intimidating behavior.

Analysis and Discussion

The group launched into Marie's issue of purpose and overall self-determination. Her quizzical and genuine manner of pre-

senting the dilemma of her impact in the workplace on program development for African-American families and the
secondary issue of her impact in her immediate family sparked
the interest of the group. Her need to be affirmed and the
desire to be recognized for her intellectual worth became central to the essence of her soul. The pain of Marie's struggle was
dissected, synthesized, and interpreted by the group; and her
experience stimulated the group leader's memory of a personal
incident. Internally the group leader found herself wondering
about her own past efforts in trying to move an establishment
in the direction of developing certain programming, some that
were culturally appropriate and effective. Appealing to the
"people in power," often White European-Americans, she
found herself losing focus (for she knew what worked in the
African-American community) as she appealed to their willingness to relinquish some of the power. Or at least she felt she
had a better clue than the White power holders who were the
ultimate decision makers since they had absolutely no idea
what it's like to live under the endless pressure of a racist and
sexist society. Marie very articulately described one of her
encounters with a supervisor. The wonderment of her effectiveness showed through with each carefully chosen word as
she described the specific incident. She was very convincing as
she unraveled the details of the story, yet some self-doubt
flashed that flavored the otherwise very astute rendition.

Rarely had the group leader encountered a sister who had
so many redeeming qualities but needed affirmation and
assurance that the path she had chosen for herself was a sound
one. Marie's strong and firm facial features matched her
impeccable taste in clothes. Her tall, slender figure left no
question that this mother worked at maintaining a toned body
and a clear head. However, as she shared the details of the
event, her voice softened. The words came out no less descrip-
tive, but her eyes seemed to drift off, viewing the scene as an
outsider. The intensity mounted with each emotion-laden
word, and one sentence built on another. Her volume did not
change as she recounted:

Marie: My boss just stood there as if she was literally looking
through me. Expressionless.

Marie's words were carefully placed. She revealed the step
she made into verbal aggressive behavior. The glaze that

entered her eyes was a metaphor for her attempt to maintain control in the midst of her description of losing control. Her experience of invisibility had tipped the scales and set her on edge. The agony of needing to appear to be maintaining control when having lost control was a tremendous burden that Marie had risked to reveal to the group of African-American women who, with the exception of one other group member, she had not known prior to the group meeting. The suspense in the room was pervasive. The speculation on managing anger became an additional focus.

Finding myself, as a group leader, struggling to switch the focus from myself and the many fantasies of getting revenge on the countless European-Americans who had tried to discount me in the past was playing havoc on my mind. Utilizing self-disclosure in as appropriate a fashion as possible, without revealing my total infuriation of the events I had many times experienced, we began to break through the isolation Marie experienced. Her words hung there, begging for the mystical connection that binds us together as African-American women. Each painfully shared word was cradled by members of the group and the air was filled with ringing truths such as "I know what you mean" and "That doesn't sound crazy to me." The members shared as the group leaders encouraged self-disclosure and moved the group gently into the use of immediacy.

Group Leader: Marie, take a moment to ask someone in this group how they view you.

An intense working silence filled the room. Marie's eyes traveled back to the room as if they were still focused on the incredible, overwhelming event she had just finished describing. Her body went through a transformation, and she appeared to shift into a less tense state.

Group Leader: Are you aware that your body has shifted?
Marie: Gee, no. I knew something had happened but I was focused on the event. I felt like I relived it again!

With this statement, Marie's body stiffened, but as she spoke, more of the visible tension left her body.

Marie carefully reviewed each person in the group and picked the person to whom she wanted to direct her question. Her eyes dropped to the floor as if to metaphorically pick herself up, after suffering the dejection, to say to her chosen comrade:

Marie: Am I crazy or is this what's happening? Did I become invisible to this woman (my boss)?

The group member seemed to take a moment to bring Marie's experience into focus since she was mentally viewing many similar experiences, and speaking directly and assuredly she said:

Vy: No! You are not crazy. You had become a part of the woodwork in your boss's mind because she could not handle what you were saying.

A look of "I/we needed to hear that" settled on Marie and spread to the other group members. The group began to process the idea of staying connected to a central belief: We have the power to determine our own reality, forge our own ideas, and challenge an entity that discounts our inalienable rights to just "be."

Marie's struggle fascinated me. The roots of oppression seemed extraordinarily dominant. Immediacy, reality based on a pragmatic examination of events, and cognitive behavioral restructuring, offered Marie an opportunity to decrease significantly the personalization of perceived intentions and allowed her to approach similar situations from a position of empowerment rather than the devalued position of the "crazy Black woman."

How Purpose and Direction Impact Marie and the Group

The trust that was established in the earliest stages of our group because of the similarities in race and gender fostered the building of cohesiveness. We shared meaningful aspects of our experiences of oppression and discrimination based on race and/or gender, but often felt uncertain as to which aspect was being targeted or whether both had been. Regardless of the target, the importance lay in the bonding.

The group jointly developed goals to enhance cohesion. We agreed to work together to determine the meaning of life as it pertains to our color and gender. Since the issues of acceptance or rejection and the concern about "being like other people in the group" surfaced early, we decided to make a collage for an initial activity. (Our development of certain techniques like this is based on more than 50 *Images of Me* groups.)

The collage, entitled "I Am a Significant Part of the Group," was constructured as a "T" with the words "I am a significant part of the group" across the top of the "T." Strategically placed around the "T" were pictures of African-American women of various hues, dress, professions, emotions, and so on. Puzzle pieces, big enough for each member of the group, were cut from the initial board: Each group member selected a piece of the puzzle and wrote on the front— "What I expect from the group"—and on the back— "What I bring to the group." The members were encouraged to share their thoughts and feelings associated with these responses and were invited to put their pieces back into the puzzle after speaking. We discussed the total product made of pieces akin to the group and its individual members to highlight our individual and collective ideology.

First, we talked about the dynamics of putting the piece back into the puzzle; for example, what happens when one member elects not to put her piece into the puzzle? This question enabled group leaders to deal with issues of: (1) belonging to a group, (2) willingness to make commitments, (3) discomfort with revealing self to others, (4) fear of rejection, (5) fear of relationships, and (6) manipulative behaviors. Second, we asked about what happens when a piece of the puzzle is not put into the puzzle properly? This question allowed us to focus on feelings of loss, incompleteness, discomfort, anger (at the puzzle piece not fitting the expected spot), confusion, and apathy (not caring whether one fits in or not). Third, we asked about the connections among the women in the puzzle (i.e., pictures of African-American women). This question helped us focus on the issues of similarities in perceived careers, skin colors, economic levels, and educational levels. It also allowed the leaders to question the effect of perceptions. We asked, "What happens when you fit your piece into the puzzle but decide not to talk about your piece and not allow your puzzle piece to be seen (disclosed)?"

Ultimately, this activity enabled the group leaders to work through (1) fear of disclosure, (2) feelings of unworthiness, (3) feelings of not fitting into a group (because one feels that their problems are not as serious as those of other members of the group), and (4) resentment (about membership in a therapy group). There are many additional scenarios: The list is virtually endless. The puzzle activity stimulated issues that were dealt with in the group, and the conclusions reached by them involved processing the puzzle pieces, as addressed in Chapter 8.

Strengths and Areas of Concern

In view of what has been shared thus far, we ask what are the strengths of *Images of Me* and other groups that carry similar themes (i.e., groups for African-American women facilitated by African-American professionals), and focus on only one specific topic such as the workplace? A strong reason for the group's success since its inception has been the similarity in the race and gender of all members, including the group leaders. Culturally sensitive and competent techniques and strategies, such as immediacy, directiveness, and challenge, were identified and employed at the appropriate times. Further, the concept of linear thinking was not forced on participants who generally value circular thinking. The idea of assimilation, the reality of existing in an African-American world and a European-American world is addressed but not forced. Beliefs, values, and appreciation are held and understood for the power of the "pull" of the force of the motherland (Africa), and come out in values such as cooperation, family centeredness, collective behavior, consciousness, and so on.

One area of concern that group leaders run into when leading an African-American women's group in a relatively small community is the chance that members know each other from previous settings. Another area deals with the levels of professional attainment and higher education—some groups contained members who had degrees ranging from advanced ones to GEDs. While this issue was raised on one occasion, it has not noticeably affected the interaction of the group. The group's criteria are to be African-American, employed, and female. Just remember, caution must be used when dealing with women from a small community who may have varying levels of education.

Summary

Nia, celebrated on the fifth day of the Kwanzaa holidays, is a concept that emphasizes how we are to work together to restore the greatness of our people. We need to take the time to learn about our leaders and our proud history by reading and naming historical heroines and heroes. On special occasions, such as holidays or in our everyday life, we also should dress like our African ancestors. As African-American women, we are, as noted, connected to a great heritage and legacy of richness. Our stumbling can be attributed to a lack of vision or awareness of our history.

Throughout the group, issues of identity are touched on at various levels, with the group leaders assisting members to become more mindful of our everlasting connection to African history. Awareness of our great history allows issues, such as self-worth, to be challenged. Oppression and the constant degradation of African-Americans has caused us to doubt our abilities. We share the knowledge of various African and African-American personalities who have influenced us: We invite them to our group by sharing writings or the areas of life they represent. Poems were read, skits acted out, and words of inspiration absorbed. In short, the purpose of Nia lies in acts of sharing knowledge and celebrating our heritage.

After an activity involving candles, readings, and the wearing of African outfits actualized her, Marie described feeling discounted and invisible as if she didn't exist. Reaching back into her history, the group leader asked Marie to tell the group about the people who influenced her development as an African-American woman. Just as she was invited to tell her story, Marie began to physically sit up, and grew in stature. The minimal cues that could be seen in her expressions showed joy and affirmation. The people who influenced her were both male and female. The beginning of the healing for the *Images of Me* group participants began when the members elected to participate in a group for African-American women. The healing continues.

Too little attention is given to the development of the African-American woman in the area of careers (Evans & Herr, 1991). The level of aspiration is affected by such factors as single parenting, divorce, and ability level; that is, how well can one develop managerial skills to head a household (Buehler & Hogan, 1980). The ability to financially care for one's own needs and those of the family greatly impact on the level of satisfaction in family involvement (Bould, 1977). Sexism and racism affect the career development of African-American women and not until equality is reached will the African-American woman reach levels of achievement. Actively embracing the model of feminist identity and its contributions to women will facilitate upward mobility, and incorporating this same feminist identity into the participants while immersing the group in cultural roots and heritage moves them to a sharper sense of pride—what it means to be African-American and female (Downing & Roush, 1985).

Self-esteem rose when concepts of sisterhood were incorporated into the group. Brown (1993) discussed the necessity for going deeper than a mere objective examination of discriminatory events if one is to get at the emotional response to them. Looking at experiences of discrimination on an emotional level facilitated change. Shipp (1983) concurred that "group work is most effective with African-American women who operate from an Afrocentric approach" (p. 108). Emerging as victors from the vicissitudes of life is the result of culturally trained therapists who utilize modalities that best suit their clients, as seen in the *Images of Me* group.

The initial stage highlights the principle of Umoja (unity); Chapter 5 describes it and walks readers through critical events. The effectiveness of group cohesiveness assists group leaders in creating a sense of Umoja.

References

Bould, S. (1977). Female headed families: Personal fate control and the provider role. *Journal of Marriage and Family, 39*, 339–349.

Brown, J. F. (1993). Helping Black women build high self-esteem. *American Counselor, 2*, 9–11.

Buehler, C., & Hogan, J. (1980). Managerial behavior and stress in families headed by divorced women: A proposed framework. *Family Relations, 29*, 525–553.

Downing, N. E., & Roush, K. L. (1985). From passive acceptance to active commitment: A model of feminist identity development for women. *The Counseling Psychologist, 13*(4), 695–709.

Evans, K. M., & Herr, E. L. (1991). The influence of racism and sexism in the career development of African-American women. *Journal of Multicultural Counseling and Development, 19*(3), 130–135.

Harris, N. (1992). Afrocentrism—Concept and method: A philosophical basis for an Afrocentric orientation. *The Western Journal of Black Studies, 16*(3), 154–159.

Hoyt-Goldsmith, D. (1993). *Celebrating Kwanzaa.* New York: Holiday House Publishing.

Phillips, F. (1990). NTU psychotherapy, an Afrocentric approach. *Journal of Black Psychology, 17*(1), 53–74.

Shipp, P. (1983). Counseling Blacks: A group approach. *Personnel and Guidance Journal, 62*(2), 108–111.

5

The Initial Stage—Umoja

Umoja, the first principle celebrated during Kwanzaa, means unity (harmony). "For many people, this principle is the most important part of the entire Kwanzaa celebration" (Hoyt-Goldsmith, 1993, p. 11). We are challenged to strive for and maintain unity within the family, community, nation, and ethnic group (Karenga, 1988, p. 7). As discussed in Chapter 2, unity can be seen on many levels. The examples demonstrate the great strides made by a parent group that took action to build community and ensure their children were well served in the educational system. A small idea sparked a mass gathering and protest, or a sister searching for the small particle that would ensure peace rather than continuing the fight over vague aspects that only divided the family. The sister took a step back to view the situation from another angle. She made a conscious effort to stop taking her sister's insults as personal attacks; this new point of view gave her the energy to assist in the care of their elderly mother. Success came from relating on an interpersonal level and establishing a win–win situation. She was the individual who repaired her hurts from the inside out, and began the journey to find her own power and settle the inner turmoil. The intrapersonal level is easily accessible to us when we follow the example outlined in the testimony of the sister who explained the shift from collapsing under societal oppression and its negative messages to internally building on our inherited God-given greatness.

Developing Group Cohesiveness

Being united makes us stronger because we all can work together (Hoyt-Goldsmith, 1993, p. 10). Umoja is established and nurtured in the group setting once cohesiveness has been developed among the group members. It is a factor that one of the group members had assumed, in a manner of speaking, when she relayed a sad experience to the group and gave her reason for seeking help. The group members assisted her in sharing her story in a safe environment; Shari had been robbed and she needed to tell people who cared.

Shari: I was at lunch with three friends of mine in a section of town where construction was going on. I paid the bill with cash. We do that for each other on a rotating basis. No one can order more than ten dollars worth. We like to pretend we are treating each other, but really we're just paying for our own lunch in the end.... Well, I was on my way to my car after having said good-bye to my friends. The noise of the construction surrounded us so we couldn't hear very well. This guy ran up to me and snatched my purse! I yelled but couldn't be heard over the noise of the construction. I felt horrible.... it was a Black guy. I never thought that could happen to me. I had just gone to the bank; he got the remaining $250.00.

I've never been robbed before. I never thought it could happen to me. I intentionally refused to develop a negative opinion of our Black youth. I always speak to them because I believe they need to know we still care. Then this happens. ... It is all I could think about. Sure, I was mad because that money had to last me three weeks. The police later found my purse—of course, no money and a missing credit card. Well, he couldn't use it because I put a stop on the account. The credit card was how he got caught.

The robbery changed everything for Shari. She had had an idea of "a people unified," one that included caring for and protecting one another. She felt comfortable around her brother and sister African-Americans. She had been shielded from the realities of urban life when she lived in the suburbs, and had only recently worked downtown, traveling through the city with ease. Shari had been traumatized in more than one way by the incident: The robbery was scary enough, but the fact that it was perpetrated by an African-American made the experience all the more galling.

In the eyes of some, it was a simple assault. Shari was unhurt and had the keys for her car in hand. Even though Shari didn't receive a scratch, she felt it was much more serious. It made her feel unsafe, and she became distant, and lonely. The group had the task of restoring her trust in herself and her people. The young man's trial was scheduled in a couple of weeks, and Shari felt very nervous about testifying. She found herself returning to the spot where it happened, standing in the same place, even walking into the restaurant and sitting at the same table, all the while thinking, "Why would a kid do such a desperate thing? Where have we failed?"

The group's task was to restore the trust Shari had lost. The trust had to develop on many levels—the main level was the one between her and the African-American community Shari had believed in all her life. The group needed to restore her hope of building community.

Shari: This kid goes to trial and I am expected to attend the hearing. I tried to get out of the requirement of being there but my attorney would not hear of it. My attorney said, "He did the crime, so he must do the time." I think there are many more alternatives to "paying for a crime" than going to jail.

The next week Shari shared with the group her prayer of finding an alternative solution to jail.

Shari: I believe in consequences for behaviors but they need to be lessons, not just punishment. I began thinking more seriously about a comment the group leader made about unity. I remember the urgency in her voice when she shared the Kwanzaa principle. I want you to tell me what you think of my idea.... How about having this kid do 250 hours, an hour for every dollar stole, of community work at ten churches or recreation centers in the city? I could work with the courts to supervise the jobs. While he will not report to me directly, he will have to get the message that I know it's "pay-up time."

The group shared their opinions. They were mostly supportive:

> I think that's smart but I don't know if I would go so far as to have to see him every time.
>
> You are brave, you are brave! What makes you think you can just treat this kid like he's your own? I like the alternative to jail, but are you sure you want to supervise?
>
> That's the best I've heard in a long time. I guess prayer is working in this guy's favor!
>
> I wish I had that kind of faith and bravery. You are taking a chance but I bet it pays off. Maybe, just maybe, this kid might think twice the next time he considers going outside of the law.
>
> We need to do more of that kind of reconciliation more often.
>
> Well, worst things have happened, so your idea may prevent the child from getting exposed to the professionals in jail who really know about crime. You know what they say, "If you want to guarantee he will learn a better way to commit his crime, just send him to jail."

Some comments were warnings and others out-and-out criticisms:

> Shari, please think about that. I think you are making a mistake.
>
> Don't do it. Don't do it. . . . Are you trying to save the world or something?
>
> You can't "work" the criminal out of them. You're living in a fantasy world. I really wouldn't do that even if you paid me.

Umoja is an essential part of any group interaction. Cohesion is the basis for communication. African-Americans' efforts to devise creative ways to build a bridge impacts tremendously on the community. After all, Shari could have chosen to be punitive but, instead, designed a way to heal while still holding the young man accountable: She, and countless others, want to make a difference and initiate healing. The safety of the group environment permitted Shari to work out a solution that gave both sides a chance to resolve the incident with integrity.

Group cohesiveness is approached from the perspective of African-American scholars. African-Americans have taken the initiative in the healing process for the betterment of the community under the guidance of these reflective scholars who lead the way. Lee (1991) described these "thinkers," W. Curtis Banks, Fredrick Harper, Wade Nobels, and Clemont Vontress, as equal contemporaries of Carl Rogers, Albert Ellis, and Fritz Perls. They lead us to the entryway, instilling us with the idea that Black culture, with its African origins, is qualitatively different from European-based White culture. In addition, Linda James Meyers, Joseph White, Barbara J. Shade, Harriette Pipes McAdoo, and Nancy Boyd-Franklin (1970s and 1980s) developed, expanded, and enhanced the facilitation of knowledge. Lee (1991) stated that the validity of theories and techniques grounded in European and European-American cultural traditions have to be questioned when applied to counseling interactions for African-Americans.

Rebuilding our community requires the motivation to build "bridges" instead of forging ahead and operating within the framework set by the current legal system, which can be cruel and especially punitive to African-Americans. The legal system created by White authorities here in America imprisons African-Americans at a higher rate than it imprisons Whites. By designing the consequence for her attacker, Shari spurned the traditional judicial system, and in so doing created a positive belief system about people of color rather than a negative belief that denigrated color and strove to "control" or "limit" their advancement. She certainly "questioned" the legal system and put in place a method that created healing and unity.

Keeping in mind the African proverb of unity, "I am therefore, we are" (Leslau & Leslau, 1985), African-Americans are able to develop methods and roads to healing. The proverb states essentially that what affects one affects another and therefore, what I do to you, I also do to myself. To sum up, once Shari dealt with the incident, she was able to consider the reality of our judicial system, a system that has, as noted, been unusually harsh on African-American males. Shari's openness allowed her to see the necessity of making the punishment "fit" the crime, a decision made easier by the group's support. Trust enabled the group to voice opinions without creating dissension. This group cohesion is like a "culture" in biological terms: When you have the right "culture," the proper growth will occur. Healing begins on the individual level and radiates out to the community, as an African proverb from Nigeria posits: "Before healing others, heal thyself" (Leslau & Leslau, 1985, p. 46). This group began to grow together like "ivy on the wall" as individual members developed skills in healing themselves.

Group cohesion is an essential element of the group process. All group development paths lead to group cohesion. Shari dealt with her internal fear, which helped her to relate to the group on a more personal level, thus contributing to a tight-knit atmosphere. Other members compared stories of pain and anger with the same result. A younger group member's recounting of her abusive relationship caused a member who had been quietly involved to become more verbal. The story started out as a tale of disappointment, but turned into a sad and scary experience.

Another participant, Jean, seemed like an average, hard-working, single woman. At 36, she had not been divorced too long. She said about her decision to come: "I came to find myself" which didn't seem like such an unusual goal. "I can't seem to stay focused on any one project at a time." Still relaxed and intently listening to Jean, I noticed her eye contact decrease to nil and her body stiffen. She explained that, earlier in the year, her live-in boyfriend had decided they would be married and the two decided on a civil ceremony. They went to the courthouse to place their name on the list. As they waited in the hall for the judge to finish the couple ahead of them, her spouse-to-be ran into a friend. They spent a few minutes talking and parted ways. He introduced Jean at the last moment, as if it were a last-minute thought; she shared her reaction:

Jean: I started to leave right then and there, but I thought I was making too much of the situation and simply said to him, next time introduce me right away. I didn't notice his expression change. He just said, "Sorry, okay." We were married and made no big deal of it. We just went back to our regular lives. I worked four days a week as a full-time health-care provider, which means that my days are very long. His work is seasonal. He works about nine months of the year, very long days, 12 to 15 hour days. He complains a little, but not often.

We've been together for the past three years. Nothing was different, or maybe I missed something. . . . Well anyway, I came home one day to find him sitting in his chair with a beer in his hand. He's a recovering alcoholic, 10 years next month. It was downhill from there. He became violent and had weekly extramarital affairs. He ran around so much I became scared about my safety and AIDS. Needless to say, we separated and divorced. I feel lost and so confused. I keep asking myself, "Did I miss something?" and "What's wrong with me that a man would have to drink to get away from me?"

I later learned that he had lost his job that day and found out that his daughter, from a previous marriage, was pregnant by her stepfather. He just lost it. It's months later and he's stopped drinking but he's not the same person I married."

Jean's voice began to trail off as did her gaze, and she looked quite uneasy. She began to talk more softly in shorter sentences. After some mild intervention by the group leader, Jean seemed to bring her attention back to the group. Another group member shared with Jean the difficulty of divorce and assured her that she had made the right choice to end a marriage that had become life-threatening to her.

Zena: This sadness will pass as long as you stay connected to your support system; use your support system to talk about both cheerful and sad things, and take advantage of the available therapy. You'll be okay. I've been right where you are. It will be okay.

Jean seemed to brighten a little when she realized other people shared her situation. When Bea talked about her situation, Jean even became animated. Bea related: "But I know what it's like, too." The dynamics in the group began to intensify: Members had become comfortable enough that a light-heartedness seemed to be in the air.

It was not exactly a joking kind of lightness, but a relaxed environment conducive to honest discussion of topics and issues not typically shared. "I just don't seem to pick the right kind of man," said Bea as she watched the group members' reactions. The others picked up on Bea's close examination and appeared to listen more intently. The members were fixed on hearing her discovery.

Bea: Since being in this group and with individual counseling, I think I know what that is. I keep looking for love in all the wrong places. I never seem to find it in any of the places. Having children, which I have two, gave me the chance to experience love. I think that's sad that you have to be an adult before you get a taste of love.

The group leader asked Bea to say that again using "I" instead of "you." She squirmed and smiled a little but was used to being redirected on the use of "I" instead of "you":

Bea: I don't have to feel the pain so deeply if I put it a few feet away from me by the use of "you." It's easier for me to think of it as someone else's pain. If I think about it as my pain, I feel like I'll cry endlessly. But when you [the group leader] force me to see it as my pain, it doesn't seem to be the way I imagined it. The first time I used the term that conveyed the real deal, I cried. I cried for a long time. I also stopped crying. It was just as much a relief to cry as it was to stop crying. I really stopped, so I'm taking that risk more often, using "I" but she [the group leader] is like this little bird sitting on my shoulder reminding me to use "I." It's personal and it's okay to be personal with yourself 'cause that's how you, rather than I, grow.

So, I'll say it again, . . . I think that's sad that I have to be an adult before I get a taste of love. . . .

Bea took a deep breath, almost surprised she didn't cry. She continued:

Bea: My mother is a drug addict. She has been one all my life. I understand the only time she didn't use them was when she was pregnant with me. Back then, she only used alcohol before she discovered she was pregnant with me. These last five years, it's been crack, cocaine, and alcohol. I tried to pretend she didn't exist since I am an only child, but having children myself made me think more about my family. She wanted to be a part of my children's lives too. It's crazy but, ... I let her be in their lives.

Since entering therapy, I've learned that I've grown up without the necessary means to mature into a healthy, well-balanced adult. I keep expecting the men in my life to love me like a mother would. Since I'm used to pain and hurt, I began thinking the pain and hurt was love. I know that sounds screwed up, but that's the best I can explain it. Love meant feeling hurt and pain, so I picked the losers, the ones who didn't have a clue about loving. They couldn't love themselves, couldn't love their family, and couldn't love their girlfriend. They didn't know how to love either so there we were, not even two halves trying to make a "one."

Jean, maybe there was something in your background that you could look at and learn where you've made the mistake of thinking you can "make up" for it by marrying a person who didn't seem to have the emotional maturity, either. It helped me to hear your story because I know I'm still growing in that department. Saying it out loud to the group is scary but I'm really tired of carrying it by myself. Thanks for listening and thanks, Jean, for telling us about your situation. I also believe that it's going to be all right. Learning to love ourselves really is the place to start. God is our "blueprint" because He set the standard. It is so-o-o-o-o-o helpful to know I am not alone in this effort. I have God and I have this group.

The group had progressed to a point where deeper issues were disclosed.

Gross and Capuzzi (1992) conceptualized the stages groups go through, based on the problem-solving behaviors exhibited. Group cohesion allows more productive interaction as members make the transition from small talk or general conversation to dealing with more salient material (Yalom, 1985). For example, the initial nature of conversation among members tends to be about general interests of the group or small talk about the community, and the like, but the more salient material concerns specifics about members' motives for participating in a psychotherapy group, their goals, and expectations.

Group cohesion is formed very early on by African-American women. Jean and Bea made disclosures about personal and deep issues by the second session. Some of the women were in individual counseling with one of the two group facilitators. While the comfort level may have been enhanced by familiarity with one person in the group, the fact remains that early disclosure proved a consistent occurrence.

Factors that lead to the early cohesiveness in the group are common race, gender, and a sense of Umoja; early cohesion allows the group to influence growth. Yalom (1985) spoke of the "the various pathways through which group cohesiveness exerts a therapeutic influence." He further explained how successful therapy, as mentioned, by the relationship between therapist and patient, one that needs to contain trust, warmth, empathic understanding, and acceptance. Although Yalom supports the long-established idea that the quality of the relationship is independent of the individual therapist's theoretical preference or approach, the authors of this book emphatically maintain that the quality of the relationship is not independent of the therapist's belief system but, in the case of *Images of Me*, the therapist's belief system and theoretical approach is essential to the quality of the relationship.

As illustrated by the processing of Shari's robbery experience, had the therapist not appreciated the "collective self," viewing life as connected and believing in the African proverb "we are, therefore I am," he or she may have risked missing the value of Shari's becoming involved in the young man's consequences. Shari did not need to be "vindicated"; instead, she needed to reconcile the crime internally and understand her role in assisting the young man in reorienting his thinking and subsequent actions. The therapist must be sensitive to cultural issues and be cognizant of the part culture plays in the healing of African-Americans. Racial and cultural sensitivity, as components of the Afrocentric school of conviction, establish relational quality. The relationship pivots on two factors: race and gender. Group cohesiveness is guided by the issues shared between the group leader and members. It is enriched and open to therapeutic impact or intervention by the group members who share in common race and gender.

Cohesion in Spite of Hostility

The group developed cohesion in spite of the underlying hostility. The underlying hostility felt was a natural group phenomenon in that many of the women participating shared a great deal of intensity. One element Mary disliked was getting counseling. A group member said it well: "I hate being in this counseling because it means I have to 'fix' me when I didn't 'break' me." She spoke of the early childhood trauma experienced while living with an active alcoholic. Another group member spoke about the societal oppression of African-Americans, on the whole: "I work hard and all I get is negativity from my White co-workers. I'm the only African-American in the whole office. I have to hear racial slurs and have promotions or transfers denied with no recourse. You're right, I'm mad. I stay mad and will be mad until I complete my education in three months and get the hell out of that place." The group member discussed the frustration of racism on the job.

The underlying hostility in the group sessions could be attributed to a number of factors such as early childhood trauma and workplace discrimination. Other elements ranged across the spectrum. An acknowledgment that the group made was that African-Americans tend to take their anger and frustration out on each other. The topic of "Black-on-Black" crime shed light on the hostility we express toward each other in extreme cases. The group pledged to build community between themselves as tension mounted rather than allowing the resentment to build.

Group Commonality

The group shared a commonality that spanned a century and perhaps because of the effects of recent hurts, alienation, rejection, abandonment, and so on. Group cohesion was enhanced by sharing of events that occurred during the week or of that very day. Sometimes the hurt had little to do with race; statements made by a group member coming to terms with the fact that her "dream" of a close relationship with her sister would not come true or the rejection suffered by a group participant who had just learned of her partner's infidelity, or the frightened look on a group member's face as she reflected on the feeling of a "motherless" life and the abandonment she had experienced, illustrated this reality.

Harmony in Spite of Racial Issues

Acceptance and approval—given when it came to race—the internalized, racist ideas of skin color were flushed out in group. Harmony was threatened by society's racist statement about skin color. The destructiveness of valuing lighter skin tones found its way into the group at various times. A group member talked about the difference made by her parents when it came to her and her brother:

Zoe: My brother is lighter than me. My parents were more lenient on him than they were with me. He is younger than me, did poorer in school, and caused them a lot of grief. You could say he got away with "murder" in some cases. I remember when we were in high school, he borrowed the car and parked it in front of our house to run in for a second, so he said. The rule in our house was "never park the car on the street in front of the house during rush hour and Friday and Saturday night, park in the driveway." You see, the street we lived on was heavily traveled during those hours and accidents were a given. Growing up, we couldn't play in the frontyard during those hours.

Don't you know, the car was hit just ten minutes after he came into the house and, don't you know, he got off with just not using the car for the week! If that were me, I would have had to pay for the damages, the entire family, uncles and aunts, would have heard about it before the six o'clock news came on, and I would have not only been unable to use the car for at least a month, but I would have been grounded for that time too. They still let him go out that night with a friend of his!!! Maybe there was favoritism because of him being a male, but it came across to me as "color."

I recall conversations within the family about color, who was cute and who was troublesome. Maybe they didn't know what kind of messages they were sending, but it came across as "if you're light, you're all right; but if you're dark, shut up and go somewhere so I don't have to be bothered with you." I had a lot of examples to verify my impressions since my family was a rainbow of colors just like Reverend Jesse Jackson's Rainbow Coalition. I find I get angry at people who are light-skinned quicker than someone of my own complexion. It wasn't 'till lately, I realized what that behavior resulted from.

The discussion of the group centered around dealing with the various hues in the group. Much discussion focused on how members had internalized negative messages; time was taken to carefully inspect and probe the inner workings of the internalized messages. Sentence-completion exercises facilitated the discussion on their reactions. Incomplete sentences were posed by the group facilitators in a free-flowing, spur-of-the-moment interaction. Some examples follow:

"When I look at you I see...."

"I get angry when I see a _____ -skinned person." (light or dark)

"My heart rate races when I see a _____ -skinned person." (light or dark)

"Your skin color makes me feel. . . ."

"I became aware of my skin color at age. . . ."

"When I first learned of my skin color I felt. . . ."

"I wish I was _____ color instead of _____ because. . . ." (light or dark)

"My skin color makes me feel. . . ."

"When people look at me, they see. . . ."

"When I look at a person, I see. . . ."

"My experience of being _____ has been. . . ." (light or dark)

"My childhood experience of skin color was. . . ."

"In regards to color, I would like to teach others about. . . ."

After completing this exercise, we underwent a ritual of cleansing and embracing our inherited beauty and greatness. We erased the mental message tapes and replaced them with positive messages that empowered us. This exercise evoked a profound reaction, and healed us.

Corey and Corey (1977) described group cohesion as the extent to which the members identify with one another. The authors' describe the willingness to become transparent with one another so that as conflicts arise, the deep level of trust allows for a working-through process.

Common Interests and Reality Enhance Cohesion

Early talk about common interests and the reality of being different from society enhanced the group cohesion. Common interest spanned many areas—mother to daughter, mother to son, mother to elders, sister to sister, sister to brother, women in the workplace, women in schools, and more. Group members also seemed to enjoy taking the time to "socialize," talking about pleasant life experiences. One group member reported:

Joi: It's nice to unwind by just talking about our positive experiences before we get to the painful stuff. I realize we have so much in common. It makes the troublesome stuff approachable. Thank God for the small talk!

Members verbalized how they felt safe in the group; they did not have to guard what they said about White people. Some sample comments:

"You know how we say White when we're in public and we want to talk about them? Well, I don't have to whisper when I'm here."

"They all relate to us as being the same, we should do that to them for a month. Let's see how that feels."

When therapists trained in multiculturalism are able to have a substantial impact on clients, they are more apt to affect change. We will examine how change occurs when cultural awareness factors are included in the effort. Sue and Sue (1990) emphasized the importance of modifying the counseling approach when working with African-Americans. Once "modifications" have been made, using differences in cultural values and cohesiveness, good interpersonal relationships usually quickly follow.

Socializing behavior was allowed to continue without interruption during the early stages of the group. Building relationships and investigating common interest occurred as early as the first meeting. The purpose for allowing the socializing stems from the African-American value of "harmonious blending" as referred to in Chapter 2. Here is an example of a first conversation:

Tania: I came here to work in the local plant. The plant was downsizing in my town and increasing in production in a number of plants in other states. I knew if I wanted a job I needed to consider a move out of state, so here I am as a result. My family came after I settled in and my husband could transfer with his company. We've been lucky, in a manner of speaking; my husband's company is large with many locations throughout the United States so when I was threatened with losing my job unless I was willing to move, I took the move. Some of the other families were not so lucky. Many moves broke families up because they needed two incomes and couldn't afford to take a break in pay to move. You know, living paycheck to paycheck.

Well, when we moved, I had house set up and schools researched for our kids completed. Some families could not move and lost their jobs with the company. Many moved like I did. We were disliked at the plant we moved to because we took jobs that were "easy" jobs. Everyone from our plant, about sixty-five of us, were called names, had cars vandalized, and you name it. All in all we stuck close together.

Another group member, hearing a familiar story chimed in with:

Sera: We came here the same way! We're from there too. My husband's job offered a transfer. It's a small world, ain't it?!!!!! My husband had family here, so the move was not too hard on us. I didn't like it because it meant leaving my family. There are four kids in my family and everybody lived within ten miles of each other. I never had to worry about a babysitter or anything like that. My husband had fifteen years with the company so he didn't want to mess that up.

You're right about the resentment the people at this plant had toward the "newcomers." We even got hate mail. It was scary at first but when nothing happened, we stopped worrying about it.

So, where did you go to church?"

The conversation went on to discuss people they knew in common and other similar events back in their hometown. It was not long into their conversation until they mentioned the importance of church and spirituality, a central part of the lives of African-Americans. Other topics of "social" conversation emphasized the connections with a familiar surrounding and now coming to a hostile environment. They comfortably shared the pleasure of having both gone through the harshness of plant "turf" issues.

Stages of the Group Process

Development is characterized by certain stages of the group process, stages that address feelings and behaviors (Corey & Corey, 1982). Thus, as group members get to know one another better, higher levels of anxiety occur. Corey and Corey (1982) outlined the rubric of the group process: It comprises such activities as establishing norms, group cohesion, learning to work cooperatively, setting up ways of solving problems, and learning to express conflict openly.

Yalom (1985) refers to the formative stages of group as those beginning long before the first meeting when proper group selection, composition, setting, and preparation are determined. He identified the primary task as determining the participant's purpose in having joined the group. Yalom believed that participants must attend to their social relationship in the group so as to create a niche for themselves that will provide the comfort necessary to achieve their primary goals. The accomplishment of the primary goal will result in a certain degree of gratification. The member enters the group with questions that reflect confusion about aspects needing clarification. According to Yalom (1985), this confusion can surface months after the first meeting, and these areas of confusion have much to do with expectations about individual roles in group and the collective group process.

Bates, Johnson, and Blaker (1982) discussed the issues of inclusion in reference to a person's ability to establish a connection with group members. They believe that openness, trust, and warmth are shared by group members who have consciously or unconsciously come to terms with their inclusion and control needs. Stated very plainly, the group member is more comfortable when her identity in the group is clearly defined and she has assessed her potential contribution to the group. Corey (1981) refers to cohesion as the attractiveness of the group for the participants. *Attractiveness* means the member's sense of belonging and solidarity. "The honest sharing of deeply significant personal experiences and struggles binds the group with others by seeing themselves in them" (Corey, 1981, p. 67), a process that is far from automatic.

Group participation by African-American women appears geared toward honest sharing of deeply significant personal experiences. The sharing of struggles in the group setting seems to occur early and often. The mention of the issue of anger is a topic that readily lends itself to the disclosing of deeply personal experiences. A 56-year-old divorced mother of three shared the following during the second session:

Barbara: I wanted to come to group because I just don't seem to get anywhere with my youngest daughter. She is sixteen and does not want to cooperate at all. There is nothing I can

mention that we can have a decent conversation about. I
know what the problem is, it's her father. He spends no time
with her. They were very close before the divorce over a year
ago, now he spends more time at work and with his new
ladyfriend.

I am furious because my daughter is hard to manage;
he's nowhere around to be found and is having fun with this
new woman as well as escapes paying child support. It's like
we don't exist anymore. I stay mad. I try to talk with my
daughter as much as I can about missing her father but I
have a hard time with it since she is in so much pain about
her Daddy not paying the attention she is used to. It hurts to
see her pain, it really does.

I think he's wrong. I don't care how much we argue, the
kids should stay out of it. It just burns me up when he drags
our daughter into our fight. She's just a kid. It's not her fault
he can't be faithful . . . I just don't understand it. He is so
irresponsible. It seems like everybody pays for his actions.

I came to this group from another group. That group was
a mixed group. The White women tried to cover up their
anger . . . at least that's what they appeared to do. I wanted
to shout my anger out and they were scared at the slightest
expression of it. After the third session of "nice talk," I
talked with the group leader about individual sessions
because I had to get this stuff out of me and she directed
me to this group.

Once I got here and saw that everybody was Black, I
knew we were going to get busy and deal with some real
hurts. I know you [speaking to the group members] understand when I say I'm mad. You don't want to smooth it over.
Don't get me wrong or anything, I don't hate White people;
they just don't know how to deal with anger, especially when
it comes from Black people.

My daughter is in pain and she's pushing me away. I'm
losing my effectiveness with her because I'm getting angry
at her reaction toward me. It's just a vicious cycle that won't
end. I'm afraid I'm going to lose my daughter to drugs or the
streets. I've got to get a hold of myself because she's all I've
got right now. The rest of my kids are all grown and doing
pretty good. She is too important to lose. I need your help.

The group rallied around her request for support, seemingly
unafraid of the issue of anger. It just automatically occurred.

Once one group member shared the deep hurt of a divorced spouse, another member followed up with her own disappointment at her failed marriage which she is choosing to stick with "for now." The second woman followed up with her own description:

Helen: I'm so mad I could spit nails. I think I'm mad at myself more than anything. Here I am retired and ready to live the life we set out to live and he is acting the fool. We had a good life, or at least I thought it was good, and now he's more worried about money than our happiness. We've worked hard all our lives. I got sick a few years ago and had to quit. It seems like he just takes me for granted. I feel trapped because where am I to go? I can't work anymore, I have regular doctor appointments and expensive medication to pay for, so I try to do extra around the house to make up for my part since I can't work anymore.

    I got fed up with his ways and decided to go on strike. I stopped cooking and cleaning. I've spent more time away from home than usual. I'll go to the library or walk around the malls. Then my car broke down. You know he refused to fix it! So I called friends to get rides from here to there. I even caught the bus a couple of times. I came to the conclusion that I will not be taken for granted anymore. When I cook, it's because I want to cook. If I clean, it's because I want to clean. No more of this hurtful treatment. My mother took it from my father and I refuse to be treated in the same manner.

    If I were younger, I would probably divorce but being my age, it doesn't make sense. We get along in many areas, such as the grandkids and the treatment of our children who are all grown and doing well. I refuse to be mistreated because of my kindness any longer. Maybe he'll come around and maybe he won't. One thing is for sure, I am going to create a peaceful life for myself. I'm tired of being angry all the time.

Cohesion appeared to be present early in this group therapy. According to Corey (1981), it is the result of group members and the leader taking steps that best lead to a group-as-a-whole feeling. Cohesion fosters action-oriented behaviors such as self-disclosure, mutuality, confrontation, risk-taking, and translation of insights into action. He adds that without cohesion, participants don't feel secure enough to maintain a high level of self-disclosure.

Self-disclosure remained somewhat of a constant from the first meeting of the group on; participants remained highly involved. This involvement took many forms: listening, offering words of encouragement, giving constructive criticism, and self-disclosing. A group member shared the following at her last meeting:

Lydia: I have attended this group in the past. I wanted to come back again to get help in understanding why I give so much to my husband and son but get little in return. I wanted to know why this seems to be a consistent theme in my life. I have read lots of self-help books to search for the answer with little satisfaction. Coming to the group initially gave me much to ponder and helped me make a few adjustments in my life.

Once I made those changes and found that they worked, I became motivated to make more changes. Hearing the stories everyone so freely shared helped me take a good look at my situation. The group was very helpful as they shared the events of their lives. I knew my solution would come from hearing others. That sounds funny to hear me say that but it's true, I had to hear how you solved your problems to stimulate my motivation to get busy on mine.

Something outside the group happened in addition to the growth I experienced inside of the group meetings. My sister and cousins have a yearly meeting to discuss family concerns. In the past, our meetings were "piss-and-moan" sessions. We didn't seem to get off of complaining about things we had no control over. One of the younger cousins suggested a very smart thing; spend the first two hours complaining and writing down the problems, and the rest of the time developing solutions. During the last two hours, together we would have a healing ritual to emphasize the spiritual aspect of our lives.

We laughed at first but knew she was right. So we hurried and said our last statements of negative things about the family and planned for the next time we would be together. We knew we would see each other, or talk throughout the year so we could complain during those times. Don't you know we came together, had a wonderful time and left so uplifted that we felt inspired to keep the negative talk to a minimum! I bet throughout the year we'll keep the negative stuff down too.

We shared our successes and learned from each other. We took the lessons to our families and they worked. I found my need to "please" lessen. My family didn't know what to make of the fact that I wasn't trying to run the house from top to bottom. I think they were happy about it in a strange sort of way. They didn't pick up the things I stopped doing. They just accepted it the way it was. If I didn't cook, they ate sandwiches and fresh veggies, or had a bowl of cereal, or something they could easily get.

They seemed relaxed about it. I'll recommend it for anybody to try once, you'll see a difference in your family right away. It is as if I put too many demands on myself, following the pattern of my mother, and the family didn't need all that. They were happy with just being together. I learned a very valuable lesson, giving "me" is more important than giving "things." If I work all day and spend the rest of the day cooking this fantastic meal or cleaning the house or redecorating a room, it never stacks up to just being together and talking about things and loving each other up. I learned I have to be available to receive the loving from my family, not busy doing other things. I had been missing the gifts of their love because I wouldn't sit still long enough to receive it. I need to hear my husband tell me he loves me, which he does not say too often, and he doesn't have the chance if I'm running around the house fussing with getting things done and complaining about no one helping. Or, I need to see my son accomplish good things in school and proudly snuggle up next to me to report the joy he experiences with his accomplishments but he can't do that if I'm not sitting down. So I am here to tell you that I sit down a whole lot these days!

More examples of group cohesiveness like this one need to be explored and researched.

Group Cohesiveness Research

Research in the area of group cohesiveness is somewhat lacking. Bednar and Kaul (1978) stated that group cohesion can be a prime therapeutic factor in groups; they further showed that successes and failures frequently come down to the existence of or lack of group cohesion. They delineated little clear and systematic research on the specific factors thought to affect cohesion. Lieberman, Yalom, and Miles (1973) indicated that attraction to the group is a determinant of outcome. Members who do not feel a sense of belonging or an attraction to the group have a high likelihood of experiencing negative outcomes.

The initial screening includes an explanation of group cohesiveness. The potential group participant is informed of this circular phenomena of the therapy group. It is couched in an Afrocentric framework, that all of life is connected, "He who learns, teaches" (Leslau & Leslau, 1985, p. 21). We emphasize the importance of receiving and giving. A dialogue in a screening session can run as follows:

Group Leader: We've talked about the goals you would like to accomplish in the group; they sound reasonable and attainable; we view the importance of learning or achieving goals as the hope of each group member. There is a significant factor that is valuable to other persons in the group, that is, to learn from your new-found knowledge. There is an African saying from the country of Ethiopia that states, "He who learns, teaches." Can you tell me how this new learning can benefit the group?

Participants' responses vary, as in the following:

"I'm interested in learning from others so it only makes sense that I also share my new found-knowledge. So, to answer your question, I hope to teach other participants by explaining how I came to certain conclusions or share with the group my failures and the lessons learned."

"I don't know how to answer your question right now. I feel so low I don't feel I have much to contribute."

"I just hope to be honest with the group and tell them how I feel about certain things. I think we are silent when we should be vocal and we let each other make unnecessary mistakes so I want to 'teach' by simply warning others of the possible pitfalls of their choices. I hope that will be helpful."

"I have learned the value of God being in my life. The group will, I hope, help me to blend what I learn from personal experiences to understand how God is speaking through me or others. So prayer is a source of peace for me and I would like to give to group members the importance of the practice of praying."

"I hope to give some levity to the group. I like to laugh. Sometimes laughter is good medicine. It makes you think of your problem with a light heart and not take yourself so seriously. Laughter helps get the stress off so you can think clearer."

The importance of giving and receiving is stressed. It is also explained that the level of satisfaction is reported by participants as a high level of involvement. The group facilitator explains:

Facilitator: Our experience has been that the amount of involvement directly correlates with the amount of satisfaction. In other words, you'll value your group participation more the more involved you are in the group. If your involvement is low you will not be satisfied with your group involvement.

Further, groups with a high cohesiveness are more apt to have a positive outcome than groups characterized by low cohesiveness. In their five-stage conceptualization of group development, Gross and Capuzzi (1992) described a third stage where interaction leads to productive group cohesion development. They see this stage as one involving blending, merging, and moving from independence to more interdependence. The group member is not lost but becomes enmeshed in the group. The researchers see Stage 3 as encompassing behaviors and activities more group-specific than member-specific. The collective group, its purposes, processes, and membership must come ahead of the individual if it is to maximize its development (Gross & Capuzzi, 1992, p. 30).

When one transforms group work in general into group work with a specific population, namely, African-American women, one needs to shift the focus to examining effective group work by delineating and expounding on group cohesiveness. Shipp (1983) noted that group counseling is the most effective approach with African-American clients. "The key to helping Black clients lies in understanding Black behavior as it integrates with African ethos" (Shipp, 1983, p. 109). The following are the values, attitudes, and behaviors Shipp specifically comments on:

1. Cooperation between and among individuals
2. Collective responsibility of individuals to his or her group
3. Interdependence among individuals
4. Commonality of individuals

Group cohesiveness is demonstrated on many levels—the family, church, and a variety of social groups (e.g., fraternities and sororities) in the African-American community. The bonding within and among these groups illustrates the key elements of interdependence, collective responsibility, commonality, and cooperation between and among individuals. Nobles (1976) discussed the emphasis the familial relationship has on reinforcing the values of family sharing and cooperation. Since this is congruent with the African-American client's beliefs, it increases the group leader's chances for instilling group responsibility. Within the sphere of group work, members acquire an awareness of their universality by sharing fears and fantasies (Shipp, 1983, p. 110) and in sharing, group members come to realize that their problems are not unique.

Ramona, a 55-year-old African-American, who is employed in the private sector, has lived all of her life in isolation. She described herself as a "loner" and preferred to have little to no interaction with others. Employment positions she has held throughout her life fed her need for isolation, for most required little or no contact with other workers. The choice to join the group was made by Ramona when she decided she needed companionship, a basic African concept. Isolation rendered her totally lacking in identity and self-esteem. Ramona had been very selective when it came to male partners: The current relationship is 11 years old. Having been married once, Ramona vowed never to marry again. She describes the experience as painful and demeaning. Both the marriage and the current relationship involve the use of alcohol and infidelity on her partner's part.

Engaging Ramona was not difficult to do, in spite of her reclusive manner. Her decision to become a part of the group was met with open and genuine warmth from other group members. Direct communication patterns enhanced her story.

Ramona: I wanted to join this group because I am tired of being alone. I have siblings but they are not close in age. My sister, next to me, is eight years younger than me. No signs of affection was given to me by my parents. I didn't receive hugs or anything like that. Materially, all my needs were met but that was all. My father was an alcoholic and my mother spent all her time tending to him, or it seemed that way to me.

Ramona had listened to another group member describe her isolated life and immediately focused on that other group member. Initially, Ramona had directed her conversation to no one in particular but quickly switched to focusing on Shari's description of isolation. A stark difference could be seen between the two individuals. Shari was gregarious and Ramona was not. The shift from speaking in general to directly speaking to Shari was not coached by the therapist. She focused her attention on Shari as she continued:

Ramona: Shari, you say you are very protective of yourself, not letting anyone close, but you seem outgoing, friendly and you like to joke a lot. You've talked to everyone in this group. Our first meeting and today, our second meeting, there isn't anything that you held back on with comments. I would never do that. I have been silent all of my life, until now. Since I hit menopause, I can't keep my mouth shut.

Shari: It might look as if I'm outgoing, but that's a front. I don't let anyone in.

Janiba: Shari, I know you from another setting and I've known you for a number of years. You were always friendly. After a while, you began to develop a friendship with me. You may not have let me all of the way in, but certainly, I wouldn't characterize you as being closed.

The comparing of experiences continued:

Janiba: I'm pretty familiar with you, Ramona, having gone to school with you. What I remember the most about you is that your body language sent the message that all doors that may have been open to get to know you were closed. You have a downward gaze. At the time you wore glasses and used them to sort of hide behind. Today, you still have the downward gaze and you wear contacts. When you talk with me, your eyelids flutter and rest in a downward gaze position.

Ramona absorbed the various comments, listening intently. This direct, nontentative manner of talking to Ramona did not intimidate her. In fact, she asked for more feedback. The cotherapist assisted the group in facilitating the use of immediacy—talking in the here and now. Shari shared with Ramona her desire to reconnect with her "sisters":

Shari: Black women make me feel strong. It's like the pumping of adrenaline through my veins. My family had its ups and downs, but the one thing I remember was the importance of connecting with one another. We would have family vacations with Mom's sisters and brothers. It was different than a family reunion because it was done on a smaller scale. Maybe three families would get together for a week's vacation, or one family would go to the other's home for the weekend. Smaller, more intimate groups. I yearn for the closeness that those gatherings fostered. Sure, my uncle was an alcoholic, and another cousin died of an overdose of heroin, but the family rallied around those hurts.

The information shared at this point in the session highlighted that value lying deep within the African ethos, interdependence among individuals. The breakdown of the family in this highly mobile society, as well as the high level of stress experienced in today's workplace, creates isolation and fosters few opportunities for building lasting or stable relationships. The strengthening components for building love and restoring the healing must be put in place. We also need to look at society's responsibility for "killing" what it considers different. A group member receives affirmation for her uniqueness and inherited beauty.

The group leaders introduced an exercise incorporating the value of interdependence to deepen and enhance sisterhood. There is music playing in the background during the reading of "Sisterhood Pledge" by Antoinette Savage (1992). The entire experience created a catharsis. The message was generally one of gratitude for two things: the return of interdependence and the introduction of the concept. A comment made later by Ramona showed her bewilderment and curiosity; Vy responded to her immediatly:

Ramona: This is so foreign to me that it leaves me with the response, "I have to think about this."

Vy: Don't bother thinking about it, just feel it. If you think about it, you'll miss the best part...the warm feelings and sense of security gotten from being connected.

The group quickly took on the responsibility for facilitating communication and interaction by functioning in a facilitator's role. Vy knew to instruct Ramona regarding the processing of the "Sisterhood Pledge." The collective responsibility of an individual to his or her group (Shipp, 1983) is indicative of an alternative reality (Jackson, 1991). In that, the women in the group were spurred to reach out and trust one another rather than guarding interactions.

Forms of Communication

The traditional (Eurocentric perspective) approach is designed along dichotomous lines—that is, that the mind and body are separate. In Africa, the Adinka tribe had no concept of "mind"; they did not compartmentalize or posit a mediating agent between the individual and his or her external world (Jackson, 1991, p. 539). The African view of the individual is one of the whole rather than the separate parts. Moving toward wholeness and healing requires that self-actualization come from the individual living in such a way that the group survives. Asserting the interests of the individual over the group would be deviant or undesirable behavior, according to Jackson.

The more directive the group experience, the more effective the facilitation of the client's involvement. The client's communication patterns need to be affirmed; direct communication is the most comfortable way of relating since tentative speech has no place in African-American groups. Members don't struggle with the expectations of being nondirective and tentative in their approach to talking with other members. Shade (1991) discussed patterns of cognition and processes of perception, and reported that essentially, we experience our world through our kinetic and tactile senses (p. 243). We connect with one another intensely; our communication patterns are strong and forward.

As therapists, we affirm the use of Black English as a communication style that will enhance group cohesiveness. Smith-erman (1991) wrote about Black English and its connection to African substratum. The moments of "testifying" within the group gave power to the experiences the women in the group had in this regard (Smitherman, 1991). Indicating the remote past through the use of the word "been," as in "She been gone," "I been doing that," gave it real power when stressed (Smitherman, 1991). Semantic inversion is turning a word into its opposite (i.e., from Mandingo, *a ka nyi ko-jugu*, literally, "it is good badly" meaning "it is very good"). Here the word "bad" refers to the highest good (Smitherman, 1991, p. 252).

Specific nonverbal communication styles and behaviors are part of the group experience for the African-American woman. Just a small gesture will take unlimited words to explain and describe. Jean had hit her limit with a teenage niece she had invited into her home so that she could escape an abusive home environment. Jean and her daughter felt threatened by the teen's abusive language and defiant behavior. Jean motioned with her foot and pointed with her fingers, one on each hand, the action to be taken. The kicking of her foot and pointing of her fingers in the same direction made the message clear, the niece was going to be kicked out.

Majors (1991) examined the expressive and performance-oriented behaviors of African-Americans. He stated that these behaviors were used to cope with the "invisibility" and frustration resulting from racism and discrimination. "Many African-American people have channeled their creative talents and energies into the construction and use of particular expressive and conspicuous styles of nonverbal behaviors (e.g., in their demeanor, gestures, clothing, hairstyles, walk, stances, and handshakes, among other areas)" (p. 271). He added that we are expressive and have colorful styles: "The behaviors not only accentuate the self used to appear urbane, they are also used to keep whites off guard about one's intentions. By the use of expressive nonverbal expressions, we exercise control, express pride, dignity, and respect for themselves" (Majors, 1991, p. 272).

The use of nonverbal behavior strengthens the connection between group members and loyalty to their culture. The solidarity its use creates enhances group cohesiveness. "The way we sit, stand, and use facial expressions, such as eye movement and other body language, all contribute to intergroup enhancement and the commonality of individuals, as group members build relationships within the group" (Shipp, 1983, p. 110).

Touching is another form of communication African-Americans utilize at a higher rate than European-Americans, regardless of gender (Majors, 1991). According to Majors, African-American women touch more than European-Americans as a way of expressing intimacy, friendship, and warmth. An illustration of this can be found in the personal material Latifa shared. She wanted to objectively share her experience of loss but, unable to fight back the tears, Latifa began to cry as she talked about the loss:

Latifa: My year has been very hard. I am an only child and had the responsibility of caring for my terminally ill mother. Since I am a nurse, I could approach it with some understanding and objectivity. The difficulty surrounded the fact that my relationship with her was poor all my life. The only person I felt close to was my paternal grandmother. Grandma knew of the strain between Mom and me. She never brought it up but had her way of letting me know everything was going to be all right. We were very close. She would hug me and hold me real close. She passed away a year ago, so I had to deal with Mom's illness by myself. [*The tears began to flow and the group members on each side of Latifa immediately put their arms around her.*] I feel incredibly alone.

Shari: It's high time you let someone into your life. Can I be there for you as a friend? I have an endless supply of hugs.

Latifa: I can't go on like this, I know. I want to be close to women like me, meaning Black women, but I fear the tension and conflict so many women complain of.

Shari: I want to try. Can I?

Group Leader: I believe we have a responsibility to work toward the unity that African-Americans spoke about during Kwanzaa. How do you see it happening here?

Latifa: I think that means I can open myself up to the possibility of making a connection with Jan and also to the community, and working through conflicts.

Shari: We need each other to build a cohesive society, but more for breaking the isolation and pain of being Black and burdened.

Group Leader: I think your invitation has been accepted, Jan. Thank you for extending your hand in friendship. Umoja—unity!

Summary

Umoja carries the encouragement as well as the burden of maintaining unity. It is a challenge and an opportunity to build community so as to prepare a future for our children. Umoja is a concept that requires present action for present and future relationships. Chapter 6 illustrates the means discussed and developed that allow unity to be realized; it moves us on to the working stage of group work. Once trust and group cohesiveness have been established, deep psychological work and development of newly acquired skills can get underway.

References

Bates, M., Johnson, C. D., & Blaker, K. E. (1982). *Group leadership: A manual for group counseling leaders* (2nd ed). Denver: Love Publishing Company.

Bednar, R. L., & Kaul, T. J. (1978). Experiential group research: Current perspectives. In S. L. Garfield & A. E. Bergin (Eds.), *Handbook of psychotherapy and behavior change* (2nd ed.) (pp. 769–816). New York: Wiley.

Corey, G. (1981). *Theory and practice of group counseling*. Monterey, CA: Brooks/Cole.

Corey, G., & Corey, M. S. (1977). *Groups: Process and practice* (2nd ed.). Monterey, CA: Brooks/Cole.

Corey, G., & Corey, M. S. (1982). *Techniques in group counseling*. Monterey, CA: Brooks/Cole.

Gross, D. R., & Capuzzi, D. (1992). *Group counseling: Stages and issues* (Ch. 2). Denver: Love Publishing Company.

Hoyt-Goldsmith, D. (1993). *Celebrating Kwanzaa*. New York: Holiday House.

Jackson, G. G. (1991). The African genesis of the black perspective in helping. In R. Jones (Ed.), *Black psychology* (3rd ed.) (pp. 533–558). Berkeley: Cobb & Henry.

Karenga, M. (1988). *The African-American holiday of Kwanzaa: A celebration of family, community and culture*. Los Angeles: Sankore Press.

Lee, C. C. (1991). Counseling African-American: From theory to practice. In R. Jones (Ed.), *Black psychology* (3rd ed.) (pp. 559–576). Berkeley: Cobb & Henry.

Leslau, W., & Leslau, C. (1985). *African proverbs* (2nd ed.). New York: Peter Pauper Press.

Lieberman, M., Yalom, I., & Miles, M. (1973). *Encounter groups—First facts*. New York: Basic Books.

Majors, R. (1991). Nonverbal behaviors and communication styles among African-Americans. In R. Jones (Ed.), *Black psychology* (3rd ed.) (pp.269–294). Berkeley: Cobb & Henry.

Nobles, W. (1976). Extended self: Rethinking the so-called Negro concept. *Journal of Black Psychology, 2*(2), 15–24.

Shade, B. J. (1991). African-American patterns of cognition. In R. Jones (Ed.), *Black psychology,* (3rd ed.) (pp. 231–248). Berkeley: Cobb & Henry.

Shipp, P. O. (1983). Counseling Blacks: A group approach. *Personnel and Guidance Journal, 62*(2), 108–111.

Smitherman, G. (1991). Talking and testifying: Black English and the Black experience. In R. Jones (Ed.), *Black psychology* (3rd ed.) (pp. 249–268). Berkeley: Cobb & Henry.

Sue, D. W., & Sue, D. (1990). *Counseling the culturally different: Theory and practice* (2nd ed.). New York: Wiley.

Yalom, I. D. (1985). *The theory and practice of group psychotherapy* (3rd ed.). New York: Basic Books.

6

The Working Stage—
Kujichugulia, Ujima,
and Imani

No knowledge about group work is more valuable than knowledge about the stages through which members go. Through such awareness, leaders are able to determine the direction the group might take, feel a sense of mastery over the group experience, select appropriate intervention strategies, diagnose problems of the group, and evaluate group effectiveness. The greatest fear of many young counselors or therapists in training is that some unexpected event may happen in the group over which they would have no control. A working knowledge and awareness of the development of the group are essential for group effectiveness and success, as are the kwanzaa principles of Kujichugulia (authenticity and self-esteem), Ujima (collective work responsibility), and Imani (faith).

Embedded in group stages are factors and forces that facilitate member and group growth and change. These healing or helping agents are generally known in counseling and psychotherapy literature as *therapeutic forces*. When leaders have knowledge and awareness of group stages and therapeutic forces and are able to apply these two concepts appropriately in group, their group experiences are usually successful. Although the concepts of group stages and therapeutic forces usually are applied with traditional clientele, they also can be used with

African-American women groups, given certain multicultural considerations including cultural values, beliefs, and behaviors.

This chapter discusses selected stages of group work, the application of specific therapeutic forces, and the interaction of culture on both. The chapter attempts to help the reader understand how to apply African-American cultural values and beliefs to traditional counseling theory and practice. The reader is also given a set of guidelines or strategies for working with African-American women in counseling and therapy groups.

Group Stages, Therapeutic Forces, and Cultural Influences

Group Stages

There are various descriptions of the stages of group development throughout social science literature. In this chapter, the writers use the group work model described by Corey (1995). This model includes four stages; however, attention is only given to the initial stage and the working stage; a brief description of them follows. The initial stage and the working stage are also illustrated later based on how they are used in the *Images of Me* group.

The Initial Stage

In the initial stage, there is a concern for member safety, security, and welfare in addition to a need for orientation about group norms and expectations. Concerns about acceptance and belonging also prevail in the early stages of a group. Wanting to make an initial favorable impression, members are quite concerned about how they manifest certain attitudes, feelings, and behaviors. Perhaps the greatest issue of concern in this stage, and the greatest challenge for group leaders, is building and maintaining trust.

The Working Stage

In the working stage, members have worked through a great deal of resistance and have developed a greater spirit of cooperation. At this point, members have become a more cohesive unit and are better prepared to help one another work through their difficulties and to bring about desired behavioral change. Because members are more trusting and more cooperative in this stage, the leaders often take a less directive role, allowing the members to function on their own. In the working stage, member commitment is high and change is much more likely to take place.

Therapeutic Forces

Operating throughout the various stages of group development are therapeutic forces. Yalom (1985) defines therapeutic forces as the qualities or factors that facilitate growth and change among group members. Knowledge and awareness of therapeutic forces enable leaders to employ appropriate strategies and techniques to help members achieve personal and group goals. Even though therapeutic forces may exist throughout the duration of the group, the function of each therapeutic force may change from one group stage to another. For example, the therapeutic force, imparting information, in the initial stage could be used for orienting the members to the group. While in the working stage, imparting information could be used for explaining group process. Appropriate application of therapeutic forces can greatly improve group effectiveness. The therapeutic forces described here are adapted from Yalom (1985):

1. *Universality*–Discovering you are not the only one with the problem.
2. *Instillation of hope*–Believing that your problem can be solved–you can get better.
3. *Imitative behavior*–Growing and learning by observing others.
4. *Imparting knowledge*–Giving information to the group.
5. *Altruism*–Experiencing growth and change by helping other people.
6. *Developing socializing techniques*–Learning how to communicate and interact with one another more effectively.
7. *Group cohesiveness*–Having a strong sense of acceptance and belonging.
8. *Catharsis*–Expressing strong feelings both negatively and positively.
9. *Existential factors*–Facing life as it is.

NOTE: Those most frequently used in the initial and working stages are discussed later in this chapter.

The Influence of Cultural Values, Beliefs, and Behaviors on Group Stages

Earlier in this chapter, the reader was provided information relative to group stages and therapeutic forces—concepts that are universally applicable for counseling and psychotherapy groups. However, when working with specific cultural groups, multicultural considerations might need to be taken. Specifically, there are certain African-American cultural values, beliefs, and behaviors that may influence how one works with African-American women in counseling and therapy groups, including the following:

1. *Nonverbal communication*—It has been observed that African-Americans look at the person to whom they are speaking but tend to look away when they are listening. Extensive eye contact should be avoided because it might be considered staring. In addition, African-Americans tend to move in closer when talking. At family gatherings and other group settings, African-Americans tend to all talk at the same time. Yet, they hear and understand what others are communicating.

2. *Views toward counseling*—In general, African-Americans have a negative attitude toward mental health counselors and counseling. Rather than seek help for mental health issues, African-Americans tend to rely on their own resources such as family, friends, and ministers from their church. Sharing family secrets with outsiders is usually not encouraged. In addition, problems African-Americans encounter are usually real problems concerning their basic survival needs rather than psychological ones. More and more, middle-class African-Americans are beginning to make use of counseling and mental health services.

3. *Time perception*—Many African-Americans are concerned about survival from day-to-day rather than being more concerned about future goals and objectives. Adhering to strict schedules (even reporting for counseling appointments on time) is often problematic.

4. *Family structure and dynamics*—Family members are extremely valuable for the survival of African-American families. The family is often an extended one, including grandparents, aunts, uncles, cousins, and so forth. Many females are heads of household due to the absence of male/father figures. However, grandparents, especially grandmothers, are responsible for rearing many African-American children. Often, it is a good idea for counseling issues to be resolved in collaboration with the client and her parents.

5. *Religion and mental health*–The church plays a major role in the lives of many African-American people. It serves as a place where members can meet their personal, social, political, spiritual and psychological needs. The minister is often the counselor to whom members take their problems. Many African-American church members believe that it is blasphemy to discuss problems with anyone other than the minister or a higher power. In other words, prayer is often viewed as the answer to problems and psychological needs.

6. *Sexuality*–There is very little tolerance for homosexuality among African-Americans. Individuals who are gay or lesbian must hide their identity or be labeled or stigmatized. In general, such individuals are frowned on and are held responsible for their condition. Gays and lesbians from the African-American community are isolated, stressed, and generally not supported.

NOTE: In the *Images of Me* group, several of these cultural influences or values are manifested through member participation. Some of these cultural considerations are discussed in the next section.

The Interaction of Group Stages, Therapeutic Forces, and Cultural Influences

An earlier section of this chapter describes the initial stage and the working stage of *Images of Me* group development based on Corey's (1995) model. The concepts of therapeutic forces in group work as advanced by Yalom (1995) were identified and discussed. We concluded our background for this chapter by identifying and discussing certain cultural influences or values, beliefs, and behaviors of African-Americans that may impact the outcome of group work with women.

The remainder of this chapter attempts to illustrate the interaction of group stages, therapeutic forces, and cultural influences relative to counseling in the *Images of Me* group. In particular, we discuss how to apply therapeutic forces and cultural values, beliefs, and behaviors in the initial stage and in the working stage of a group.

The Initial Stage

Earlier we stated that in the initial stage of group development, the main concerns are safety, security, acceptance, and
norm setting. Although certain therapeutic forces may be more
prevalent in a certain group stage, these forces may appear
throughout the life of the group. However, here we identify
those forces most prevalent in the initial stage and in the
working stage of the group. This discussion is drawn largely
from our experiences of leading *Images of Me* groups over the
past five years. For the initial stage, we illustrate how to
employ therapeutic forces such as (1) imparting information,
(2) instillation of hope, and (3) universality.

Imparting Information

Generally, when we think about therapy groups rarely do we
consider didactic information as a therapeutic entity. However, the imparting of information is very important for a
group of African-American women because many of them are
not familiar with the group therapy process and need to know
what is included and expected to learn from the experience. It
has been our experience that the more accurate information
members have about group work, the greater commitment
they will make to it, and the more valuable the experience will
be for them. In the *Images of Me* group, information has helped
to reduce anxiety, teach members about the nature of group
process, clarify expectations, demystify the therapy process,
enhance group process, and allay fears.

Because many African-American women have so little experience in counseling or therapy groups, we have found it helpful to teach them several group concepts—(1) group process, (2)
therapeutic forces, (3) boundary management or ground rules,
(4) the role of members, and (5) the role of leaders. The following
are some of the procedures we use to impart this information.

Group Process. We provide a brief definition of group process because it is used so often in a group and our group is
interpersonal in nature. Using Yalom's (1985) definition, we
tell them that *group process* deals with the nature or quality of
the relationship between or among individuals who are communicating or interacting with one another. We explain that
the process is the underlying meaning of the discussions. The
process is the opposite of the content or the spoken words. The

process is the *Why* and the *How* of the interaction. Process might also be thought of as the unexpressed feelings or motivations in the group.

To further clarify the meaning of the term "group process," we provide an illustration by relating an event that took place between two members of an *Images of Me* group. Mary is a middle-class, professional, college-educated, articulate woman; and Lillie Mae is a woman with an impoverished background and a high school dropout with seven children.

Mary: I sent my son, Michael, to a historically Black college to give him a Black experience since he has always been in predominantly White settings. Recently, Michael, who has always made good grades, has had a tremendous drop in his grade point average and is beginning to show some antisocial behavior.

Lillie Mae: Children from poor backgrounds do better in life than children from wealthier backgrounds. For example, children from low SES families struggle but turn out better. Mary, I suggest that you lighten up a little and let your son grow up and face life like everybody else.

Following this example, we raise several questions to help current group members gain a better understanding of group process. First, we ask "What do you think the feelings between Lillie Mae and Mary were?" Second, "Why do you think Lillie Mae attacked Mary's child-rearing practices?" As members speculate about the meaning of this interaction, they begin to achieve a better understanding of group process. For example, we explain that Lillie Mae may hold envious feelings toward successful African-Americans. We continue by saying, "It is also possible that Lillie Mae wished she could have provided material things for her children as Mary had been able to do." Using nonmembers as a starting point enables us to teach these concepts without putting any current member on the spot too soon.

Therapeutic Forces and Boundary Management. We also introduce definitions of therapeutic forces as the healing qualities that they too can employ toward facilitating the gowth experience for all. We explain that both the leaders and the members can play a vital role in using therapeutic forces in the group. We further explain that therapeutic forces might be better understood in terms of their application in various group stages. For instance, we say: "Imparting information, as we are doing now, is an important therapeutic force and will play a vital role in your learning and in the growth process of this group."

We use the analogy of a referee who establishes boundaries and sets limits for a basketball game to compare the role of the leader. The leaders determine what is out of bounds and what is in bounds and in general enforce the ground rules that have been established for the group. For example, disrespect for other members is considered out of bounds.

The Role of Members. For members who are not familiar with group work, we find that it is quite valuable to discuss the three roles of the group member: "Members may function in three different roles—as a client, the person who is receiving help; as a model, someone who is showing others how to work through their difficulties; and sometimes as therapist, someone who is offering advice, suggestions, or insight to fellow group members." We explain or suggest: "Members are usually in the role of client during the earlier meetings and progress to the role of model during the later stages." We state further that these roles are *interchangeable*.

To facilitate or clarify the role of members, we direct a role-play in which members can practice each role. We often place these groups in triads and have members take turns acting out each role. Following this exchange, we ask the small triad groups to share their understanding about member roles to the rest of the group. This exercise is especially important when members have no prior experience in group counseling or group therapy.

The Role of Leaders. We explain that our roles are to manage, monitor, and facilitate all aspects of the group. In addition to organizing the group, we tell them that it is our overall goal to ensure the safety of the members and to engage them in a variety of experiences or tasks designed to help them learn, grow, and change certain attitudes or behaviors they have identified as problematic. Finally, we discuss how difficult it is to practice African principles in a Eurocentric society. We encourage participants to work in concert, always for the good and welfare of other group members. Our goal as leaders is to assist members achieve their personal and group goals.

Instillation of Hope

Another crucial therapeutic force in the beginning phase of group work is the instillation of hope (Yalom, 1985). Participants who expect to get something out of the group experience usually do. Group leaders need to do a good job of convincing members that their active participation in the group will yield positive results or a good outcome. We discuss success stories by telling how previous group members overcame their difficulties. New members often begin to feel self-assured about their chances for success when they learn about the success of others. We give a great deal of attention to the instillation of hope because without it, members drop out before completing the group counseling process. Sue (1981) reported that 50 percent of ethnic minority clients do not return after the initial session while White clients' dropout rate is only 30 percent. Yalom suggested that early instillation of hope is important for keeping participants engaged until other therapeutic forces for change are enacted. Hope is doubly important for many African-American women who are already demoralized when they enter the therapy group.

Many African-American women participants have been so beaten down that they do not believe that change is possible. This belief is especially true when a group member encounters racism or sexism and does not believe that there is any hope for a solution. Lillie Mae, for example, shared with the group that a teacher had pushed her seven-year-old son and had racially stereotyped him on several other occasions. Upon reporting this incident, she was given the run-around and was accused of having a chip on her shoulder. Because she did not believe that change was possible, group leaders really had to work hard to restore her belief in the system and get her to believe that through her work in the group she could relieve some of her stress, anxiety, and pain. We assured her that she had already begun the process by participating in the group.

Couch and Childers (1987) suggested that hope may be inherent in the characteristics of effective group leaders; in particular, leaders might express hope in three ways. First, they might acknowledge the client's abilities and potential for change through group counseling. Second, leaders may express hope by stating their strong beliefs in the value of group counseling. Third, they might express hope through a sense of confidence and personal power using nonverbal means. That is, effective group leaders exude a level of confidence and personal power causing group members to believe that they are in good hands.

Hope is the centerpiece in the early stages and throughout the duration of the African-American women's group. Female group leaders symbolize hope by their presence, their confidence, and their expertise as group facilitators. These African-American leaders believe in the value of the group process and that members can grow and change when they commit themselves to the task of the group. We, as leaders of an African-American women's group, personify hope through the examples we set. Specifically, we have experienced success through the application of African principles in our personal lives by providing service to the African-American community and through showing support and cooperation as a vehicle for survival.

We, as leaders, use success experiences from earlier groups to build hope in new members by bringing "artifacts" from previous groups to show how members have grown, changed, and have been satisfied with other groups. Such artifacts include cards, letters, artworks, and other symbols from members who have had successful group experiences. We often show two pictures developed by a woman from a previous group. The first picture was a self-portrait of an African-American woman with low self-esteem, low self-confidence—in general, a lady who was about to give up on life. The second self-portrait was drawn after eight sessions in the African-American women's group. The second picture shows a strong, self-confident, and powerful African-American female who had learned how to tap into her own resources as well as to join with other sisters to work through her personal and social life stressors.

Overall, we attempt to instill hope in our group by being positive, warm, friendly and open through our personal qualities. We also communicate a positive perspective concerning the worth of the group as a form of treatment for African-American women. We are convinced that group work makes a difference, and we let members know this in no uncertain terms.

Universality

Women in the *Images of Me* group are relieved when they learn that others share the same problems they have. These women seem so relieved when they find out that women have difficulty communicating with their husbands or being appreciated by their husbands. They become so relieved that they can hardly wait to tell their stories in group.

Another illustration of universality occurred during one group meeting when Tanisha, a tall, attractive, African-American graduate student from a local university, finally spoke up in the group:

Tanisha: The College of Business is the coldest, most insensitive, and the most stressful place on earth for people of color. Students and professors stereotype me and talk down to me, treating me as though I do not belong in graduate school. I remember someone asking me if I knew a drug dealer because I wear gold jewelry. On another occasion, a professor explained a concept to me as if I were a child. In addition, I feel locked out of the mainstream of both social and academic activity. After two years in my department, I have never been invited to parties where students not only relieve stress and relax but can share information about academic survival and future job opportunities. In general, I feel isolated, alienated, and do not feel like I belong.

Tanisha had hardly finished before Latifa started to tell a similar story about what was happening to her as the only African-American in a predominantly White university counseling center:

Lalifa: Well, just let me remind you that I am the only African-American therapist in the Counseling Center on our campus and right now, I am being stifled to death. I feel like I am choking and constantly fighting to catch my breath. In essence, my White colleagues believe that the race problem will go away if we deny that one exists. For example, whenever racial issues arise, they place the blame on all factors except race. Most recently, there were two counseling positions open and three strong African-American applicants applied. Observing this, the White faculty began to have some discussion about how many people of color did the Counseling Center expect to hire. The indication to me from colleagues was that "one was enough." I really get the feeling that there is a limited role they want me to fill and not much more. The director reports that the Counseling Center promotes a multicultural perspective and supports a racial/cultural staff that is reflective of the multicultural student population.

The real problem is that the Center ties me down with so much trivia that there is hardly any time to serve the very students I was hired to serve. I could really help the Center with its mission if I could provide more counseling for African-American students, the majority of whom do not come for counseling voluntarily. Underutilization of campus resources by ethnic minority students is a major concern. You see, I could attract African-American clients if I were permitted or allowed to mingle among these students in order to build rapport and establish relationships with them. I have learned that African-American counselors in similar situations have built a thriving caseload of American-American clients when they attended student socials, participated in sports events, supported their political causes, and have been able to serve as a parent away from home for them.

Well, I guess I have rambled enough. I just know how difficult it is to be the only African-American on a staff of all White people. Oh, before I finish, I have to tell you one more problem that I encounter being the only African-American on my job. When I was hired two years ago, I was brought in at a higher salary than some of the senior staff members who had been at the Center for several years. I could feel the resentment and was asked if I would accept a lower salary to promote harmony. I simply told them that it was too bad, but that was not my problem. I stood my ground, believing that I had every right to expect to be paid the salary offered, but I had to live with the isolation and alienation, which I continue to encounter every day of my life.

Group Leader: I wonder if any other group members have been in situations where you were the only African-American?

Immediately almost every member could relate to her story. They all reported being made to feel that they did not belong; and that they were there for affirmative action purposes rather than because they had the ability and qualifications for the job. Overall, group members reported that on many occasions they felt like a "guest in a strange house" and that "as long as you are a person of color you had better get used to it."

Tanisha: I feel like the group is helping me to carry my load. I also feel a closer kinship bond, knowing that there is so much similarity among us.

To provide further support, the leader said:

Group Leader: It is easier for us to get up early every morning to go to work when we know that millions of people are also getting up.

Yalom (1985) reports that, in the beginning stages of therapy groups, the client's discomfirmation of being the only one with the problem is a powerful source of relief. Such relief is really crucial for African-American women because they often believe the feedback that they are oversensitive or that they have a chip on their shoulders. Some are also made to feel like they are "crazy."

Tanisha: What a comfort it is to realize that if I am crazy, many of my sisters, who I am learning to love and understand, are also crazy because they feel the same way I feel.

Clients exhale with relief when they learn that they are not alone and that others experience the same doubts, fears, and uncertainties as they do.

We have observed that universality is an important step toward group cohesiveness. Members come to know that the group is a unit rather than a group of rugged individuals all pulling in separate directions. We foster universality by focusing on commonalties rather than on differences, especially in the early development of the group. In fact, we look for as many opportunities as possible to show similarities of thoughts, ideas, feelings, attitudes, and behaviors. For this reason, we listen closely for common human connections and linkages as minor steps toward major growth and change.

The Working Stage

In the working stage, members come together as a cohesive unit ready to work, take risks, and, in general, to be productive. With the support of other African-American women, members are expected to be responsible for their own lives. They decide which issues they wish to work on and how to give and receive the feedback needed for personal growth and development (Corey, 1995).

The leader's main task in the working stage is to maintain the atmosphere of trust and caring that was developed earlier.

During this phase, we focus our energies more on observing and processing the interaction that takes place between and among members than on direct leadership. The group is on "automatic pilot"—essentially it carries itself as a cohesive group. Here the members take on more of the role of leaders than in the earlier stage. Although several of the therapeutic forces might be used in this stage, such as instilling hope, information giving, and so on, the major one we employ is altruism, in which members attempt to understand and help one another.

Acceptance and Belonging

A characteristic of the working stage is that members are encouraged to have a strong sense of acceptance and belonging. This therapeutic force brings members of the group even closer and contributes to their abilities to deeply explore some personal conflicts and issues. Anzella, a well-dressed, professional woman, previously had never said anything in the group.

Latifa: Anzella, it seems unfair for you to be a nonparticipant who does nothing but turn up her nose at other members.
Anzella: I have no real problems to discuss and I came to the group just to connect with and receive support from other professional Black women. Unlike most of you, I have never had any conflicts with White people in my community. I am the only African-American living in my immediate subdivision and I am the only African-American on my job. Contrary to popular belief, I receive support from White people and mostly negative criticism from African-Americans. It has been my experience that African-Americans are jealous of me due to my financial success and my overall status in the community. In fact, Black people have always given my family a hard time because we are light-skinned and are believed to have had advantages over darker-skinned African-Americans.

I grew up hearing my mother give accounts of African-American people believing that she received certain advantages and privileges due to her light-skin complexion. According to my mother, she could remember feelings of jealousy in high school when she was elected homecoming queen, in college when she was elected campus queen, and in her professional life when she received certain job promotions. It seems that this group is no different from the "bullshit" I have heard all of my life, and I was silly to expect you to be different than people from the outside world. You see, I feel your envy too, and I sense the looks from your evil eyes. In fact, I wonder if I should quietly drop out of the group and not make a big fuss out of it.

We told Anzella that we were glad she did not drop out and that it might be a good idea to check out her perception of the group by asking each member to give her feedback.

Each group member gave Anzella positive feedback and stated how important her role in the group was. Some members were quite specific in letting Anzella know that they cared about her regardless of her skin complexion and they invited her to be a group participant. Most members expressed appreciation for her willingness to discuss the issues, and told her that they knew how difficult, lonely, and limiting life could be when being stereotyped.

Sue: I grew up in a wealthy, upper-middle class family because my father was a well-known surgeon and my mother was a very successful engineer. I remember making low grades in school to be accepted by my peers, because I am light and my parents were successful professionals.

Latifa: You are just as African as anyone in the group, regardless of your skin color. You are invited to come to my home whenever you please and to call me whenever you need help or whenever you want to talk.

This discussion was a clear indication that the group had reached the working stage of development in which members could begin dealing with lifelong problems and concerns.

Group Leader: Anzella, how do you feel about the feedback you have received? You know, it is possible you might be bringing some of her childhood defenses into your life right now which might be causing you to remain distant from us. Please let the group know when you sense that any of us are reacting to you negatively due to your skin color.

This session ended on a high emotional level with members hugging Anzella and reassuring her that they were all sisters and that sisters come in a wide variety of beautiful colors. We can never remember a time in all of our group leadership when members, functioning in the role of leader/therapist, showed more understanding, love, and caring for one another. The spirit of cooperation had been established with a circle of caring sisters who from that early point were ready to deal with any problems members had. This particular group then immediately progressed further into the working stage.

Specifically, there was the cracking of the facade of a woman who gave the impression that she had it all together. She was a nonparticipant until the group demanded that she remove her mask. As soon as she self-disclosed, allowing the group to know something about her background and previous experiences, she received the acceptance and sense of belonging that allowed her to grow by leaps and bounds. More important, Anzella learned it was acceptable to be an African-American with very light skin.

The behavior of the group members during the working stage includes receiving feedback, expressing positive feelings and closeness, developing a healing capacity, and confronting (Rogers, 1970). These process patterns, as Rogers calls them, are closely linked to some of Yalom's therapeutic factors: altruism, catharsis, interpersonal learning, developing of socializing techniques, imitative behavior. Sue offered Anzella support by sharing her experience of being rejected and stereotyped. Even though therapeutic factors can be looked at separately, they operate interdependently. Two therapeutic factors that are essential during this stage are group cohesiveness and interpersonal learning. Yalom (1985) states that the type of group cohesiveness changes over the course of a group. In the beginning stages, the cohesion rests on universality and a sense of belonging, group support, and the facilitating of attendance. Later it operates through the interrelation of group esteem and self-esteem and through its role in interpersonal learning (Yalom, 1985).

The goal of the African-American women's group is to learn and grow through relationships with each other. Attempting to monitor or manage all the interactions is often quite challenging because these women often have pent-up emotions and experiences they are ready to express. We, as leaders, model altruism by expressing how wonderful it is to help other people. We also explain that people often get bogged down or depressed when they spend too much time thinking only about themselves rather than being more concerned about the welfare of others.

When we were sure that Anzella had completed her work
for the session, we invited Binta, an assistant professor at one
of the local universities, to work.

Binta: I guess I'll work. I have been putting this off long enough.
   I have been on the faculty at a southern university for four
   years but I have never felt comfortable. I never talk in faculty
   meetings and I am really afraid to voice my true feelings
   and opinions.
Group Leader: Binta, give the group an example of an issue
   about which you could not express your true feelings.

Initially, Binta could not specify because she felt she could
not express her feelings about anything without being judged
or ignored by the group. Later she was able to provide this
example:

Binta: One day I requested that my department consider hiring
   an African-American secretary since there was an opening.
   The faculty told me that I was too race conscious, that I
   really needed to think about getting tenured rather than
   being concerned about race quotas. Faculty members
   suggested that I take the chip off my shoulder and added
   that there was not enough time to find a qualified African-
   American secretary.
      On another occasion I was invited to a faculty party
   where I was offered a bowl of collard greens and a slice of
   sweet potato pie rather than being served the same snacks
   as the other guests and, as the evening progressed, the
   department chairperson played music by James Brown and
   Aretha Franklin as a means of making me feel welcome.
   However, rather than making me feel welcome, I felt
   embarrassed and found myself withdrawing even more. The
   bottom line is that I do not feel comfortable expressing my
   true feelings in the department where I work on a day-to-
   day basis. The stress is overwhelming and I don't know how
   much more I can take.
Group Leader: It must be very difficult for you to refrain from
   expressing your true feelings. Have any of the other group
   members experienced similar situations?
Callie: As a faculty member, too, I understand what you are
   saying. But everyone has a right to be heard and tenure
   should not be a barrier to open and honest expression! Binta,

you should speak up at the next faculty meeting as a beginning point.

Tanisha: I wonder if race is really the issue here. Maybe Binta is too shy to speak up in any group.

Binta became more aware that she did not express her views, even in the group of supportive African-American women. Again, members invited her to talk more, saying they valued her friendship and wanted to hear more of her ideas, thoughts, and feelings. Binta accepted the challenge and vowed to express herself more in the therapy group and more in her professional life as a faculty member. Members vowed to call on her if they noticed her slipping into a withdrawal state in which she was not expressing her feelings.

As leaders, we were concerned about the deeper meaning of her withdrawal and her reluctance to self-disclose. We asked her to speculate about times in her past when she did not feel free to communicate her feelings. In addition, we asked her if she could think of anything or any experiences in her early childhood that might be a contributing factor to her present lack of disclosure. Binta responded by telling the group that she grew up in a family in which children were not allowed to express themselves or to voice their opinions—"Children were to be seen but not heard" was the guiding principle.

As we worked with Binta, we supported and encouraged her for having shared her story with us and for having survived in such a dysfunctional family for so long. Group members agreed and suggested ways she could leave some of her old baggage behind. We suggested that Binta begin the process of speaking up and of making her own decisions in the safety and security of the African-American women's group. Through the group, Binta was able to understand her personal and interpersonal dynamics better. We told her that she could be harboring anger that she had allowed to build up so high that she was now unable to express it.

Group Leader: There is so much anger that you are afraid to express for fear it might not come out right. We would suggest that you express anger when it arises rather than wait until it builds up.

We suggest that members like Binta pay attention to feelings of anger in the group where they can receive feedback in a supportive environment.

Altruism

To illustrate altruism in the *Images of Me* group, leaders begin by telling stories about how altruism helped to bring about change in somebody's life. To illustrate the role, we tell stories of how these therapeutic forces in group have helped somebody change. One such story concerned a suicidal client who became less suicidal as a result of helping others through a tutorial program. This client, who was a medical student, was preoccupied with suicidal thoughts and had made several serious attempts. This person was an excellent student with exceptional abilities in mathematics and science. Given that the student had been seen by many therapists, her therapist decided to employ an alternative strategy; the therapist thought: "What a waste of knowledge and skills it would be if this bright, young, and talented person were to die." Therefore, the therapist proposed that she might serve as a mentor or a tutor in math and science for students in special services who were having difficulty in those courses. After only a few sessions of mentoring, the medical student was "turned on" and found real meaning in life from helping other people. She reported that she spent a great deal of her time trying to figure out how to help her mentees learn complex concepts in physics and chemistry and less time thinking about or feeling sorry for herself. Clearly, altruism is an important healing agent in the group therapy process.

We remind the group that the survival of African-Americans is clearly linked to giving and receiving help from others. Success in African-American families contains stories of how family members helped others through difficult times. Yalom (1985) reported that helping others is quite curative for group members who have been devalued and feel that they have nothing to offer. Several group members shared stories that illustrate altruism.

Binta: My story is about an African-American woman who grew up believing that she was not beautiful. It seems that she had been told since early childhood that she was ugly because she had big lips, a big nose, big feet, and kinky hair. Having just returned from Africa, I told her that I had noticed how beautiful she was and that she looked like an African queen.

Mary: Your story reminds me of some of the ways I feel about myself as not being attractive. However, when I think about myself as an African, I do feel beautiful and more accepting of myself.

Group Leader: I grew up in a small rural community in Alabama and I remember how people helped one another as a way of life carried over from African traditions. I remember how families would share farm produce with others during harvest. For example, the family who harvested potatoes would share with other families. Those who slaughtered animals for food would give a portion of their meat to neighbors in the community. Such acts of kindness lifted the spirits of people, drew them closer together, and helped them to survive the devastating effects of poverty and despair.

Ramona: I remember how altruism was manifested in ways people in my community tried to provide emotional support for one another. In one event, a 12-year-old African-American boy was accused of whistling at a White girl and was sent to reformatory school as punishment for his crime. The boy's family was devastated and deeply saddened by this event. They feared for their lives and for the life of their son. The Klu Klux Klan rode through the community threatening to burn the homes and to kill all African-American boys. Yet, in the midst of all this, the community came together and offered support for the family. Prayers were offered that the son would return home safely. Food was prepared so there would be plenty to eat for the family and guests. The men patrolled the home to ensure that no harm would come to the family. The community continued their support for this family throughout the crisis period and beyond.

Group Cohesion

MacDevitt (1987) observed several leader behaviors that are quite similar to those we use with African-American womens' groups. He suggested that cohesion could be developed in the early stages of the group by helping members feel natural and comfortable. Specifically, he suggested that leaders could report to the group early enough to socialize or participate in small talk with members. In an African-American women's group, we greet members and attempt to make them comfortable by asking them to discuss things they mentioned in the session before. Other small talk could center around their children and how they are doing; for example, we might ask a mother about her daughter who is a basketball player for her school. One small-talk discussion was about the member's son, who maintains a 3.85 grade point average. MacDevitt (1987) also believes that cohesion can be built by inviting or encouraging all members to participate. Total participation is important because the lack of it may create ambiguity, decrease investment and involvement by members, and prevent the development of group cohesion.

MacDevitt (1987) further suggested that cohesion can be developed by treating group members in a respectful manner. Included among his suggestions are being on time; letting the group make decisions; making positive remarks about individuals and the group; pointing out commonalties in clients' issues, concerns, and experiences; and pointing out successes already experienced in the group.

Strategies for Building African-American Women's Self-Confidence

One of the goals of this chapter is to help group leaders learn practical group counseling strategies to use in their work with African-American women. The first strategy we will discuss is designed to help group participants gain self-confidence in order to increase their level of functioning in their everyday lives. While this skill is not the only important one leaders need, our experience in the *Images of Me* group is that the lack of self-confidence appears most frequently and impacts the lives of women the most.

Although most people, regardless of race or cultural background, experience a lack of self-confidence in one facet of their lives or another, African-American women report that the lack of personal support and career opportunities accelerates their lack of self-confidence. This lack of self-confidence in African-American women is manifested in several ways that we have observed in the *Images of Me* groups. First, they tend to be much more reluctant to self-disclose than those women with more self-confidence. Even though they have many thoughts to discuss and many pent-up feelings to express, they tend to hold them inside. Lillie Mae, a group participant, told the group that she believed that she did not talk much because she grew up hearing her father say that men do not like women who are always running off at the mouth. She stated further that her reluctance to talk was related to her fear that she might say something stupid. Another member who grew up down South stated that she did not speak up because she had always believed that she had no right as an African-American female to express her opinions or feelings.

A second manifestation of the lack of self-confidence is the reluctance to take risks. Personal progress, in general, and personal growth and change, in particular, require a certain amount of risk-taking behavior. In the *Images of Me* group, Tanisha reported that the more willing she was to take risks, the more growth and change she experienced. She told the group how frightened she was to tell the group that she had sent her baby South to live with her mother because she did not want the responsibility of bringing up a child alone. To her surprise, the group understood her dilemma and offered their support. She later told the group how freeing it was to stop lying about what had happened to her baby and how pleased she was to be understood, accepted, and supported by the group. Clearly, risk-taking is a desirable quality that is directly linked to self-confidence.

Hardly anyone would argue that risk-taking is essential for progress in almost every field of human endeavor. In the field of business, those who are afraid to take risks rarely ever progress to larger and more profitable businesses. We have all observed that the winning teams in sports are those that are willing to take more risks. Basketball team members who have a high level of self-confidence are the most willing to attempt three-point shots. These are also the players you want to handle the ball when the game is on the line. Clearly, in our *Images of Me* group, the participants who are the greatest risk-takers are the most self-confident and experience the greatest amount of change, growth, and learning.

Given that having self-confidence is important among African-American women, how then can a group be used to help clients build self-confidence? To answer this question, we use an activity called understanding and building self-confidence. These sessions usually include (1) assessing self-confidence, (2) providing information about self-confidence, (3) developing action plans to increase self-confidence, and (4) displaying self-confidence as one of the essential qualities.

Assessing Self-Confidence

We usually begin this session with a few general comments about the role of self-confidence in our lives. Then we explain that we will be conducting a brief Self-Confidence Inventory to make each participant more aware of aspects of their lives where they are strong in self-confidence and areas of their lives where they are weak in self-confidence. We use the Parker and Armstrong-West Self-Confidence Inventory (unpublished) for assessing their levels of self-confidence. This inventory is a 25-item Likert-type scale consisting of a series of hypothetical situations that people encounter. A copy of the Self-Confidence Inventory, along with scoring instructions, is in the Appendix at the end of this chapter. Additional information concerning the use of this instrument for counseling or research can be obtained by contacting the authors.

It has been our experience that a great deal of data is created for group process following the administration of this examination. Participants receive immediate feedback because we allow them to score their own inventories using the scoring instructions. The following is a list of some of the frequently asked questions for general processing:

1. How did you feel while completing the inventory?
2. With which situations or scenarios did you identify the most?
3. With which situations or scenarios did you identify the least?
4. Which item reminded you of a significant event in your life?
5. To what extent did your perceived level of self-confidence match your level of self-confidence as indicated on Parker and Armstrong-West Self-Confidence Inventory?
6. Scanning your inventory results, which self-confidence area is your strongest?

We usually end this session by reminding participants that these results should be used to raise awareness and to indicate areas of our lives in which they can work harder toward becoming more self-confident. These results should not be used for categorizing or stereotyping. In the next session, we focus on providing information about the concepts that make up self-confidence and the strategies we use for building self-confidence.

Providing Information About Self-Confidence

An important therapy mechanism in group work is information giving. Applying that concept to building self-confidence in the *Images of Me* group, we provide a definition of self-confidence and identify its five key components. First, we explain that in order to understand the meaning of self-confidence, you need to know the definitions of self-concept and self-esteem. Giving a general definition of self-concept, we explain that it is the overall big picture we have of ourselves, resulting from both positive and negative feedback we have received throughout our lives. In general, *self-concept* is an accumulation of perceptions of the self that may not be agreed on by others. *Self-esteem*, which is a subset of the self-concept, is a personal judgment about the individual's worth that can be strongly influenced by the opinions of others. While not situation-specific, areas of one's self-esteem may vary; for example, a person could have very high self-esteem socially but low self-esteem academically or athletically.

Finally, we define self-confidence as a subset of self-concept and self-esteem in which the individual has varying degrees of being self-assured and having faith in herself. Some qualities of self-confidence are judgmental, very situation-specific, and influenced by many social variables. For example, an individual can have low self-confidence in her ability to play racquetball, moderate self-confidence in her ability to host a party, and very high self-confidence in her ability to do well on chemistry examinations.

We continue the information-giving process by teaching group members the five components of self-confidence and use each component as a tool for engaging members in building self-confidence. Descriptions of the five components, and the implementation of them by using various action plans, follow.

Seeing Oneself as Capable

The first component of self-confidence is seeing oneself as capable or believing that one can do things as well as or better than others in her group. We then ask members to think about groups to which they belong (church, social clubs, work, family and so forth) and to rate how capable they view themselves in various groups. Invariably, group members say that they feel more capable in certain situations than in others.

The overall goal of this session is to help group members to see themselves as capable. We facilitate the attainment of this goal by asking members to think about things in their lives that they do well and about which they are proud. We also ask them to work on their issues as a means of becoming more capable. For example, we encourage participants who have problems expressing themselves to give a five-minute speech on a topic of their choice before the group. Others are given creative tasks to accomplish based on the nature of their problem.

A final technique we use to help members see themselves as capable is to help them use self-talk. We usually initiate this strategy by saying that many people practice self-talk as a normal way of day-to-day functioning. One rule is to change "I can't" statements into "I can" statements. We ask each group member to share a time when she used self-talk to overcome a negative experience or a negative thought. One of the leaders shared that she almost always begins her day with self-talk. For example, she tells herself that she has done it before and there is no reason she cannot do it again, referring to many tasks she has to perform. We usually end this segment with free discussion in which members share experiences about feeling capable and offer advice or suggestions to others.

Feeling a Sense of Belonging

The second component of self-confidence is feeling a sense of belonging. In other words, the individual feels like she is a part of the group rather than feeling like a bother to the group. Belonging and acceptance are essential aspects of self-confidence. African-American women who have achieved the most have worked in collaboration and cooperation with other African-American women the most. As we stated earlier in this book, group interaction and sharing are valuable because it is a natural model for people of African ancestry.

As group leaders, we encourage and promote group or team work as often as possible. For example, we ask members with certain skills to help other members who can benefit from them. In one group, we asked Anzella if she would be willing to help Lillie Mae work through some problems with her computer. We also facilitate the sense of belonging by asking members to make everybody else aware of special information or skills that can be used to help others.

Being Optimistic About the Future

The third component of self-confidence is being optimistic about the future or holding a positive outlook on life, believing that everything will turn out fine. We explain to the group that if we only focus on the problems of life, we would never find solutions. The "I Can" philosophy is encouraged and promoted and, in general, negative self-talk is not reinforced. We further facilitate optimism by asking group members to visualize having worked through the problems or difficulties they present in the group. With these directions, members take turns fantasizing about better life conditions in every aspect of their lives. Most of the members see themselves as more powerful, with more control over their own lives, and, in general, feel better about themselves. Tanisha said that she looks forward to the day when she can spend more time being good to herself and not feel guilty about it. Anzella reported that she visualized herself being at peace with herself and not apologizing to anyone for having a light complexion. She stated further that she was not responsible for her skin color and that she plans to appreciate herself just as she is for the rest of her life.

In the last part of this session, we ask members to develop personal action plans designed to ensure a positive outcome in the achievement of their personal growth goals. Each member's action plan should consist of answers to questions like the following:

- What key actions are needed to accomplish the plan?
- Who will perform the action?
- When will the action take place?
- What challenges will be encountered in carrying out the action plan?
- How will you know whether your action plan for being optimistic about the future has been successful?

Members present their answers to these questions and we facilitate discussion and interaction among all members.

Being Able to Cope with Failure

The fourth component of self-confidence is being able to cope with failure. Another way to view this component is to think of a failure experience as an opportunity for learning, growth, and change. We tell participants in the *Images of Me* group that in order for an individual to make progress, she must be willing or to be free to fail.

We explore the concept of failure first by asking members to discuss past failure experiences and how they dealt with them. We also ask members to generate ways that those experiences could have been handled better. We illustrate by sharing some of our own failure experiences as group leaders. For example, one of the leaders told the group that she submitted an article to a journal for publication but the article was rejected. She told the group that she was hurt that the article was not accepted because she had worked long and hard developing it. However, after a few days of contemplation, she rethought the process and asked some of her friends to look the article over for their observations. Later, her friends offered suggestions that helped to improve the quality of the manuscript, which was later published in one of the leading journals in her profession. Ultimately, her article was rated as one of the most cited articles in the field of counseling over the past five years. The lesson here is that failure can propel the individual to greater heights if she remains open, flexible, and optimistic.

Following this model by the leader, other group members continued to tell their stories of both failed and successful experiences. One of these sessions ended with a member stating:

Anzella: You know, I think that I have learned a valuable lesson from this. Being afraid to fail has kept me on the fence most of my adult life. For example, I did not try out for the college debating team because I was afraid that if I had not been selected, I would have been seen as a failure. After college, I did not apply for a job as a marketing specialist at a leading pharmaceutical company, even though I was well qualified, because I was afraid that the company would not like my work. Instead, I took at position far below my educational and training levels. For these reasons, I have hated myself for not reaching out and challenging myself to achieve what I really deserved. This group has helped me to face my fears and it has provided me with the love and support I need to move forward.

Having the Appropriate Source of Reinforcement

The fifth component of self-confidence is having the appropriate source of reinforcement in role models with whom the individual can identify. The value of role models for personal growth and development for people in general is well known in social science literature. Role models for African-American women are crucial and critical as African-American women of the present age seek to venture into every field of human endeavor. Role models for African-American women are also important to counteract the myriad of problems put upon them by society, in general, and the media, in particular. A number of writers have shown how the media has portrayed African-American women in stereotypic roles as strong, bosomy, authoritarian Black females who are given only minor roles in films and other media (Bond, 1979; Collier, 1974; Reid, 1979). It is no secret that advertising has served as a vehicle for transmitting ideologies related to Black inferiority and White supremacy. Unfortunately, African-American women believe many of the lessons taught to them by the media and have spent countless hours trying to unlearn many negative lessons.

Another problem for the African-American female is that she is expected to strive for the ideals of White beauty. One aspect of White beauty is thinness and, as a result, more and more African-American women, as well as other minority women, are dieting. Root (1990) said:

> Dieting also appears to be a strategy women rather than men use to increase self-esteem, obtain privileges, increase credibility in the workforce, and contend with conflicting gender-role proscriptions.... Although this strategy appears to be superficial, mythology, fairy [sic] tales, television, movies, and advertising lead women to believe that thinness is beauty, success, power, and acceptance and, therefore, dieting is a viable strategy (p. 526a).

Clearly, the media is an inappropriate source of reinforcement for African-American women. For this reason, we hold open and honest discussions about how women are exploited and stereotyped in the media and we have a dialog about which role models are more appropriate for building self-confidence in African-American women. In this regard, we celebrate the works of historical African-American female role models such as Mary McCleod Bethune, Harriet Tubman, Harriet Beecher Stowe, and many others. We also celebrate the life and works of current models such as Rosa Parks, Angela Davis, Hatlie Lou

Hammer, Linda Whittington-Clark, Sherlon P. Brown, and many others. Although we discuss many questions concerning their lives, our main question is "What can we learn from these African-American role models' lives to enhance our level of self-confidence?"

To further assist women in the *Images of Me* group with counteracting stereotypes, we follow the suggestions and guidelines offered by Copeland (1977) and Boyd-Franklin (1987). Copeland suggested that counselors need to understand their client's frame of reference and to be able to build trust. She also suggested that counselors must also serve as advocates and attempt to change clients' oppressive environment. Copeland's (1977) final suggestion is to use and reinforce the client so that she can feel confident and in control of her life. Boyd-Franklin also offered a few guidelines for African-American women in group. She suggested that support groups are effective. Like Boyd-Franklin suggested, our group provides an opportunity for African-American women to experience sisterhood while they learn to work together in harmony and to trust one another. Finally, the group encourages support, insight, self-exploration, and behavior change.

Summary

It has been our experience that African-American women carry the tremendous burden of racism and sexism, both of which they inherit at birth. They undergo a great deal of mistreatment from their families and from the community at large. By the time they show up in the therapist's office, or in a therapy group, many are ready to explode. Yet, without prodding by leaders or other members, they persist in concealing their true problems or wearing a mask declaring that their problems are quite insignificant. It is our duty as group leaders to help them get through the initial stage of being accepted, and feeling secure.

Our next challenge is to help them move through the transition stage (being resistant, being competitive, and trying to determine their place in the group) in which they begin work toward *Kuumba*—they are encouraged to do whatever is possible to create beauty in the community that they are a significant part of. The transition stage is the make-or-break stage because too often members will drop out if transition issues are not handled with expert precision. We think of this stage as the "darkest hour before dawn" or as "the light at the end of the tunnel." When we enter the working stage, we place the group, in aeronautic terms, "on automatic pilot." Because the norms have been established, the boundaries have been set, expectations are clear, and safety has been ensured, the group is ready to do what groups do best, and that is solve problems deeply rooted in interpersonal relations.

The next chapter focuses on the termination stage of group development, including a general assessment of what members have gained from the group and what steps they need to take next. In addition, there is a discussion of reality testing to determine the extent to which members are ready to apply the skills learned in the *Images of Me* group to the outside world.

References

Bond, J. C. (1975). The media image of Black women. *Freedom Ways, 15*(1), 34–37.

Boyd-Franklin, N. (1987). Group therapy for Black women: A therapeutic support model. *American Journal of Orthopsychiatry, 57*(3), 394–401.

Collier, E. (1974). "Black" shows for White viewers. *Freedom Ways, 14*(3), 209–217.

Copeland, E. J. (1977). Counseling Black women with negative self-concepts. *Personnel and Guidance Journal, 55*(7), 397–400.

Corey, G. (1995). *Theory and practice of group counseling* (4th Ed.). Pacific Grove, CA: Brooks/Cole.

Couch, R. D., & Childers, J. H., Jr. (1987). Leadership strategies for instilling and maintaining hope in group counseling. *Journal for Specialists in Group Work, 12*(4), 138–143.

MacDevitt, J. W. (1987). Conceptualizing therapeutic components of group counseling. *Journal for Specialists in Group Work, 12*(2),76–84.

Reid, P. T. (1979). Racial stereotyping on television: A comparison of the behavior of both Black and White television characters. *Journal of Applied Psychology, 64*, 465–471.

Rogers, C. R. (1970). *Carl Rogers on encounter groups*. New York: Harper & Row.

Root, M. P. (1990). Disordered eating in women of color. *Sex Roles, 22*(7/8), 525–535.

Sue, D. W. (1981). *Counseling the culturally different: Theory and practice*. New York: Wiley.

Yalom, I. D. (1985). *The theory and practice of group psychotherapy*. New York: Basic Books.

Appendix

SELF-CONFIDENCE INVENTORY
(10TH GRADE THROUGH ADULT LEVEL)

Grade/Classification _____ Age ____ Race ____ Sex ____

Directions: Listed below is a series of hypothetical situations in which people find themselves at one time or another. Place yourself in each situation, then select *one* of the four responses based on your *initial* reaction.

1. If employees in my work setting were given the option of selecting a new assignment or keeping their regular assignments, I would choose the new assignment.

   1 – Strongly Agree   2 – Agree   3 – Disagree   4 – Strongly Disagree

2. I tend to be a loner rather than an active member of any specific group.

   1 – Strongly Agree   2 – Agree   3 – Disagree   4 – Strongly Disagree

3. Even though legislation dictates equal occupational opportunities for all, there still are certain restrictions in the job market for applicants. Regardless, I will enter the occupation of my choice.

   1 – Strongly Agree   2 – Agree   3 – Disagree   4 – Strongly Disagree

4. If the principal of my school announced that I had been granted a scholarship for my leadership abilities, for the most part my friends, relatives, and significant others would ignore my achievement.

   1 – Strongly Agree   2 – Agree   3 – Disagree   4 – Strongly Disagree

5. My philosophy in life is "if at first you don't succeed, try, try again."

   1 – Strongly Agree   2 – Agree   3 – Disagree   4 – Strongly Disagree

6. Among my peers and friends I usually am one of the followers rather than the leader.

   1 – Strongly Agree   2 – Agree   3 – Disagree   4 – Strongly Disagree

7. Two pick-up teams are getting ready to play a game. There are more people around than are needed for the teams. Somebody has to get left out. I feel sure that I wouldn't be left out.

   1 – Strongly Agree   2 – Agree   3 – Disagree   4 – Strongly Disagree

8. As I plan for my future work, I become keenly aware of serious limitations in career options. I realize I have to be realistic and enter a lesser occupation where I can be assured of success in the future.

   1 – Strongly Agree   2 – Agree   3 – Disagree   4 – Strongly Disagree

9. I would look to parents, friends, relatives, and professionals for help if I needed moral support rather than relying totally on myself.

   1 – Strongly Agree   2 – Agree   3 – Disagree   4 – Strongly Disagree

10. If I went out for an athletic team one year and did not make it, I probably would not try out again.

    1 – Strongly Agree   2 – Agree   3 – Disagree   4 – Strongly Disagree

11. As a student in the classroom, I usually view myself as a better than average student.

    1 – Strongly Agree   2 – Agree   3 – Disagree   4 – Strongly Disagree

12. If members of my unit learned about a special opportunity to save money, they probably would not tell me about it.

    1 – Strongly Agree   2 – Agree   3 – Disagree   4 – Strongly Disagree

13. As I look ahead and think about what the future holds for me, I feel good about doing this because I am pretty sure that I will reach my goals, and these goals are important to me.

    1 – Strongly Agree   2 – Agree   3 – Disagree   4 – Strongly Disagree

14. The first test in a class usually determines how I will do in that course. If I don't do well on the first exam, I usually become discouraged, and it is difficult to bring up my grade on subsequent exams.

    1 – Strongly Agree   2 – Agree   3 – Disagree   4 – Strongly Disagree

15. There are several people in my life who are very confident in my ability to succeed.

    1 – Strongly Agree   2 – Agree   3 – Disagree   4 – Strongly Disagree

16. I would prefer to have a job doing something that I've done before rather than one in which I have to learn new skills.

    1 – Strongly Agree   2 – Agree   3 – Disagree   4 – Strongly Disagree

17. I am a member of several groups and have been able to establish some good friendships through my participation in these groups.

    1 – Strongly Agree   2 – Agree   3 – Disagree   4 – Strongly Disagree

18. Many of the difficulties that people encounter from day to day are grounded in various sources. Some people are strangled by the system while others overcome the system and succeed. I believe that the system determines my success or failure.

    1 – Strongly Agree   2 – Agree   3 – Disagree   4 – Strongly Disagree

19. In a school setting, I often feel frustrated and incapable of understanding the task assigned.

    1 – Strongly Agree   2 – Agree   3 – Disagree   4 – Strongly Disagree

20. When I encounter a task that is very difficult to do, the challenge of mastering it motivates me to tackle it again.

    1 – Strongly Agree   2 – Agree   3 – Disagree   4 – Strongly Disagree

21. I am the only new group member of a highly selected group whose purpose is to study problems in school or at work. I believe that I was chosen for reasons other than my abilities.

    1 – Strongly Agree   2 – Agree   3 – Disagree   4 – Strongly Disagree

22. My friends see me as being a talented individual.

    1 – Strongly Agree   2 – Agree   3 – Disagree   4 – Strongly Disagree

23. If 60 percent of the employees where I work receive bonus pay for top job performance, I would be awarded a bonus.

    1 – Strongly Agree   2 – Agree   3 – Disagree   4 – Strongly Disagree

24. If I were in trouble and needed moral support, I would find it difficult to trust others to help me.

    1 – Strongly Agree   2 – Agree   3 – Disagree   4 – Strongly Disagree

25. If I were hired to fill a vacancy where underrepresented groups (minorities, women, persons with handicapping conditions, elderly persons, and so forth) had been encouraged to apply, my friends, parents, and co-workers still would think that I would succeed.

    1 – Strongly Agree   2 – Agree   3 – Disagree   4 – Strongly Disagree

Scoring Instructions

1. The Self-Confidence Inventory utilizes a four-point Likert-type scale for responses.

2. Each item has a minimum score of 1 and a maximum score of 4.

3. For items worded in a positive manner (affirms self-confident attitude or behavior), strongly agree = 4, agree = 3, disagree = 2, and strongly disagree = 1.

4. For items worded in a negative manner (affirms an attitude or behavior which is *not* indicative of self-confidence), strongly agree = 1, agree = 2, disagree = 3, and strongly disagree = 4.

5. Since there are 25 items on this SCI, the minimum score that can be attained on the instrument is 25 (if all responses = 1). The maximum score is 100 (all responses = 4).

Scoring

The following items have the positively weighted scores: 1, 3, 5, 7, 9, 11, 13, 15, 17, 20, 22, 23, and 25. These items use scoring delineated in #3.

The remaining items have the negatively weighted scores: 2, 4, 6, 8, 10, 12, 14, 16, 18, 19, 21, and 24. For these items, use scoring described in #4.

7

Terminating the *Images of Me* Group—Kuumba

We began discussing stages of group development by using the analogy of the flight of an airplane. We pointed out that in the initial stage, the plane is carefully and meticulously prepared for take off. In the transition phase, the plane struggles against the forces of gravity and, using all the energy it can muster, becomes airborne. In the working or cohesiveness stage, the plane reaches a cruising altitude and flies smoothly except for occasional turbulence. In the final stage, the pilot prepares the crew and passengers for a safe landing. In a similar way, the final stage of group development is vitally important for assisting group members in reaching their destination or goals for which they joined the group. Corey (1995) suggested that no group leadership skills are more important than helping members identify skills they have learned throughout the group experience and transferring those skills to the outside world. Corey (1995) stated further that termination is a time to integrate, summarize, pull together, and to interpret the group experience. The Kawanzaa principle of *Kuumba* (creativity, a new reality) applies to this stage.

This chapter outlines and discusses the application of several principles or concepts of group therapy we have found to be essential in terminating African-American women's groups. While several of the concepts or interventions have been discussed in earlier chapters, we will discuss them in this chapter relative to their application to the termination phase of the

Images of Me group. In particular, we will discuss applying boundary management to termination of a group, leadership functions in terminating groups, therapeutic forces in the termination stage, creative techniques for the termination stage, and terminating individuals and the entire group.

Applying Boundary Management to Termination of a Group

Singer, Astrachan, Gould, and Klien (1975) proposed that certain limits or boundaries must be established and managed if group experiences are to be effective. The boundary-management process should be initiated before the group begins its work and needs to continue throughout the duration of the group, playing a vital role after the completion of all group sessions. Boundary management might be thought of as a process of fine-tuning the group experience by setting limits on the nature of the group's task, the role of the members, the role of the leaders, and the time of the activities. The application of boundary-management principles sends a message to African-American women that group work or therapy is more than a general rap session. Rather, it is a set of organized and synthesized activities guided by the group's purpose and by the mode offered to the group. Given well-orchestrated boundaries, the group's outcome level is more predictable.

Boundary management plays a key role in the termination stage of group work. First, those boundaries we apply in the African-American women's group center around member and leader roles (tasks). Members' roles consist of the following:

- Confronting their feelings about separation
- Completing unfinished business or work
- Evaluating the effectiveness of the group
- Practicing how to apply what they have learned to the outside world

Leaders' roles usually include the following:

- Preparing members for termination
- Helping members deal with unfinished work
- Helping members determine how they can apply their newly learned skills to the outside world

- Teaching members how to give one another constructive and meaningful feedback

These roles are illustrated at the end of this chapter where we describe the actual terminating experience of selected individuals and groups.

Managing the group's task is very complex and critical during the termination stage of the group. In particular, we really have to work hard at managing the emotional levels of members who hold their feelings inside until the last meeting of the group. While we encourage expression of feelings (negative or positive), we do not encourage expression of negative feeling during the last meeting of the group. For example, toward the end of one final session, Vy decided to blast Callie for a comment she had made several weeks earlier. We blocked her bashing immediately because we viewed her comment as an act of aggression. Second, her statements did not assist Callie toward behavior change. Third, with less than 15 minutes before group termination, it was not possible to bring closure to this newly introduced issue. Although we did not permit Vy to work through her negative feelings about Callie in group, we invited her to do individual work with us or with some other therapist.

Given the catastrophes of the 1960s group movements (nude encounter groups, drug abuse disguised as therapy, group sex, orgies, and so on), we set strict limits on all phases of the group process to minimize chaos, and to help members receive the respect they deserve, for them to feel secure, and for them to achieve the objectives for which they joined the group initially. We pay close attention to boundary management in the termination phase because we do not want group members to introduce new issues that we cannot explore or address fully. We learned from one of our earlier groups what can happen when a member is permitted to introduce an emotion-loaded problem and issue in a final group session.

> During the final session of a group meeting, Kate stunned the group by telling us that she had finally decided to kill her father. She perceived this to be the only avenue or way she would ever have peace. Even though the group members and leaders were shocked, one of the leaders managed to inform her of the ethical and legal issues surrounding her statement.

The leaders informed Kate that we were required to inform authorities as well as her father whom she had vowed to kill. Kate essentially ignored the leaders and continued to scream, stating that she was tired of her father's abuse of her mother. She told the group that her father was a minister who believed that women should be obedient to their husbands. Therefore, whenever her mother was thought to be disobedient to her father in the slightest manner, he would physically abuse her, citing verses from the Bible to justify his action. Whenever her father tried to whip her mother, Kate would hide in the closet until his rage was over. She told the group that her father told her to keep her mouth closed about what went on in their house lest he would give her a whipping she would never forget. She declared that she hated her father more than anything in this world. She began shouting and screaming about the Bible and God and everything connected with her father.

By this time the members were frightened to death and the leaders were petrified. One member became so frightened that she ran out of the group room. Another member retreated to the corner of the room and curled into a fetal position. Still other members took on a caretaker's role and began to offer suggestions in the form of alternative things she could do rather than kill her father. For example, one member suggested that Kate should talk with her family to try to improve the level of communication. Others suggested that the family should hold meetings to work out difficulties. One member told Kate that she needed to pray and ask God to remove these thoughts from her mind. She reminded Kate of the commandment, "Thou shalt not kill."

This session ended with members feeling frightened, overwhelmed, angry, and sad. One member stated that while the group had been successful, the final meeting was dominated by one member who had not contributed much. She expressed her anger toward the leaders for allowing the group to get out of control. She stated that she did not feel safe in the group. She told us that somehow she felt responsible for Kate but was helpless to do anything about it.

In retrospect, there were several things we, as leaders, could have done to lead the group more effectively, including the following:

1. In the screening process, we could have determined that Kate was not appropriate for our group and could have "deselected" her.
2. When Kate declared that she had decided to kill her father, we should have explained the legal ramifications of such statements and that we would talk with her further after the group session.
3. Given Kate's state of depression, it would have been appropriate to order a psychiatric evaluation. Kate seemed incoherent and, at times, seemed out of touch with reality.
4. Given group members the opportunity to offer support for Kate after the group meeting was over.
5. As leaders, we should have reminded the group that introduction of new "loaded" material was out-of-bounds and could have restated the purpose of the final termination stage of group work.

Specifically, we should have told them that the final session was designed to summarize the work we had already done, to evaluate the extent that goals had been achieved, to determine what additional work needed to be done, and to devise a plan for follow-up activity.

Leadership Functions in Terminating Groups

The reader is reminded that the leadership function varies throughout the life of the group. The focus of this section's discussion is on the application of selected leadership functions in the termination stage of a group.

Lieberman, Yalom, and Miles (1973) identified four leadership functions in group work. Even though they described these functions more than two decades ago, they are still quite relevant to work with African-American women's groups. The four functions they described are (1) executive functions (2) caring, (3) emotional stimulation, and (4) meaning attribution. The application of these functions varies throughout the group process. Although we use all four of them, we have found that caring, emotional stimulation, and meaning attribution are the most important leadership functions during the termination stage.

Caring

Group leaders look for many different and practical ways to show caring for the members. In every session, we acknowledge their presence and tell them with our eyes that we are pleased that they are members of the group. We also show caring by remembering small details about their lives or about their family members. Above all, we demonstrate care for members by showing respect, warmth, and high regard. Another way to demonstrate caring is through our belief that these women have the power and ability to help themselves and to help others. We reiterate time and time again to these women that their contributions to the African-American collective is essential to the welfare and well-being of us all.

While we show our care for members by celebrating their birthdays and other significant life events, we also show that we care by working hard to help members solve their problems, grow, learn, and change. The following are some of the session-by-session comments leaders can make to manifest caring:

"Callie, here is the book I promised I would bring and share. It might help you understand some of those control issues you have been trying to understand."

"Mary, how did the conversation with your neighbor go?"

"Anzella, good evening. Good to see you. Hope everything is going well."

Even though the word *caring* seems simplistic, we cannot overemphasize the importance of its role in the effectiveness of group work. Caring is having an understanding and a deep feeling for other people. Through caring, group members can work through their past feelings of hurt, shame, guilt, joy, anger, and frustration. We are convinced that members do better when we show them that we care about them. Not only do we care for group members in the *Images of Me* group, but we encourage and promote caring for members and others. We try to impress on members that their change and growth require an atmosphere characterized by love, acceptance, and caring. In this termination phase, we tell the group that growth and change could not have occurred without the care that members have shown toward one another.

Love, care, acceptance, and belonging are especially important in our group due to the wide range of complex problems and issues the various members present. It has been our experience that members begin to really care for other members when they share their pain, struggles, excitement, and fears in an *Images of Me* group. In some ways it stands to reason that it is easier to love and care for people you know than for those you do not know, as in the following example:

Mary Frances, a member of one of our earlier groups, moved to the Northeast from the South shortly after a tragic auto accident in which her mother and three sisters had been killed. Mary Frances was scared of those new Northeastern people and vowed to keep her family's tragedy a secret. Keeping everything inside, she clung to her husband, not allowing him freedom to meet new friends or to adjust to his new environment. In addition, having hurt feelings about the loss of her family, she vowed never to return to her hometown in the South.

One might guess that life was quite difficult for Mary Frances, given she was afraid to meet new people in the city but did not want to return home down South because the painful memories were more than she could bear. Having suffered severe depression for many years, Mary Frances's doctor recommended that she should seek psychological counseling in a group setting where she could interact and interpersonalize with others.

When Mary Frances reported to the *Images of Me* group, we had never observed a person so withdrawn. In addition to having lost her family of origin, her husband had passed away recently after a massive stroke. Even though Mary Frances was depressed and under a great deal of stress, she was a delightful person whom the leaders and members really adored. Members liked her because she had a great sense of humor, had a winning smile, and was always willing to help others. Having those qualities, the group fell in love with her and began an ongoing process of caring for her. The more Mary Frances opened up and shared her life story with the group, the more the group accepted her and helped her feel a sense of belonging.

Of all the leadership functions we have employed, it has been our observation that none is more important than caring.

Group members, like plants in a garden, blossom when they are nourished and are given appropriate care. Mary Frances is a different person from the withdrawn, non-self-disclosing, non-trusting woman who came to our group initially with no hope and little confidence in her ability to adjust to life in her new Northeastern community. Although all her problems have not been worked through, she is much more self-confident, more self-disclosing, and is well on her way to complete recovery.

Emotional Stimulation

Emotional stimulation refers to factors or forces used to energize the group or to keep the group moving. This function is critical because the African-American women's group quite often gets bogged down or depressed and needs hope to keep going. Essentially, we use these three variables to energize the group: the personal attributes of the leaders as motivating forces, African-American literature, and selected group interventions.

The leader as a technique is well known in counseling and psychotherapy literature. Brown, Lipford-Sanders, and Shaw (1995) presented a model for group counseling with female African-American university students on a predominantly White campus. This group, called Kujichagulia, uses an Afrocentric approach designed to empower, motivate, and energize African-American women to be successful in the university community. Brown et al. (1995) indicated that the leaders themselves exude a high level of energy, interest, and enthusiasm which is often contagious. We as leaders try our best to be cheerful, both physically and emotionally, in order to raise the emotional level of members. We put forth a special effort to dress in a manner that radiates energy and cheer. Group leaders have been classified as either plums or prunes. We insist on being plums that are full of juice and the vitality needed to stimulate women who need the best we can offer to work through their presenting problems and issues. We can think of no greater way to stimulate African-American women in their efforts toward achieving their goal than through our own positive example. As leaders, we have to be good human beings who make every attempt possible to model good physical and mental health.

A second way to stimulate the interest of African-American women in a group is through literature, especially through the works of African-American women writers. These writers are motivating and stimulating because they mirror the issues in the lives of group members so closely. The following is a list of some of the typical African-American literature we use:

- *I Know Why the Caged Bird Sings* by Maya Angelou–Illustrates the life experiences and stages of development of a young African-American girl who grew up in the South (Angelou, 1969).
- *Song of Solomon* by Toni Morrison–Shows the value of self-understanding and self-knowledge toward optimal development of African-American women (Morrison, 1977).
- *A Piece of Mine* by J. California Cooper–Points out the realities of oppression among African-American females and how they can use their inner strengths and power to overcome such depression (Copper, 1984).
- *Their Eyes Were Watching God* by Zora Neale Hurston–Illustrates how certain women seek to find happiness through their relationships with different men. These women discover later that they can find peace and happiness within themselves (Hurston, 1937).

These are only a few of the literary works we discuss, many of which have special meaning to African-American women since most of their problems and issues are interpersonally related. In selecting the works, we attempt to focus on those that are appropriate for the particular stage of the group's development. For instance, in the termination phase, we focus on the aspect of the novel that resembles what the member will encounter when she returns to the outside world.

A third way to stimulate the interests of African-American women in group is through selected interventions. Here, we describe an intervention strategy designed to stimulate interest and to begin to bring closure to the group. We call this "The Tunnel to the Future," which is a two-part activity designed to make participants aware of the realities of returning to the real world after the group. In the first part, we ask group members to generate a list of barriers or forces that make adjustment to the real world more difficult. In the process of generating this list, a great deal of discussion is usually generated about societal factors and forces that would make the return to "real life" more challenging. Making the list also generates a great deal of discussion about the environmental factors and forces with which many African-American women interact. The following are eight of the most common factors:

1. *Self-doubt*–The belief that they will relapse into being the same as they were before they joined the group.
2. *Racism and sexism*–In our society, racism and sexism seem to prevail no matter how hard we fight against them. Some members thought they would always hold outgroup status in White America.
3. *Lack of support and encouragement*–Often husbands, other family members, and significant others do not support African-American women who have changed some major aspect of their lives.
4. *Lack of a mechanism for venting thoughts and feelings*– Unlike the group, the outside world often does not lend an empathic ear.
5. *Peer group pressure*–There is often pressure to conform to the wishes and desires of peers.
6. *Racial/ethnic identity conflicts*–Some members believed that no matter what they did, they would always have to seek a balance of being not Black enough or of being too Black.
7. *Struggling to understand* what it means to be a strong African-American woman.
8. *Self-acceptance*–The ability of the African-American woman to accept herself as beautiful, intelligent, and productive is an ongoing challenge in a society where standards of beauty are based on White norms and standards of power are established by middle-class White males.

After this list of predicted problems has been generated and discussed, we invite group members to role-play these problems as part two of the activity. We prepare members for the roles they will play by practicing the role of each problem to be played. We use the go-around in the group to practice each problem. We, the leaders, begin by modeling how we want the rest of the group to practice. Beginning with the first problem, self-doubt, we say, "No matter how many group meetings you may attend, you're still no good." Then we invite group members to model the voice of self-doubt. Some of their self-doubt comments follow:

Cameal: You're still going to be looked over for faculty raises, no matter how hard you work.

Binta: You are never going to have enough courage to speak up for yourself. You are not strong enough to be a real Sista anyway.

Janiba: Once an Oreo, always an Oreo. So, go on back to White America where you belong.

Mary: Face it, you were not attractive then, and you are not attractive now, and you will not be attractive in the future.

Ramona: What's wrong with being alone? Perhaps you were born to be alone, so why don't you accept it?

Shari: If you want real peace, you need to leave that all-White setting. But you are not going to leave because you think that White is right and you are better off there, no matter how bad you are treated.

Sue: You are still a rich girl so don't kid yourself by trying to mingle with the poor.

After practicing self-doubt, we ask members to take the other seven problems to role-play in the next phase of the activity. When each member has selected one of the problems to role-play, we direct them to form two lines (a tunnel) with enough room in the center for one person or group member to walk through. The two lines of group members, facing one another, represent (with their voices and actions) all the factors and forces group members will encounter when the group has terminated. We ask each group member to think about her role and how she will project it when the identified member or protagonist walks through the "Tunnel to the Future." When we sense that the members who form the tunnel have formulated their words and actions, we direct one member at a time to walk slowly through the tunnel where she will encounter all the factors, forces, and blocks to successful functioning in the "real world." We often blindfold the protagonist in order to focus more on the sense of hearing the voices.

As the member slowly walks through the tunnel , she hears the voices, some in low quiet sounds and others in loud screams. For example, as one participant entered the tunnel, she heard a voice saying, "OK, Sista, welcome to the real world. This is the real deal—the group can't help you now." Another voice of self-doubt shouted, "You are not going to make it. You might as well stop right here and stop fooling yourself." Before she could take another step, she heard a quiet voice saying softly, "You never had courage to stand up. What makes you think you have courage now? Sista, I've been knowing you a long time and I know you are not strong enough to make it." Suddenly a painful voice shouted in the tunnel, stunning the protagonist and nearly caused her to freeze. That cold, mean voice said, "Go back to White America where you belong. You don't belong among the sistas. Besides, you can't be trusted any more. Once an Oreo, always an Oreo."

When one member walks completely through the tunnel, she moves to one side of the line and becomes a voice to send a message to the next member who comes through the tunnel. When all participants have walked through, they usually feel exhausted because they often encounter multiple problems represented in the role-plays by many voices. That is, when the members from the *Images of Me* group think of multiple problems such as racism, sexism, economics, family issues, and job-related problems, they become overwhelmed and often hopeless. The thought of facing so many real-world issues was so powerful and frightening that one member turned around and rushed out of the tunnel.

This group experience stimulates a great deal of thoughts, feelings, and data for discussion purposes. Here are some of the questions we raise for processing the experience for group participants:

- Think of the problem you selected to role-play and tell why you selected it.
- How did you feel in your role as one of the future problems and as the protagonist, the person walking through the tunnel?
- While walking through the tunnel, what did you want to do?
- What future problems, factors, or challenges were most difficult for you to encounter?
- What do you believe would make it more bearable for you to deal with life issues and problems after the group?
- What did you learn from this experience?

Through the processing of these questions, African-American female group members learn many valuable lessons and report that they are much better prepared to deal with post-group issues. Several members expressed feelings of being surprised by the strong feelings that were generated even though the activity was only a role-play.

Cameal: I found myself in the middle of the tunnel and I could not decide whether to go forward or backward.

The Voices: They are still not going to give you the raises you deserve, no matter how hard you work.

Another Voice: They think you make too much money to be an African-American woman anyway, so don't be misled by false promises from that *Images of Me* group. White folks are putting all African-Americans back in their places. If you don't believe me, just wait to see what is going to happen to Mr. O. J. Simpson.

Leader: Hearing all this, I turned around. I'll have to admit this was one of the most powerful experiences I have had in all of the group work we have done.

Having heard these expressions, we believe that the purpose of the group experience had been achieved. We simply wanted group members to think deeper about problems and issues they could face following the termination of the group. We not only wanted to raise issues they would face in the future, but we wanted to offer support; encouragement; and strategies to help them deal with such future problems, issues, and concerns.

Meaning Attribution

Meaning attribution is a process of explaining or analyzing the group interactions or group dynamics; it is an attempt to answer certain "why" questions concerning feelings, attitudes, and certain behaviors. Even though meaning attribution is one of the most powerful leadership functions, it also can be the most dangerous. In particular, attempting to give meaning to another person's experience without adequate training and with knowledge of the clients background or worldview can cause misdiagnosis, which could easily lead to mistreatment and possibly stereotyping. Stereotyping or labeling especially during the group termination phase can be hurtful because there may not be time or opportunity to help the member recover.

Finally, experience has shown us that meaning attribution needs to be used with extreme caution in the *Images of Me* group. We tell members that our hunches must be validated by them before they can have real meaning.

Therapeutic Forces in the Termination Stage

In Chapter 6, we discussed the application of therapeutic forces in the initial stage and in the working stage of the *Images of Me* group. Therapeutic forces also play a vital role in the termination stage, the focus of this chapter. One of the most important therapeutic forces in the termination phase is giving and receiving feedback and offering support. Members are encouraged to support one another throughout the group, but especially at the termination phase. We have found that a phone call from one member to another can be a lifesaver for women who are trying to raise teenage boys, many of whom are constantly in trouble at school and in their communities. Other women need support to work through family issues, particularly if they are trying to separate from an abusive husband or boyfriend. Still others need acceptance and support for day-to-day problems and issues that people generally encounter.

Support, a key therapeutic factor, is especially necessary when women are preparing to leave the group and return to the outside world. They need both member and leader support for reality testing. An example of reality testing occurred one week before the group termination with Mary, a member who struggled to claim her own identity.

Mary: My husband is a well-known, highly visible city official who does not respect or value me as a highly functioning individual. At social gatherings, he places me in a corner while he socializes with other women. At the end of the evening, he gives me the "It's time to go home" look and expects me to follow him home.

After Mary discussed her dilemma with the group, we encouraged her to rehearse what she would say and do when this happens again. Even though she had practiced, she reported to the group that she was unable to confront her husband when he repeated the behavior.

The group members offered suggestions Mary could use to deal with this situation. Many of the women shared their stories of how they broke their own psychological barrier of being neglected or abused. We, the group leaders, offered support and discussed how difficult it is to bring about change. However, Mary was encouraged to believe that she could work through the challenge when the time was right.

We stated earlier in this section that giving and receiving feedback is one of the most important therapy factors in terminating the group experience. Feedback among group members is considered a key factor in promoting interpersonal learning. Rhode and Stockton (1992) found that using structured feedback activities assisted in the achievement of group goals. They suggested that in order for members to benefit from feedback, they must be willing to listen to a wide variety of reactions that others have concerning their behavior. They further suggested that there be a balance between positive and negative feedback. An important point about feedback, which we stress in the *Images of Me* group, is to make sure that members care about one another before giving feedback. We have observed the powerful impact group participants have when they hear how their behavior has influenced others positively. Most group leaders would agree that feedback is an important way members learn, grow, and work through difficult problems and issues. Corey (1995) identified the following nine points for providing feedback:

1. Reaction to specific behavior is better than general feedback.
2. Feedback given in a clear, concise, understandable, and in a direct manner, is better than some interpretive feedback.
3. Positive feedback is almost always more helpful than negative or corrective feedback. Positive feedback is believed to be more conducive to behavior and attitude change.
4. When feedback is difficult or is of a sensitive nature, it must be done in a caring and a nonjudgmental manner, lest the participant becomes defensive and the opportunity for growth is inhibited.
5. Negative feedback is more useful when there is a focus on specific behavior and when the group has developed a strong sense of cohesion.

6. Group members are skeptical about giving negative feedback for fear of rejection and misunderstanding.
7. Negative or corrective feedback is more acceptable if the speaker says how the particular behavior makes her feel.
8. Immediate feedback is more valuable than feedback resulting from pent-up anger.
9. Feedback from leaders is usually of higher quality but is often less acceptable by group members.

The Communication Interaction Index

The Communication Interaction Index (CII) is a mechanism for giving and receiving feedback, one of the most powerful tools or strategies in the *Images of Me* group. African-American women consistently say that they want and need honest and genuine feedback if they hope to grow, change, and learn. Many of these women say that because they have experienced so much "B.S." in their lives, they will not tolerate it in their groups.

Being sensitive to the need for honest and genuine feedback for women in our group, we ask them to participate in a feedback activity called the pre- and post-CII (see Figures 7.1 and 7.2).The purpose of the CII is to monitor the feelings of closeness members have for one another. In the early sessions, we ask all group members to make judgments about how close they feel to one another. We give the following simple instructions:

1. Write your name on the diagram (Figure 7.1) in the innermost circle.
2. Write the names of all other group members in the smaller circles surrounding yourself.
3. Mark an X on the line between you and each surrounding member depending on how close you feel to that member. The closer you feel toward a member, the closer you mark the X to yourself.
4. After you have judged your degree of closeness to each member, seal the paper in an envelope and don't look at it again until directed to do so by the group leader.

In the process of the group's development, members either are drawn closer together, gravitate further apart, or they remain about the same. The CII enables us to plot the group

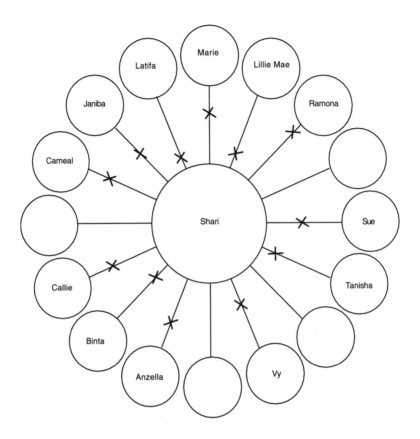

FIGURE 7.1   Pre-Communication Interaction Index

members' degrees of closeness. We spend a great deal of time promoting and facilitating closeness among group members using a variety of group counseling mechanisms and therapeutic factors and forces. It is through this closeness that members begin to trust one another, which enables them to experience group cohesion, in general, and to self-disclose their thoughts and feelings, in particular.

Toward the ending phase of termination, we ask participants to fill out the post-CII by following these directions:

1. Write your name on the diagram (Figure 7.2) in the innermost circle.

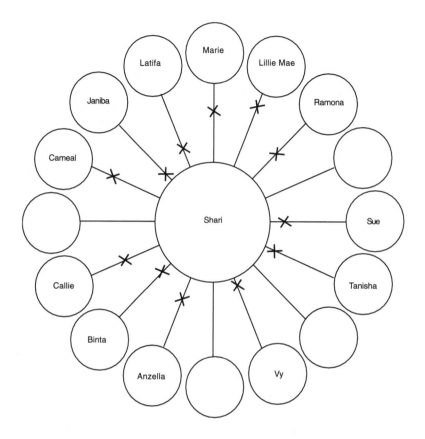

FIGURE 7.2   Post-Communication Interaction Index

2. Write the names of all other group members in the smaller circles surrounding yourself.
3. Mark an X on the line between you and each surrounding member, depending on how close you feel to that member.
4. Now, look at your pre-CII results and compare that diagram to the post-CII results.
5. Observe the results, and answer the following questions:
   - For which members were your ratings between pre- and post-CII about the same and why?
   - For which members were your ratings radically different (either closer or further away)? Why?
   - What surprised you the most concerning your ratings of group members?

Processing the CII Results

This pre–post activity generates a great deal of data for group discussion and feedback among group members and between leaders and group members. We instruct members to use caution and sensitivity when sharing and discussing their results. In particular, we ask them to use the nine guidelines already mentioned for giving and receiving feedback. Most of this group's members gave positive feedback to one another and to the leaders. In general, members stated that they felt closer to everyone and even closer to members with whom they had worked on projects. Some of the following feedback was offered:

Ramona to Mary: I am pleased to see that you no longer think of yourself as unattractive.

Mary to Ramona: Thank you. Your support and encouragement are always appreciated.

Tanisha to Sue: Believe it or not, Sue, your positive attitude and openness to all people has helped to change my attitudes toward wealthy, middle-class African-Americans.

Sue to Tanisha: Thank you, Tanisha, and I know that you would not say those things if you did not believe them.

As members give one another feedback, we monitor the process closely and reframe comments or feedback that is vague. We especially encourage members to focus on as much specific behavior as possible. Leaders should be cautious about feedback they give individual members so that other members do not feel left out. We commend all members for their courage toward growth and change because we know how difficult the change process can be. For members who may not have achieved their goals, leaders need to encourage them to keep working or trying. In the process, we also invite them to give us feedback about how we conducted the group or about any personal reactions they may have had.

Creative (Kuumba) Techniques for the Termination Stage

A major concern in delivery of mental health services to ethnic minority clients is underutilization and/or premature termination. Leong (1992) provided guidelines for minimizing premature termination among Asian-American clients in group counseling. We strongly believe that these guidelines parallel premature termination guidelines for African-American women's groups. The following are Leong's (1992) guidelines for group leaders:

1. Take time to learn Asian (African-American) values. Group counselors need to be aware of cultural variations in the counseling process.
2. Approach interpersonal problems from a collective rather from an individual orientation.
3. Provide some measure of structure in the group rather than conduct the group in an open-ended, nondirectional, laissez-faire manner. Leong suggests that Asian group members could serve as "cultural informants" for group leaders. African-Americans can also serve as cultural informants, given the myriad of cultures within the African community.
4. Use Asian-Americans outside the group to assist with Asian-American group members. African-American group leaders may turn to the church, community organizations, and social groups for assistance with group members.
5. Leaders need to exercise a great deal of patience with Asian-American (African-American) clients by not expecting them to share feelings about their experiences too quickly and candidly. Open communication too soon violates both groups' cultural norms.
6. Group counselors need to change their approach to be congruent with Asian-American (African-American) cultural orientation.
7. Group leaders should not overemphasize the focus on cultural differences because many differences exist among Asian-Americans (African-Americans).

Even though these guidelines were developed to minimize premature termination among Asian-American groups, they can also be used to reduce premature termination for African-American women in group counseling. Not until we have established a secure and stable group can we focus on termination.

Having led African-American women's groups for several years, we have learned that termination should begin at the initial session. We have found it helpful to discuss termination in every session so that members will not wait until the end of the sessions to begin to work on their issues. In other words, termination is seen as a constant reminder for members to get busy or get to work toward solving their problems. Although we use a wide range of termination interventions and techniques, the three we use most often are discussed briefly here: discussion questions, role-plays, and drawings and other art forms.

Discussion Questions

In order to summarize and evaluate the group experiences, we raise several discussion questions, including the following:

1. What did the group mean to you?
2. Are there things you'd like to say to others?
3. How do you feel about saying good-bye?
4. What decisions have you made?
5. Where do you want to go from here?
6. To what extent did you achieve your purpose?

Each of these questions is discussed carefully with each member having an opportunity to express herself. Often, it takes one or more sessions to complete the discussion of these questions.

Role-Plays

A key intervention strategy for all stages of group development is the role-play. Role-plays assist in the transition from talk to action, or from theory to practice, or from insight to action. Psychodramatic procedures are broadly used in a wide variety of group modes and group experiences ranging form guidance groups to therapy groups. We have found role-plays to be quite helpful for the ending or termination stage of the group. The following are a couple ways we use role-plays:

1. We ask group participants to role-play some of the situations they expect to encounter after leaving the group. Shari and Mary role-played a strained relationship with their husbands resulting from their new-found sense of independence. Anzella and Marie role-played strong feelings of freedom and security, having learned that they can be whole persons without having to be in a committed relationship or having to be married.

2. Other members role-played how they would be different at the end of the group. For example, Mary role-played being in more social settings where she interacted with more people rather than being shy and withdrawn. She saw herself being more assertive, imagining herself initiating conversations with new and different people.

Drawings and Other Art Forms

Some group members are able to visualize the meaning of the group experience through drawings and other art forms. We have asked women to draw pictures or symbols that reflect what the group has meant to them. In other termination assignments, we have asked members to make a collage that shows how they have grown and changed. The amount of insight we gain and the data we collect about participant growth are remarkable.

Terminating Individuals and the Entire Group

Thus far, we have discussed boundary-management issues, leadership functions, therapeutic forces, and creative group intervention strategies in the termination stage of *Images of Me* groups. In the remainder of this chapter, we will share with the reader procedures we use to terminate individual group members as well as terminate the entire *Images of Me* group. Case vignettes taken from *Images of Me* groups will be used to illustrate the termination process.

During the termination phase, we help group members identify what they have learned and discuss how they will apply these newly acquired skills in their lives outside the group. We also ask them to identify incomplete work they might want to continue in the future. On several occasions, we ask members to practice or demonstrate a particular skill they have learned as part of the termination. For example, we asked Latifa to give feedback to all members of the group because she had problems communicating with others in a direct, honest, and open manner. Latifa has been working hard since the group started on expressing her feelings rather than being so intellectual. Therefore, we asked Latifa to take some time to get in touch with her feelings toward each group member and to express those feelings.

The following is a brief excerpt of Latifa's feedback to each person in the group, including the group leaders. The procedure began with Latifa standing in front of each member and leader, expressing her feelings toward them. She began by talking to one of the leaders:

Latifa: I feel blessed to have you as a friend, yet I feel afraid of you because you are my boss and the group leader. [*She added.*] The more I interact with you, the more I know that you care about me.

Leader to Latifa: I really do care about you and hope that our relationship will continue to grow. [*Latifa hugged the leader and thanked her again for caring.*]

Latifa moved to a second member and said:

Latifa to Anzella: I have been angry with you throughout the entire group. I believe that you needed a great deal and I thought you were being insincere. I am pleased that you have become more open and have begun to share more about yourself in the group.

Latifa to Cameal: I feel real good about our most recent interaction. You came to church with me and afterward you put your arms around me and said we were soul sisters. I am glad we are in this group together. It gives us an opportunity to see one another on different levels. [*Latifa finished by saying.*] I hope we can be friends long after the group terminates.

Latifa to Vy: Vy, you have been kind of like a mystery to me. I like you because you really have worked hard for yourself and others.

Latifa to Ramona: This may seem weird, Ramona, but throughout this group I have had an issue with you I did not know how to handle. You see, I have a close friend whose husband had an affair with a woman named Ramona. I am wondering if you are that woman.

Ramona: [her immediate reply]: I am not the one.

Latifa was relieved and thanked her over and over again. She was pleased to learn that the woman who had caused her close friend so much grief was not a member of the group. She also expressed regret that she had held her feelings inside for so long.

Group Leader: Latifa, you are doing a great job, continue.
Latifa to Ramona: You made me nervous because you acted as though you wanted something from me that I was not able to give.
Ramona: I wondered about the nature of your discomfort and questioned whether it had anything to do with my reaching out to you.

Although the two women could not reach a clear understanding concerning their interpersonal perception, they were open to continuing their relationship.

Latifa to Binta: Binta, I like you. You are sweet and well-spoken.

Binta returned the compliment and the two women hugged one another and they both cried tears of joy.

Latifa to Lillie Mae: Lillie Mae, you are so pretty and I love the way you dress. I have been touched by all the things you have shared. The way you recovered from your divorce and moved on with your life was a lesson for us all.
Latifa to Janiba (the co-leader): Janiba, sometimes I really don't like you and that's because you challenge me and that makes me feel uncomfortable. I don't like you but I love you. Through my contact with you in this group, I have experienced spiritual growth, social growth, and personal growth.

After each feedback, we raised several process questions, the most common one being, "How do you feel?" Latifa disclosed, "I was uncomfortable but became more comfortable as I went along." We, the leaders, explained that interpersonal communication is uncomfortable when we do it infrequently. We encouraged Latifa to keep issues fresh by expressing them when they arise rather than when they are old and rancid, telling her that the more she expressed herself, the easier the task would become. The opportunity for interpersonal feedback was offered to all group members and it has proved to be one of the most productive tasks of the experience.

Termination is an integral part of group therapy and, if managed effectively, can be an important force in the process of change. Most clients terminate therapy with some goals achieved and some not achieved. Many women who have participated in *Images of Me* groups learn that the change that takes place within themselves can create additional problems. That is, many women outgrow their partners or spouses and often finding themselves on different maturity levels. For example, Ramona shared this with the group:

Ramona: I did not know how poor communication was between me and my husband until I joined the group. I rarely expressed my true feelings to my husband unless he "pushed me into a corner" or made me extremely upset. In the past, I needed to be very angry before I could express my true feelings. However, having been in the group for several months, I have been invited to speak up and was reinforced and supported by group members and leaders when I expressed my true feelings or thoughts. I have become increasingly intolerant of my husband who believes that it is "cool"' to hide his feelings and that it is "wimpish" to let others know what his true feelings are. Unfortunately, being in the group has caused me to give serious thought to leaving my husband.

Although therapists should encourage advanced members to terminate the group when their work is finished, many therapists will keep certain members around due to their ability to co-lead in an unofficial capacity. Yalom (1985) described some of his advanced members who became so skilled that they could offer sound advice or make valid interpretations of the group process. He suggested that when members reach this stage of maturity in the group, the leaders should use termination as an integral part of their growth and learning process. In our African-American women's groups, we are cautious about becoming too dependent on the leadership of advanced members. We often notice that they become impatient with certain members who do not change as rapidly as they believe they should. When this happens, we reclaim the leadership for fear some of the newer members might feel overwhelmed and may even drop out.

Neophyte group leaders often are surprised to learn that some group members do not want to leave the group whether they are ready or not. We have had members pretend that their conditions have worsened in order to remain in the group longer. For some members, the group is their major source for interpersonal interaction and support. Therefore, thoughts of termination bring about feelings of sadness, fear, and alienation. One such example took place in a recent support group.

Mary had joined the group because she had strong feelings of isolation, alienation, and a lack of support. She had moved to the vicinity with her husband, whom she had recently divorced. Her only friends and source of support were her husband's relatives and friends who were natives of that city. Since the divorce, she really felt cut off and isolated and told the group that she felt like a "guest in a strange house." Her goals in the group were to gain self-confidence, to feel a greater sense of belonging and to build a stronger support base among people in this new city. Her alienation was further compounded because she lived in a wealthy, upper-middle-class subdivision where no other African-American families lived. She told the group:

Mary: Now, with no African-American husband and no children, I feel alone and afraid in this cold and insensitive world. Without my husband, I feel like a nobody.

As group leaders, we have never known a client who worked so hard and progressed so quickly. She was sensitive to her own dynamics as well as the dynamics of the other women. She listened respectfully to others which led a better interpersonal understanding, communication, and support. She was a model group member in every way. She attended all sessions and served as a model of hope for other group members. One of her specific goals was to make connections with women from the African-American community where her social, political, and spiritual needs could be met. Mary reached not only this goal but many others as well.

When we noticed that it was clearly time for Mary to terminate, we asked her to summarize her achievements and practice some of the communication skills she had learned in the group. The following are some of the specific termination questions we raised with Mary:

- What has the group meant to you?
- Are there things you'd like to say to anyone here?
- How do you feel about saying good-bye?

- How do you believe you will be different?
- What decision have you made?
- Where can you go from here?
- To what extent did you achieve your goals?

Mary responded to these questions in a way that we were certain she had reached such a level of maturity that there was nothing more the group could offer her. We reinforced her for all the good work she had done and encouraged her to apply the skills she learned from the group in the real world.

Having one session remaining, we gave Mary one last homework assignment which was to wrap up any unfinished business that could be handled in the final session. We instructed her that such issues must be related to past work rather than introduce new problems that could not be adequately handled in the last session. We further informed her that if new issues arose, she could perhaps join another group or work it out through individual therapy.

During the final session Mary made a complete turn around, seeming to regress back to the first session. Leaders and members were surprised by her behavior. She appeared to be in a stupor and a somewhat depressed mood. Observing her appearance and behavior, we attempted to connect with her and to find out what had happened since the last meeting. She talked in a low sad voice:

Mary: I am going to be all alone in a large, cold, insensitive city where no one loves or cares about me. Every time I place my trust in people, they end up leaving me. My grandmother, whom I loved, died and left me with an uncaring mother and an abusive stepfather. My husband brought me from my hometown down South to a Midwestern city filled with cold, insensitive people only to divorce me for no understandable reason.

Leaving the group reminds her of all the times she has been left behind. We explained that leaving the group often causes feelings of sadness, doubt, and fear because the group has been a loving and caring family of individuals who have nourished her to health. We assured Mary that many clients experience feelings at termination and those feelings are signs of readiness for new challenges to be undertaken in the real world. We invited group members to give Mary feedback and encouraged her to face life and function in life as she had so skillfully functioned in the group. One member started:

Joi: Mary, I know you are going to make it because you are one of the most courageous people I know. You are kind, warm, and caring, and I don't know anyone who would not enjoy being your friend. If you think I am lying, just call me and we can get together for lunch or dinner or we can go to the fitness center together.

Another Member: I agree, but there is something else I like about you, Mary. I especially like your intellect. You introduced the group to African-American literature from the new Renaissance period. You are so knowledgeable about Black writers such as Du Bois, James Weldon Johnson, Claude McKay, Langston Hughes, Countee Cullens, Zora Neale Hurston, Gwendolyn Brooks, and many others. In fact, I would love to be in a reading group with you. I know that it is time for you to leave this group but I want you to know that I love you, I appreciate you, and I know that things are going to work out just fine.

At this point, Mary raised herself up from her depressed state and acknowledged all the wonderful gifts the group had given her. As this final session ended, Mary gave everybody a hug, wished everybody well, and said good bye-to all.

Yalom (1985) suggested that some socially isolated clients might delay termination in order to use the group for their social needs—for developing a social life for themselves—rather than for personal growth. He suggested that group leaders should emphasize transfer of learning and encourage clients to practice skills outside the group. Yalom (1985) further asserted that some members delay termination to be guaranteed that they will never again experience difficulty. In this case, he suggested that group leaders must let members know that such guarantees are not possible and delayed treatment does not improve the clients' circumstances because there is always a certain amount of risk involved in life and there cannot be absolute guarantees.

The reality of termination is problematic for many group members especially African-American women who have suffered the need to belong for such a long time. The need to belong to the group or to the family is a significant aspect of the

African-American way of life. Therefore, when many African-American women terminate, they become very sensitive to abandonment and often believe that the solution to their problems is being connected with the therapists and the group. These women believe that the group will provide a home for them as long as they have problems; they resist getting well to avoid abandonment. In these cases, we attempt to help the members understand the dynamics of their reluctance to terminate and encourage them to move forward. Very rarely does it help to deny or delay termination. Yalom (1985) stated that a departing member can be a ray of hope for the remaining members. Specifically, it serves to remind them of the importance of time, so members should get busy working on their own issues. He also suggested that the loss of a departing member can serve as a vehicle for dealing with issues of loss, separation, and so forth.

Finally, we as leaders find it helpful to process our own feelings about terminating group members. Sometimes, we find ourselves struggling to become more comfortable letting members go after they have finished. Too often, we want members to be perfect before we think they are ready for termination. In addition, leaders may deny termination to certain members due to the major contributions they make to the group experience. For example, some experienced members are great norm setters and great models for behaviors we want members to learn. Certain group members can expertly employ leadership functions such as caring, emotional stimulation, and meaning attribution (Lieberman et al., 1973). Yet, no matter how valuable a member is, leaders must let her go when the psychotherapeutic process is complete. We, as leaders, have to remind ourselves of these principles because there are members who we come to love dearly; they sometimes become such a part of our family that we are reluctant to let go.

Our previous discussion was about terminating individual members from a group. Now, here are a few comments about terminating the entire group. Most terminations involve an entire group which may have lasted anywhere from six to nine months. Usually, it is good to terminate the group at a given time unless the majority of the members tend to be ready sooner. Although termination practices vary from group to group, we tend to follow these nine general principles and practices:

1. Remind members of the termination process early in the group so they will not wait until the end to work toward achieving their goals.
2. Even though group members often find it difficult to terminate, the leader must still focus on ending the group and encouraging the members to move ahead with their lives. We invite members to determine how they would like to say good-bye.
3. When members continuously deny termination, we make them aware of their attitudes or behaviors and interpret or give meaning to their reluctance.
4. Invite group members to decide how they want the group to end since the group is theirs.
5. Having group members share past experiences in the group is one way to help them deal with the pain over the loss of the group.
6. Members express positive feelings and closeness rather than negative feelings. The expression of negative feelings during the final session usually does not serve a useful purpose.
7. Encourage each group member to demonstrate one skill she has learned that could be applied outside the group. (Many of our members demonstrate or role-play confrontation with a significant other.)
8. Basic to our final meeting are personal testimonials about what the group has meant to them. In almost every case, these African-American women discuss how nourishing and empowering it is to connect with other women with issues similar to their own.
9. As Yalom (1985) recommended, we as leaders facilitate the group process by sharing our own feelings about separating from the group. We disclose some of the critical moments from the group, including both low points and high points. However, we try to end the group with words of encouragement or hope.

We also invite the members to leave a legacy, or a gift, or words of wisdom for the group. From these simple directives, members offer a wide range of supportive thoughts and ideas to individual members and to the entire group. Some of the typical comments from members follow:

"Believe in yourself."

"Don't allow others to define who you are."

"Know that no matter how difficult things become, you are never alone."

"Take risk, nothing beats a failure but a try."

"Lighten up and enjoy life."

"Remember that you can eat an elephant if you take one bite at a time."

The group usually ends with members and leaders saying good-bye to one another in their own styles, including hugs, kisses, handshakes, and verbal exchanges. Most groups end in a very positive manner characterized by hope, optimism, and a spirit of achievement.

Summary

To complete our analogy of group stages being similar to a plane that prepares to take off, flies to its destination, and lands, our African-American women's group has had another safe flight. The termination phase just described was a preparation for a safe landing. These women can now deplane and go about their lives; as some pilots often say: "The safe part of the journey is now over." We have provided a safe and secure place for members to explore many issues and conflicts in their lives. The turbulences in the sky were transition points, which were used to help members grow and change. The strain of the engine to lift the plane to even higher altitudes represented members' attempts to trust one another, to establish their places in the group, to test the leaders' competence for leading the group, and to determine how much risk they were willing to take in the group.

At cruising altitude, group members are directed to move about the cabin because the captain has given them permission by turning off the fasten seat belts sign. Members feel safe enough to explore their issues. They feel safe enough to trust the group process and to take more growth-engendering risks. The time is right for group cohesion, for a spirit of cooperation, and for interpersonal support at the highest level.

When nearing the destination, the pilot prepares the crew and the passengers for landing and within a short period of time, the plane touches the ground. The touching of the ground symbolizes the reality of going back into the real world with new attitudes, behaviors, and outlooks. The touching of the ground symbolizes that each member must take control of her life because the pilots (or leaders) give up control. The touching of the ground is a reminder that members need to take responsibility for their own lives. We have given these members our best leadership by creating a therapeutic environment characterized by a group of caring African-American women who care about one another, who feel a strong sense of African connectedness, and who offer unselfish support and encouragement.

References

Angelou, M. (1969). *I know why the caged bird sings.* New York: Random House.

Brown, S. P., Lipford-Sanders, J., & Shaw, M. (1995). Kujichagulia: Uncovering the secrets of the heart—Group work with African-American women on predominately white campuses. *Journal for Specialists in Group Work, 20*(3), 151–158.

Cooper, J. C. (1984). *A piece of mine.* Navarro, CA: Wild Tree Press.

Corey, G. (1995) *Theory and practice of group counseling* (4th ed.). Pacific Grove, CA: Brooks/Cole.

Hurston, Z. N. (1937). *Their eyes were watching God.* Philadelphia: J. B. Lippincott Company.

Leong, F. T. L. (1992). Guidelines for minimizing premature termination among Asian-American clients in group counseling. *Journal for Specialists in Group Work, 17*(4), 218–228.

Lieberman, M., Yalom, I. D., & Miles, M. (1973). *Encounter groups: First facts.* New York: Basic Books.

Morrison, T. (1977). *Song of Solomon.* New York: Knopf.

Rhode, R., & Stockton, R. (1992). The effects of structured feedback on goal attainment, attraction to the group and satisfaction with the group in small group counseling. *Journal of Group Psychotherapy, Psychodrama, and Sociometry, 44*(4), 172–180.

Singer, D., Astrachan, B. M., Gould, L. J., & Klien, E. B. (1975). Boundary management in psychological work with groups. *Journal of Applied Behavioral Science, 11*(2), 137–176.

Yalom, I. D. (1985). *The theory and practice of group psychotherapy* (3rd ed.). New York: Basic Books, Inc.

8

Empowering African-
American Women
to Embrace Accurate
Images—Kujichagulia

Kujichagulia, the Swahili word for self-determination and empowerment, embraces the expression of feelings, ideas about self-image and worth, and the ability to make a difference in a world of racism and sexism from an Afrocentric perspective. Regardless of educational and socioeconomic levels, *Images of Me* groups' participants tend to derive a sense of empowerment from participation in an Afrocentrically oriented group.

African-American women have found strength and success through their use of support networks with family and other African-American females. Over time, the professional literature has offered information to support the usefulness of therapeutic groups to assist with the empowerment of African-American females. In this chapter, we offer a concise summary of two major constructs, group dynamics and therapeutic forces, of group work from an Afrocentric worldview. Group dynamics are the attitudes and interactions of both group leaders and group members. Therapeutic forces are specific conditions within the group that influence both group dynamics and group process. We discuss the relevance of each construct to enhancing African-American women's appreciation of their bicultural (racial and gender) assets. We challenge the reader to view group work from an Afrocentric perspective while working with African-American women and to understand the importance of this perspective to empowering these women as they ask and answer the familiar questions, "Am I crazy or is this what's happening?" and "Is this for real?"

An Afrocentric Perspective of Major Group Constructs

Some traditional Western group counseling services are helpful, regardless of race or gender. This helpfulness, in part, is due, to the group leaders' ability to recognize and operationalize the three dimensions of multicultural competence—personal awareness, knowledge of the population being served, and skills appropriate for the population being served—as they provide group services to women and non-European-Americans. These leaders actualize group theory in ways that show an appreciation for the life experiences and worldviews of both individual and collective group members.

It is important, however, to note that some group counseling experiences are oppressive in that leaders adhere to basic assumptions, values, beliefs, and customs that are very different from those of group members who are women and members who are racially and ethnically different from the European-American population. An outcome of oppressive behavior, lack of recognition of life experiences and worldview, and limited multicultural competence by group leaders may be attributed to the small number of racially diverse populations who elect to remain in counseling using traditional interventions. Group leaders who wish to empower all group members, particularly those who are oppressed, must identify ways to promote the development of identity and pride within group members. A guide to assist group leaders in developing their multicultural helping skills is the monograph, "Operationalization of the Multicultural Competencies," by Arredondo, Toporek, Brown, Jones, Locke, Sanchez, and Stadler (1996, January), which has been endorsed by the Association for Multicultural Counseling and Development and the Association for Counselor Education and Supervision.

The Afrocentric approach is increasingly recommended as an effective and practical intervention, particularly with African-Americans (Jackson & Sears, 1992; Nobles, 1990; Parham, 1993; Robinson & Howard-Hamilton, 1994). Moreover, counseling African-American women from an Afrocentric perspective increasingly has been found to be effective (Brown, 1993; Brown, 1994; Brown, Sanders, & Shaw, 1995; Gainor, 1992). Brown et al. (1995) presented an effective group therapy model for African-American females, led by African-American women and designed around the theme of Kujichagulia. In this group, a primary focus of group leaders is to assist African-American females on predominantly White college campuses uncover the secrets of their hearts. Of significance are secrets that relate to the group members' cognitive and emotional experiences and how these experiences influence their individual and collective racial and gender identities and images.

Group work is recognized as an effective therapeutic tool to psychologically, socially, and spiritually empower African-American women. Group work with these women is enhanced by a clear understanding of group dynamics and therapeutic forces operating within the group, particularly from an Afrocentric perspective. A common theme undergirding the dynamics and therapeutic forces operating in *Images of Me* groups is self-determination. *Kujichagulia*, literally, means to define for oneself, create for oneself, and speak for oneself, instead of being defined, named, and spoken for by others; it captures the mindset espoused by both group leaders and members. Kujichagulia connotes an Afrocentric approach to group counseling and cognitively and affectively embraces values such as community, spirituality, and interdependence. Although some of these values are inherent to the group process (e.g., community and interdependence) from an Afrocentric perspective, the interrelatedness of dynamics and forces needs to be reviewed when working with African-American women. Further, questions about dynamics, forces, and the influence of life experiences, such as race and gender, on African-American women in groups need to be posed. Sample questions, which group leaders striving toward this end might pose, include the following:

- What thematic dynamics of life experience must I know in order to empower these African-American women to embrace accurate images of themselves?
- How are specific historical and contemporary sociopolitical forces around race and gender significant to the current

life experiences and subsequent image building of African-American females?
• How do I free African-American women to individually and collectively walk in the newness of their empowerment created around images of their strong and positive African and female legacies?

Group Dynamics

Group dynamics are the physical interactions and the reciprocal psychological, emotional, spiritual, and cultural forces operating between group members and group leaders. Practitioners who understand the intertwining of these forces are well positioned to identify (1) the nature of the group, (2) how interactions between members and leaders affect the development and progression of the group, and (3) the cultural (e.g., racial and gender) implications of these forces on group dynamics (Capuzzi & Gross, 1992; Gladding, 1991; Jacobs, Harvill, & Masson, 1994; Sue & Sue, 1990). While working with African-American women, questions like the following may be operating to influence group dynamics related to the development and progression of the group as members and leaders interact:

How do the verbal and nonverbal communication patterns of African-American women influence the dynamics of the group?
What influence does race and gender have on the dynamics of the group?

Callie and a group leader provide an example of the influence of verbal and nonverbal communication patterns on the psychological and emotional progression and development of *Images of Me* group members:

Callie: Binta, I like the way you speak with conviction! You say exactly what you think and feel. I always know that when I hear from you, I hear the truth!
Group Leader: Callie, what did you see and hear that helped you believe that Binta is truthful?
Callie: She...
Group Leader: Speak directly to Binta and use "I" terms.

Callie: Binta, I noticed you looked me in the eye when you
talked to me. You touched my hand while you were sharing
your feelings, which made me feel connected to you. When
you wanted to emphasize a point, you raised your voice. I
heard and felt your emotion. I like that.

Group Leader: You know that we, as African-Americans and
women, have an appreciation for feeling life and expressing
our feelings. We can use this value as a tool to promote our
growth and pride during group.

Callie: Yes, but you know I find that sometimes when I show
my feelings and speak my mind at the university, I tend to
upset people. At least that's what it seems like to me.

Group Leader: I wonder what influence race and/or gender
might have on your experience, Callie. What do you think,
group? What images come to mind for you?

Marie: I feel the energy, the emotion in group and I like it. It
feels familiar to me. When I go to church, I feel energy and
emotion. When I'm at home interacting with my family, I
feel energy and emotion. Energy and emotion are a part of
who I am! My spirit feels freed!

Binta: I feel connected to you, like we are sisters, when you
share your world and emotions with me. Yet, I know the
influence that speaking your words and thoughts can have
in the White world. Remember, we talked earlier in group
about the differences in the values of the European-American and African-American worldview. I guess what we are
talking about now is an example of how the different values
are viewed from those two perspectives. We don't have to
give up ourselves and our values, but we do have to be aware
of the values and worldviews of others. We can define for
ourselves who we are as African-American females and at
the same time we can respect the worldviews and values of
others. I see myself as a strong Black woman who values
others as well.

Cultural forces, such as African traditions, have implications on group dynamics. Ideas are the substance of behavior
in an African tradition, which means that truth lies in the congruence between what a person says and what a person does.
Group leaders seeking to understand the intertwining of physical interactions and the reciprocal psychological and emotional forces between group members might ask, "How is what
one group member says congruent with what the member is

doing?" Put another way, "Is the group member 'talking the talk and walking the walk'?" What's the influence of a member's incongruent behavior on other group members? Do group members seem confused, angry, or indifferent to the member who says one thing and does something else?

Callie, a professor and outspoken member of an *Images of Me* group, shares her words and her behaviors around a specific experience at her university. Another group member demonstrates the implications of incongruent behavior as perceived and experienced from her worldview. The group leader searches for the implications of cultural forces on group dynamics; in this case, the influence of a member's incongruent behavior on another group member.

Callie: I always speak up for women, no matter what. Recently I served on the faculty search committee at my university. We had four candidates—three men and one woman. I am the only woman on the faculty in our department, so I was very excited about the upcoming interviews. We needed another woman!

Binta: I know what that's like. I am only one of two females on the faculty at my university. So what did you do?

Callie: Well, on paper the female was well qualified and I was sure she would be one of the final candidates. When we interviewed her, I discovered she was a White female and, to me, seemed rather aggressive.

Anzella: Sounds to me like you're jealous, Callie. After all, you pride yourself in saying what you think and what you feel. How did you vote?

Callie: No, I'm not jealous of the sister. I did not vote for her; I voted for one of the men.

Group Leader: Anzella, you seem confused and upset with Callie. What's going on with you right now?

Anzella: Callie, you are saying that you always stand up for women. You had a qualified White woman candidate and you ditched her! Sounds to me like you are saying one thing and doing another!

Group Leader: Go on, Anzella, you still seem upset.

Anzella: You are basing your actions on her being a White woman. I am angry because it reminds me of what I experienced most of my life because of my complexion. Blacks have been jealous of my light skin, and I feel like I missed out on a lot because I'm light.

With African-American women, the forces of group dynamics can be subtle and simultaneously blatant. Not only individual but also cultural communication patterns, feelings, experiences, and self-images, as well as images of others who are African-American and women, are reflected in physical interactions and reciprocal psychological and emotional behaviors. Binta and Marie reflect the power of group dynamics as they discuss images of African-American women.

Binta: When I look at you, my sista, I see myself. I'm Black, my lips are large, I say what I think, and I don't take no stuff off of nobody!

Marie: You know, Binta, I'm sick and tired of you calling me your sister. We are not sisters and we don't look alike. I don't even like the way you, "say what you think." But I have to admit that I won't let people walk over me either. I guess, in that respect, we are alike.

This is an example of a significant and frequent dynamic observed in numerous *Images of Me* groups, the desire for connectedness. That is, exhibition of direct and/or indirect behaviors to confirm a thought/feeling of normalcy—I'm okay because you are the same/I am because we are. We are, thus, I am. While there is an obvious specification of individuality exhibited in Marie's words, there is also a sense of connectedness to Binta when she says "I guess, in that respect, we are alike." Binta asserts her connectedness to Marie early in her statement, ". . . . I see myself."

Another group dynamic is communication patterns such as knowing who talks to whom, the frequency of speech during sessions, and explicit as well as implicit nonverbal behaviors and messages. In the beginning stages (almost from session one) of *Images of Me* groups, we have noticed a pattern of members quickly becoming comfortable, speaking early and frequently, talking to each other, and exhibiting clear nonverbal behaviors and messages. Members often share intimate stories, challenge each others' beliefs and attitudes, and express deep feelings. A dialogue among three *Images of Me* members during the first session exemplifies this comfort and freedom around verbal and nonverbal communication patterns.

Latifa: When I was a young girl, I guess I was about nine or ten, my mother and I went to the doctor because I had chicken pox. Mother was concerned that the bumps I had were not healing properly. I'll never forget this incident because it was one of the early experiences I relate to who I am as a Black person. Our family doctor was a White male and we had visited him many times prior to this. But this time he showed us another side of himself. He asked my mother how he could tell if the bumps I had were related to my disease since my skin is so dark.

Marie: It sounds to me like you are making more of this than you should have. After all, if he did not know, how else was he to find out but to ask your mother?

Callie: I am concerned about what impact your doctor's words had on you as a small child. You heard those words too.

Group Leader: Callie, you seem to be connecting with Latifa. I've even noticed as you talk to her that your voice is picking up pace. What's going on?

Callie: As I shared before, it's important to me that women are lifted up and empowered. To me this process begins in childhood. Latifa is sharing an example of someone tearing down her image as a Black person.

Group Leader: So you're feeling. . . . ?

Latifa: Well, I think it's clear that I was hurt.

Group Leader: Hold on a minute, Latifa, Callie seems to be struggling here. Callie, you're feeling. . . . ?

Callie: I am pissed off! How dare he be so insensitive! He's hurting another Black child, and in particular a young Black female!

Group Leader: Latifa, I cut you off. I'm sorry, please continue.

Latifa: Well, that incident is still very real in my mind. But you know what? I also remember how my mother dealt with the doctor. She put him in his place right there and then. She didn't hold her tongue nor did she hide her emotions. That made me feel more secure and validated.

Callie: Yeah, I bet she did! We, as African-American women, tend to say what we think and what we feel. I like that about us! Yet, at times this kind of behavior tends to get me in trouble. People seem to take it the wrong way. They seem to lose focus. It's as if they take it personally.

If, for some reason, the group fails to begin to work as quickly as previously mentioned, we use an exercise—*Kujichagulia: You Are an Important Part of This Group*—to get the group working and bonding. In addition, this exercise has been an effective tool to promote and quickly observe group dynamics such as specific verbal and nonverbal communication patterns. A large puzzle is placed on the floor in the center of the group. The background for the puzzle is a collage of African-American females that depicts the diversity in socioeconomic status, roles, and physical features such as coloring, hairstyles, and so on. The center of the collage reads "You Are an Important Part of This Group." Each member, including the group leaders, is given a puzzle part and told to write on one side of it her response to the question "What do I expect to get from this experience?"

Along with her expectations for the group, each member is asked to write the name she wishes to be referred to by the group for the remainder of the group experience. On the opposite side of her puzzle piece, each member is asked to respond to the question "What do I bring to the group?" After all members have responded to both questions, each member is invited to take her puzzle piece and work with the group to put the puzzle together. Quickly and clearly, communication patterns emerge such as who verbally or nonverbally takes control, who verbally and/or nonverbally gives up control, who talks to whom and with what behavioral characteristics (e.g., directly or indirectly, with emotion or without emotion).

Practitioners who recognize the traditional requisite skills and behaviors for effective group work and the significance of Afrocentric values on creating a group atmosphere in tune with the life experiences of African-American women use interventions which promote interactions, connectedness, and energy exchanges between group members and leaders. The Kujichagulia exercise embraces and therapeutically uses these Afrocentric values. Another way to embrace and therapeutically use Afrocentric values is to notice, address, and validate nonverbal communication. In the previous example of the dynamics between Marie and Binta, the group leader notices Marie's nonverbal language and senses unshared feelings associated with Marie's words. She encourages Marie to address the emotion implied in her statement and to voice her nonverbal behavior.

Group Leader: Marie, while you were talking to Binta, your
 voice became louder than it usually is, your head swayed,
 and you put your hands on your hip as if you are angry. Tell
 Binta what you are feeling.

After Marie shares with Binta, the leader recognizes an opportunity to educate the group about the values reflective of themelves as members of the female gender and descendents of the African culture.

Group Leader: It's *us* to feel and to connect. As descendents of Africa, we have a history and appreciation for connectedness, cooperation, and the power of the group working together for the sake of the group. As women, we have a strong appreciation for connectedness, cooperation, and the strength of the group. So it makes sense that in our individual ways we embrace connectedness while, at the same time, demanding our individuality. But, we see ourselves as individuals who are a part of a group working on behalf of the group, not so much as individuals working alone to promote personal success.

To further understand the ethnic and gender components of self, the leader offers an opportunity for the group to delve deeper into who they are as individuals (a woman, an African-American), who they are as individuals who value being a part of a group (a member of the African-American community and a member of the female gender). A critical focus is the identification of values, experiences, feelings, and behaviors that seem important individually and collectively.

Techniques that have proved effective and are consistent with the interactive nature of African-Americans and women are videos of African-American women (e.g., *Images and Realities: African-American Women*). Viewing the video in group enables the sharing of common and individual experiences. After viewing the tape, the group is invited to share and process the content of the video. A primary focus is identifying and working through observed physical behaviors and interactions as well as psychological, emotional, spiritual, and cultural forces noticed in the video. Then, each member is invited to apply her observations to herself (the individual), to the group as a whole, and to her life (e.g., at home, in church, on the job) relative to thematic behaviors, interactions, emotions, spirituality, and cultural forces.

Over and over again, we have noticed that the *Images of Me* participants' sense of empowerment has been heightened by their understanding of personal and collective images of African-American women. Use of these images encourages them to work toward a definition of self as well as a comparison of how personal self-definitions do or do not relate to societal gender and racial images. More often than not, images embraced by numerous African-American women relate to values—such as a belief in the interconnectedness of things; an appreciation for harmony; and a sense of self-worth measured by contributions to family, other people, and the community—indicative of their African heritage and female gender.

Practitioners with a clear understanding of the attitudes and interactions around real-life experiences, such as race and gender, operating in groups are better positioned to build an effective helping foundation and atmosphere. Crucial to the effectiveness of the foundation and atmosphere are therapeutic forces operating within the group. Of significance are two questions:

> How do therapeutic forces, such as the desire to feel safe and accepted within group, influence the empowerment of African-American women?
>
> How do therapeutic forces interrelate with group dynamics, and foster empowerment for African-American women?

The Interaction of Therapeutic Forces and Group Dynamics

The specific conditions within the group, which influence attitudes and interactions of group members and leaders, are significant in helping members share and address experiences of racism and sexism and in enhancing a sense of empowerment within a society that tends to devalue African-Americans and women.

Lillie Mae: I hear people say that I must be a superwoman because I have to fight racism and sexism. I am strong and I fight the "isms" well. But I get tired of fighting and often angry that I have to work twice as hard just to show others, and even at times myself, that I am competent. Sometimes I just have to go and be with my own folks, just to remind myself that I'm okay.

Janiba: It is so hard to be an African-American female. Sometimes I feel so drained.

Ramona: When I'm at work, I feel like I'm in a sea of faceless people!

Shari: It's comforting to be in the company of my sisters. To be with women who look like me, think like me, feel like me. I don't have to explain myself. I can be me and be heard and understood.

Jacobs, Harvill, and Masson (1994) shared the 16 forces that they think group leaders need to consider and address as they work to offer positive group experiences. Of the 16 forces, three are of particular interest at this time. Two of the three forces, adequacy of the setting and leader's attitude, are briefly addressed here. The third—leaders' experiences in group work, in this case culturally competent group work—is discussed in more detail later. Each force is addressed from an Afrocentric perspective.

Adequacy of the Setting

The matter of where a group for African-American women should be conducted is an important question. The ideal situation is to offer the group in a location convenient for all group members. If the helping professional's office is not conveniently located, alternative sites include a church or a community center. In addition to general considerations, such as proper lighting and placement of chairs, to facilitate the development of a comfortable overall environment that sends the message "you are welcomed and appreciated," we suggest that group leaders intentionally select and have available African-American female forms of arts—wall decorations, music, magazines, books, videos, and printed materials. Intentional selection of these kinds of art forms promotes education and enhances access to individual and collective psychological, spiritual, and emotional experiences for group members. The following have been helpful in creating a counseling setting that emphasizes an appreciation for African-American females:

1. The use of magazines, such as *Ebony*, *Jet*, and *Essence,* have assisted group members to generate concrete examples of their individual and collective values, reflect on the diverse images of themselves, and promote discussions about African-American women.

2. Music has fostered the identification and actualization of issues, behaviors, and struggles common to women and Afri-

can-Americans. Group leaders who use music are encouraged to select classical and/or contemporary music that serves a specific function and sets a specific tone. For example, music (artists) that helps to promote the identification of issues and behaviors related to specific roles for women, relationships, and intimacy include: "I'm Every Woman," Whitney Houston; "Ladies First," Queen Latifa; "Count on Me," Whitney Houston and CeCe Winans; "How Could You Call Her Baby?" Shanna; and "Sex Is on My Mind," Blulight. Music that promotes strength and interconnectedness includes spirituals such as "When I Think about Jesus" and "Mama's Song," Kirk Franklin and the Family; and "You Are the Source of My Strength," author unknown. Music that creates atmosphere and promotes relaxation includes jazz by various artists such as Kenny G and Rachelle Ferell.

   3. Books—*Song of Solomon* by Toni Morrison, *Daddy's Little Girls* by T. D. Jakes, and *Waiting to Exhale* by Terry McMillan—and television movies, such as *The Women of Brewster Place* and *There Are No Children Here* starring Oprah Winfrey, create yet another opportunity for group members to see themselves reflected in the helping environment, generate appropriate images of African-American women, affirm their individual identities, and promote the development of collective pride in being members of the African-American female population and legacy.

Leader's Attitude

The leader's feelings and attitudes about leading a group, particularly a group of African-American women, affect how effectively the group will function. If the leader believes that people are people and women are women, regardless of race and ethnicity, an antitherapeutic force may be created. That is, a leader with this attitude will, at best, struggle with providing African-American women tools to identify and embrace accurate images related to their African and female heritages. Operating from a "we are all people" stance inhibits a leader's ability to be open to the differences as well as the similarities among multicultural and diverse populations and women. While it is true that we are all people, a leader operating from this position falls short of seeing and working with the total person (i.e., a person who needs to deal with a gender or race issue, comes from a specific socioeconomic background, has a specific lifestyle orientation, and so on) and consequently falls short of being able to promote individual and collective empowerment around cognitively and affectively defining for self, creating for self, and speaking for self, instead of being defined, named, and spoken for by others.

More specifically, the leader with an attitude of universality (we are all the same) is more prone to ignore, not hear or sense issues around race and gender that are significant to African-American women's growth and development. For example, a leader insensitive to or unknowledgeable about racism may not hear in Lillie Mae's previous statement ("Sometimes I just have to go and be with my own folks ....") the power and affirmation that she experiences when she joins a group of African-American women. Instead, the leader may interpret Lillie Mae's statement as her need to isolate and not deal with her issues.

On the other hand, a group leader who assumes a specific attitude about the realities of culture is more open to seeing and more comfortable with people's differences and similarities. Of critical importance is the fact that this leader does not view difference as deficiency, but sees difference as what it is, just difference. Such a leader believes that people are people, in that we share common characteristics such as the need for love, food, and safety. At the same time, this leader knows that people have cultural, racial, and ethnic differences and similarities which influence the expression of common characteristics and the effective meeting of needs.

From this perspective, a group leader is better able to promote an Afrocentric approach to group work, to elevate the concept of Kujichagulia among group members, and to foster the individual and collective empowerment of group members. A leader who is sensitive to and knowledgeable about racism will hear Lillie Mae's pride in her people and the sense of strength received when she is in the company of her own. Such a leader will be open to the reality that even though Lillie Mae seeks to segregate herself, at times, she is not necessarily needing to isolate from, deny, and/or fail to appreciate the multiculturalism that exists in the world. For her, this behavior is a way to recapture her strength and heritage, revive her spirit, and better herself for productive daily living.

Chapter 9 provides more detailed information and discussion about group leaders' characteristics and challenges as they lead groups, particularly groups comprised of members who share similar life histories, worldviews, and experiences.

Leaders' Experiences in Providing Culturally Competent Group Work

For new group leaders, regardless of the group's focus, experience with group process, leader behavior, and so on is important. However, when leading a group for African-American women, additional awareness, knowledge, and skills are also important. Sue, Arredondo, and McDavis (1992) offered specific cross-cultural competencies that need to be used when working with diversity. Among their suggestions, which are certainly applicable to group leaders, is the need for group leaders to understand as many of their personal biases, beliefs, values, and attitudes regarding race (in this case African-Americans) and gender as possible. Group leaders (regardless of race and ethnicity) working with African-American women need to feel comfortable with emerging differences between themselves and their clients. Culturally skilled group leaders know and/or are open to learning about their own and others' racial and cultural heritages and how these heritages influence their decisions and biases within groups. As leaders, they must understand how oppression, racism, and discrimination affect not only them and their work, but also how these realities affect African-American women.

Culturally competent group leaders know that regardless of geographic location, socioeconomic level, and educational achievement, African-American women carry within an inner movie screen on which are projected incessant images casting who they are, who they should be, and who they will become. These images are often confusing, sometimes distorted, and frequenty throw African-American women off balance so that many lose sight of their bicultural identities and fail to embrace who they are as women and who they are as members of the African-American communtity. The persistent flashing of inaccurate images of African-Americans and of women agitates the confusion, distortion, and imbalanced experiences.

Frequently, African-American women are portrayed as competitive, aggressive matriarchs and victims (Fleming, 1983; Jordan, 1991; Mitchell, 1991). Often beauty is defined by standards of the dominant culture so that physical characteristics such as coarse, curly hair, typical of numerous African-American females, is seen as unattractive. The emotional vibrance (directly voicing and expressing feelings) of numerous

African-Americans is frequently misunderstood and often constricted. When viewed through traditional Eurocentric lenses, her personalized, caring, and relationship-oriented approach to life is enigmatic. Yet, two unwavering flaws projected onto the screen of life for African-American women and encompassing their existence are racism and sexism. Finally, culturally competent group leaders understand the positive and negative, individual and collective challenges of African-American women around issues of race and gender and address racial and gender contributions to African-American women's mental health and sense of empowerment.

Culturally competent helping professionals strive to identify and use strategies that promote psychological and emotional success in the lives of African-American women, and thereby, empower these women to unveil and address hidden issues directing their behavior (Brown, 1993; Brown et al., 1995). Racial and gender issues are sometimes likened to secrets, thoughts, feelings, and perspectives that are kept to one's self and not openly shared. Intrinsic to secrets are factors, such as cultural heritage and cultural scripts, that contain guidelines and expectations for living as defined by the African-American community. These secrets influence verbal and nonverbal communication; personal, social, and professional life experiences; and the desire to explore frustrations, disappointments, and questions around significant issues like race and gender. African-American women must be supported and encouraged to unveil, analyze, and work through those secrets that create discomfort and discover those secrets that foster empowerment in order to promote effective interrelatedness between group dynamics and therapeutic forces.

As the search for effective therapeutic interventions with racially diverse populations and women persists, group work is becoming an effective tool to help African-American women with their development and to empower them against life challenges like racism and sexism (Brown et al., 1995; Jackson & Sears, 1992; Nayman, 1983). Regardless of educational and socioeconomic levels, *Images of Me* participants have, more often than not, derived a sense of empowerment from participation in a group that urges the interrelatedness of group dynamics and therapeutic forces from an Afrocentric worldview. Let's join the group as members share thoughts and feelings.

Binta: Five months ago I felt like I was isolated and alone. I was afraid to speak up and even go anywhere. Now, in just ten sessions, I am feeling connected with my sisters.

Shari: For me, the group has been like a rebirth. I feel stronger and can go back to work with more peace in my heart, and I feel less angry with my White colleagues. I don't have to give others power over defining who I am. I'm proud to be a Black woman.

Callie: I have learned that when I say what I think and feel, I'm reflecting a value related to my African heritage. I know that I need to be more sensitive to the values and the worldview of the European-Americans in my university but I don't have to accept the "aggressive" label that has been given me. Aggression suggests that I am not okay. I AM OKAY! People holding a similar value for direct thoughts and feelings, like many of my African-American sisters, appreciate my behavior and label my direct behavior more positively.

Anzella: I am recognizing that not all African-Americans see my light complexion as something to be jealous of. That is extremely important to me. African-American women come in all shades, each holding her own beauty and value. I think what has been most significant for me, though, is recognizing how to confront my African-Amerian sisters about our differences and still maintain a relationship. I have a lot more growing to do as I struggle with the "pull" related to skin color among us. But I now recognize that I have more control over that pull than I thought. I do not have to accept what others may say and/or think about what is beautiful about us as women! That's a gift I will cherish.

Marie: I am becoming a stronger woman. I realize that race matters but the question remains, How do I as an African-American woman deal with race? I have learned to cope and deal with situations and not analyze everything. I have learned to take things as they are. In doing this, I have learned to respect myself and others regardless of race. Racism has been and will always be a part of my life. I cannot allow myself to hurt anymore. Accepting, dealing, and educating are key to healing the pain I have endured in my lifetime. I want to be strong. I want to be positive. I want to endure all of what the world offers me. It is a continuing battle that I must face every day. I believe that with the strength of the Lord and the support of my family, I can achieve anything. I realize this and now it is time to heal.

Embracing Accurate Images

Empowerment for African-American women is viewed through gender, cultural, and racial lenses. Significant to the construction of these lenses are their life experience and assets. Counselors, educators, supervisors, and counseling students working to empower African-American women are encouraged to view empowerment through (1) the lenses of African-American women, (2) self-determination, and (3) the embracing of bicultural assets.

Empowerment as Seen Through African-American Women's Lenses

"Will African-American women ever get ahead?" is a question frequently posed as African-American women mature and define their images for themselves. Inherent in this question, however, is an uncertainty about personal and collective power. Yet, as these women respond to this question, it is essential for them to understand the concept of empowerment and how empowerment applies to them as African-Americans, as females, and particularly, to them as African-American females. Hall (1992) defined empowerment as "individual and collective strengthening of negotiating position in relation to the negotiating position of other people; development, growth, and maturation of real talents and aptitudes; recognition and responsibility as an equal" (p. 121). Thus, as African-American women pose and respond to the preceding question, they must recognize their personal and collective realities with regard to their negotiating position, talents, aptitudes, and equality.

Empowered African-American women have a sense of control over their lives. They know and are comfortable with who they are (their personalities, gender, and race), what they think (their cognitions), what they feel (their emotions), and what drives their behavior (their motivation and cultural heritage). Examples of empowerment voiced in *Images of Me* groups are: "I'm proud to be an African-American woman and I want people to see my Blackness and my femaleness"; "I think African-American women, because of our history of oppression, can teach others who are oppressed to survive in the face of oppression"; "My faith in God and my determination to not give in to being told that I'm a second-class person because I'm a Black female keeps me going"; and "When I get angry about my experiences on the job, I call a 'sista' (another African-American female) and ask her if she thinks I'm crazy and aggressive. I hear her share similar experiences, and that helps me feel better. I'm ready to go back to work and face the racism."

Empowerment Through Self-Determination—Kujichagulia

One form of empowerment emanates from the common cultural and gender realities of *Images of Me* participants. As African-Americans, awareness of self as an ethnic person and of the connection between self and people sharing common backgrounds, characteristics, and experiences is important in promoting the ethnic consciousness, self-determination, and positive images of African-American women. In addition, there is a sense of empowerment evidenced by their racial and gender similarities and often an assumption of familiarity, which seems to heighten comfort, determination, and affirmation. Connection, familiarity, and determination are realized (sometimes consciously and, at other times, unconsciously) through embracing both African and female values such as collective survival (we/sisterhood) and a "being" orientation to life (I/we are important because we exist). A fundamental strategy to empower African-American women participating in *Images of Me* has been to urge each person, as a unique individual and as a group member, to foster interdependence on the group through embracing the concept of "I am because we are, we are therefore I am"—thus, validating each member's part in the group as a viable link to the sisterhood. Through sisterhood and collective survival, self-determination is affirmed as participants work to define for themselves, as African-American women, who they are, what they think, what they feel, and what drives them.

In the search for effective methodologies to empower and promote self-determination among African-American women, multicultural counseling is both practical and therapeutic (Harris, 1992; Sue & Sue, 1990). *Multicultural counseling*, as defined here, is counseling built on a foundation grounded in culturally appropriate interventions, such as group work, which are (1) considered necessary to treatment planning; and (2) relevant to the needs and issues of the specific group being counseled, in this case African-American women. Remembering that the African-American self-concept is authenticated in terms of others with a worldview that is holistic, interdependent, and oriented to collective endurance, the selection of empowerment strategies undergirding such values and perspectives is crucial.

A therapeutic approach which we have found useful with numerous members of *Images of Me* is Gestalt therapy. The term Gestalt suggests the wholeness of the individual but the individual is a whole in the context of a group resembling a family and a community. Gestalt techniques, such as active leader involvement, enlisting group members' feedback, and use of confrontational skills, have proved effective in promoting greater awareness of self-defeating behaviors as a way to enhance self-determination and empowerment. Let's visit an *Images of Me* group and observe leaders using Gestalt techniques within the context of racial and gender cultural values to empower a group member who is struggling with being affirmed and heard on her job.

Marie: My colleagues seem not to hear me when I express myself and, before I know it, I feel invisible in their midst. This happens to me a lot.

Group Leader: Marie, you work in a predominantly White environment that seems to value European-American verbal and nonverbal communication behaviors. It sounds like employees at your workplace are encouraged to speak directly while simultaneously controlling the expression of their feelings, but you seem to embrace communication behaviors that are more Afrocentric in nature. You seem to speak directly and express your emotions while you are speaking.

The goal of the leader at this juncture is to help Marie communicate biculturally. Although she does speak directly (shares her thoughts and feelings), she does not control the expression of her feelings because she values being animated and emotional when she speaks. Her direct and emotionally vital communication style seems to cause her colleagues to ignore her; they perceive her as "out of control."

Group Leader: Marie, it is important for you to be able to recognize the values that are at play here. We've discussed common values of the European-American culture, particularly the White, middle-class male culture. One value that is held

in esteem is to control one's emotions. Remember, we are
not saying one set of values is more or less important than
another set of values. Our purpose is to focus on what you
are sharing now and identify values clearly evident in your
experience. A common European-American value is to keep
your emotions in tact.

Marie: Yes, I remember us talking about differences and similarities in values, but when I'm at home I am not seen this way.

Group Leader: Let's take it slowly. When you are at home, what
are the values that seem to be important and acted on? How
do these values relate to our African heritage?

Marie: Well, we get involved with each other.

Group Leader: Meaning?

Marie: It's not uncommon to hear us raising our voices, but we
aren't always fighting. In fact, we are just emotionally
engaged in what's going on.

Group Leader: Sounds like you're saying that, in your family,
getting involved means you may raise your voice and become
more animated in your mannerisms.

Marie: Yes!

Group Leader: Okay, let's keep it moving slowly. Focus on how
the White employees in your work environment tend to
relate to each other. What do you notice?

Marie: When they are relating and trying to make a point, they
speak directly and may even raise their voices. But I have
noticed that often, when they raise their voices, they seem
angry. That is, they begin to attack each other, or I've
noticed that some become defensive as if they have to
explain what's going on.

Group Leader: Okay, stay slow now! Let's look through what I
like to call bifocal lenses. That is, let's look at the same situation and look at it from two worldviews. The first view is
from your worldview in which you embrace Afrocentric values such as direct speech, animation, and emotional vitality.
The second view is from a European-American perspective
in which values such as direct speech and control of emotions are valued. What do you notice?

Marie must understand traditional European-American
communication and recognize that this communication style
may be different from traditional African-American communication. Further, she must be encouraged to appreciate that
both styles of communication are viable. As such, she may

need to practice one system at work and the other system out-side of her work environment. To facilitate Marie's potential for being heard and having an appreciation for her ethnic/racial roots, we engage in role-playing. Marie is asked to assume her typical communication style and one of the group leaders assumes the role of her supervisor. The two engage in dialogue, initially to see how Marie presents herself. The co-leader and other group members (1) observe Marie's nonverbal and verbal behaviors as she interacts with her supervisor, looking for and interpreting the meanings of gestures, posture, and movement in communication through culturally diverse lenses; (2) enlist group members' feedback, and (3) use con-frontational skills to promote greater awareness of self-defeat-ing behaviors.

As she speaks, the group members process their interpre-tations and experiences of Marie's direct speech and animated nonverbal language. It becomes clear that Marie sends a strong and intense message (e.g., "I want to move this meeting along, time is quickly passing and I am getting frustrated!"). The group shares and practices alternative communication styles which are more sensitive to the values of Marie's Euro-pean-American work environment and may increase her abil-ity to be heard (e.g., "I am feeling frustrated that we are not moving as quickly on this issue as I had hoped. What can we do to speed the process up?"). The group, however, sends Marie an important message:

Group Members: We understand your communication style and we were not intimidated, frightened, and/or confused. In fact, we can relate to and appreciate your intense feelings, direct speech, and animation; but, our collective experiences in Eurocentric work environments that promote traditional values, such as direct speech, limited emotional vitality, and limited animation, have shown us the value in behaving biculturally.

In this scenario, self-determination emerges as Marie is validated for her traditional Afrocentric communication style and is shown that her behavior is familiar to and understood by those sharing an appreciation for similar communication styles. Marie begins to confirm for herself that she is not crazy, invisible, nor deficient in any way. At the same time, Marie is empowered to recognize the value of communication at her workplace and to identify ways to facilitate being heard and seen within that environment.

Empowerment Through Embracing Bicultural Assets

Another mode of empowerment is affirmation of the interrelationship between racism and sexism. Both race and gender overlap in the lives of African-American women and can create stressors at various points. One stressor is the influence of socialization within the dominant culture, as well as within the African-American culture, which is reflected as a combination of value systems indicative of both cultures. For example, derivatives of the African worldview may be heard in the statement, "I am because we are," rather than the European worldview, "I think, therefore, I am." "I am because we are" sends the message that the individual is not as important as the group and the individual is encouraged to look beyond her own personal needs to consider what is in the best interest of the group.

The European-American worldview places value on individualism and every member of the group is presumed to have something to contribute and is expected to do so. African culture responds to the spirit rather than the letter of the law. Afrocentric lenses—laws, rules, or social structures—do not exist as abstract entities with a life of their own. Instead, they are created as tools that may be modified or discarded when they no longer serve their purpose. Personal style and attributes are also valued in the Afrocentric worldview. The European-American worldview holds status or offices in esteem. Valuing of personal attributes over material accomplishments also reflects African cultural roots. In addition, African-Americans have a heightened sensitivity to nonverbal communication, which may be a result of living in a hostile environment where attention to subtle cues can mean the difference between life and death.

The history of African people reflects a preference for oral or auditory as opposed to written communication. African-American women are not socialized to expect marriage to relieve them of the need to work; their financial contribution to the household is usually presumed necessary. The role of mother is an important one but is accompanied by tasks that aren't required of White women. Motherhood isn't limited to biological mothers (extended family concept). The African-American family is a crucial barrier against racism in the dominant culture and mothers are charged with the task of teaching their children mechanisms of mastery over racism. More important, the images (conscious and unconscious) of the significance of both the female and racial characteristics of African-American women (individually or collectively) promote empowerment when recognized and affirmed.

Summary

In this chapter, we have discussed two constructs important to effective group work, group dynamics and therapeutic forces, as they interrelate to the Afrocentric worldview. We canvassed the influence of personal and collective attitudes and interactions of group leaders and group members on enhancing images of self and images of other women, in part, identifying and embracing the bicultural (racial and gender) assets of African-American women. We stressed the importance of viewing group work from an Afrocentric perspective to promote and foster empowerment of African-American women as they pose and answer two common questions: "Am I crazy or is this what's happening?" and "Is this for real?" We offered a theme of Kujichagulia (Swahili for self-determination) to guide group work. Kujichagulia embraces the life experiences and realities of African-American women and facilitates empowerment by helping them to define for themselves who they are, what behaviors (verbal and nonverbal) relate to their cultural and gender backgrounds, and what individual and collective images they wish to embrace as they address real issues such as cultural images, racism, and sexism.

As previously mentioned, to date *Images of Me* (the group) has been co-lead by African-American females. These leaders share a history, worldviews, and life experiences characteristic of African-Americans and females. Critical to their effectiveness is what they do to personally and professionally ensure that their racial and gender parallels enhance, not distort, their effectiveness as group leaders. Chapter 9 discusses the necessity for support for group leaders while they simultaneously and effectively promote the psychological, emotional, and spiritual development of their sisters—African-American females. We propose that group leaders use the principles of Ujima and Kuumba to support each other.

References

Arredondo, P., Toporek, R., Brown, S., Jones, J., Locke, D., Sanchez, J., & Stadler, H. (1996). Operationalization of the multicultural counseling competencies—A monograph. Alexandria, VA: The Association for Multicultural Counseling and Development, a division of the American Counseling Association.

Brown, J. F. (1993). Helping Black women build high self-esteem. *American Counselor, 2*, 9–11.

Brown, S., Sanders, J., & Shaw, M. (1995). Kujichagulia—Uncovering the secrets of the heart: Group work with African-American women on predominanty White campuses. *Journal for Specialists in Group Work, 20*(3), 151–158.

Brown, S. P. (1994). *Images of Me*: Group work with African-American women on predominantly White campuses. *Journal of College Student Personnel, 35*(2), 150–151.

Capuzzi, D., & Gross, D. R. (1992). *Introduction to group counseling.* Denver: Love Publishing Company.

Fleming, J. (1983). Black women in Black and White college environments: The making of a matriarch. *Journal of Social Issues, 39*, 41–54.

Gainor, K. A. (1992). Internalized oppression as a barrier to effective group work with Black women. *Journal for Specialists in Group Work, 17*, 235–242.

Gladding, S. T. (1991). *Group work: A counseling specialty.* New York: Merrill.

Hall, C. M. (1992). *Women and empowerment: Strategies for increasing autonomy.* Washington, DC: Hemisphere Publishing.

Harris, D. J. (1992). A cultural model for assessing the growth and development of the African-American female. *Journal of Multicultural Counseling and Development, 20*(4), 158–167.

Jackson, A. P., & Sears, S. J. (1992). Implications of an Afrocentric worldview in reducing stress for African-American women. *Journal of Counseling and Development, 71*, 184–190.

Jacobs, E. E., Harvill, R. L., & Masson, R. L. (1994). *Group counseling: Strategies and skills* (2nd ed.). Pacific Grove, CA: Brooks/Cole.

Jordan, J. M. (1991). Counseling African-American women: Sisterfriends. In C. Lee & B. Richardson (Eds.), *Multicultural issues in counseling: New approaches to diversity* (pp. 49–63). Alexandria, VA: American Association for Counseling and Development.

Mitchell, J. C. (1991). Counseling needs of African-American students on predominantly White college campuses. *College Student Journal, 25*, 192–197.

Nayman, R. L. (1983, March). Group work with Black women: Some issues and guidelines. *Journal for Specialists in Group Work, 8,* 31–38.

Nobles, W. (1990). *Afrocentric psychology. Toward its reclamation, reascension, and revitalization.* Oakland, CA: A Black Family Institute Publication.

Parham, T. A. (1993). *Psychological storms: The African-American struggle for identity.* Chicago: African-American Images.

Robinson, T., & Howard-Hamilton, M. (1994). An Afrocentric paradigm: Foundation for a healthy self-image and healthy interpersonal relationships. *Journal of Mental Health Counseling, 16*(3), 327–339.

Sue, D. W., Arredondo, P., & McDavis, R. J. (1992). Multicultural counseling competencies and standards: A call to the profession. *Journal of Multicultural Counseling and Development, 20,* 64–80.

Sue, D. W., & Sue, D. (1990). *Counseling the culturally different: Theory and practice.* New York: John Wiley and Sons.

9

Group Leaders Need Support—Ujima and Kuumba—as They Lead

Ethical and culturally appropriate practices are requisites for effective helping services offered to any client. Group work is no exception. In the provision of effective service to group members, group leaders are somewhat like airline pilots. Leaders pilot group members from places of mental, emotional, spiritual, and physical challenge, hasten their journey through the group experience, and enhance the quality of life at new individual and collective destinations. The Nguzo Saba principles of *Ujima* (balance, mutual interdependence, active togetherness) and *Kuumba* (creativity, creative labor) are important to remember. Leaders who work with racially and ethnically diverse clients are challenged to use the type of awareness, knowledge, and skills necessary to work within the context of their client's worldviews (Newlon & Arciniega, 1992; Sue, Arredondo, & McDavis, 1992; Sue & Sue, 1990).

Culturally competent group leaders understand and appreciate the life experiences of their group members and pilot group sessions using professional behaviors and group practices consistent with those life experiences. Although they have been trained to engage in professional group leadership behaviors, a critical and often underaddressed reality is that group leaders (pilots) are also human beings. They also have, among other life factors, personal life experiences related to their gender and racial/ethnic heritage, cultures, and world-views. Some, for example, are women with attitudes, values, and beliefs about how people (other women) ought to interact and create as they journey together.

A dimension of group work that is often not addressed is the parallel between the worldviews and life experiences of group leaders and group members. Of significance is the parallel between leaders and members who share a cultural, racial, and gender history. An important consideration is the effect of this history on the leaders' need for support while promoting the mental health of group members. For example, what issues might African-American female group leaders have as they lead groups comprised of African-American females? If leaders value interdependence and collective behavior, how do issues influence their personal and professional behaviors within and outside of group? How might leaders emotionally, professionally, and spiritually support each other as they lead groups for African-American females.

It is not uncommon for African-American females who lead groups comprised of African-American females, such as *Images of Me*, to experience issues, realities, and interconnections that trigger their need for therapeutic support. The purpose of this chapter is to discuss the necessity for support for group leaders who are female and African-American while they simultaneously promote the psychological, emotional, and spiritual development of other African-American females. However, note that other group leaders who are different from the general society and viewed as minorities (e.g., females, persons of color other than African-Americans) may also experience the need for support when working with a group comprised of minorities. The need for support is related to the experience of oppression common to minorities living in a society that fails to value their differences.

As leaders and members of a minority culture which provides both a script for living and a map for interpreting reality, they must examine the influence of their culture as it relates to their professional philosophies and behaviors. This examination is meant to enhance personal awareness of "cultural baggage" regardless of its form—prejudices, biases, stereotypes, and so on—and then identify and engage in appropriate group leadership behaviors. In this chapter, distinct awarenesses, knowledge, and skills necessary for group leaders to work effectively with African-American females are explored. The reader is reminded that while *Images of Me* is a group for African-American women, which to date has been lead by African-American females, much of what is discussed and outlined may be applicable to group leaders who are not African-American and female but are sensitive to and understand the world-views and life experiences of African-American females.

Multicultural Counseling Competencies: Ujima and Group Leaders

The Association for Multicultural Counseling and Development (AMCD) approved in 1995, and both AMCD and the Association for Counselor Education and Supervision recently endorsed, a monograph entitled "Operationalization of the Multicultural Counseling Competencies" (Arredondo, Toporek, Brown, Jones, Locke, Sanchez, & Stadler, 1996). The monograph outlines specific awarenesses, knowledge, and skills required of culturally competent counselors working in cross-cultural situations. A three-dimensional tool (A, B, and C), entitled the Dimensions of Personal Identity Model (Arredondo & Glauner, 1992), is introduced in the monograph to examine individual differences and shared identities.

Dimension A creates the images we have of people and includes biological characteristics, such as gender, race, and ethnicity, which are neither modified nor controlled easily. Dimension B includes realities, such as education, income, and religion, and is presented as a possible outcome of what occurs due to Dimensions A and C. That is, what happens to people relative to their Dimension B (e.g., education) is influenced by some characteristic(s) of Dimension A (e.g., gender) and the major political, historical, sociocultural, and economic legacies of Dimension C (e.g., the Civil Rights Movement). Dimension C reflects the universality of people. It places each individual in an historical, political, sociocultural, and economic context and recognizes that sociopolitical, global, and environmental events impact personal culture and life experiences. To illustrate, an African-American female (Dimension A) group leader who marched in the Civil Rights Movement to fight for the rights of Blacks and women (Dimension C) decided a way to continue helping people live more productive and healthy lives was to pursue a Ph.D. and become a licensed professional clinical counselor (Dimension B). As leaders help group members create and develop positive images of themselves as African-American females, leaders are challenged by *Ujima*; they are challenged to create balance, mutual interdependence, and active togetherness.

Throughout this book we have discussed the skills and competencies required of group leaders working effectively with African-American females. Leaders who work with group members that share dimensions of personal identity must be culturally aware, knowledgeable, and skillful in examining their own identities. For example, *Images of Me* co-leaders discuss their cultural heritage around gender, race, and religion. They underscore their awareness and sensitivity to their heritage and the subsequent influence on personal experiences as group leaders.

Group Leader A: Each time I lead an *Images of Me* group I am reminded of how proud I am to be African-American. My father taught me to be proud of us (African-Americans), to know and live the values important to us as a people, and not to let anyone take that pride and those values away from me. It is significant for me to be able to help other African-American females come to grips with who they are as African-Americans and females. I embrace the opportunity to assist group members identify more productive ways to interact with other African-American women as well as other racial and ethnic women. My belief in and knowledge of common values held by African-Americans and women, such as a relational orientation to life, fosters my ability and conviction to use counseling behaviors and skills to promote an Afrocentric approach to life.

Group Leader B: I know what you mean! I feel such a connection with my sisters and find that religion is a common value which helps group members develop strength and focus. African-Americans have a history of strength derived from faith. That attitude of "power in God" is an exciting reality for me and it's affirming to see it actualized within group members too. Thus, it's natural for me to help group members develop skills to draw on their spirituality and religion as tools to enhance the quality of their lives.

However, developing cultural awareness, knowledge, and skill is an ongoing process. Thus, leaders may find that there are periods of time when they are more or less aware, knowledgeable, and skillful, particularly when working with group members sharing similar personal identities. Skills of seeking balance and providing feedback are significant during the maturation process. Leaders who do not recognize and work through the balance between their cultural backgrounds and experiences on their psychological processes during group sessions may find that they inappropriately distance themselves from or over connect with group members. In either case, to promote leadership effectiveness, leaders need support in identifying and working through shared dimensions, as in the following example:

Group Leader A: There are some group members that seem to blatantly resist the concept that values are influenced by gender and race. Like the other day, Anzella refused to acknowledge any pride in being African-American and seems to have little knowledge of her cultural values. I tried as hard as I knew how to help her get in touch with who she is. She chose to join a group for Black women, led by Black women, so it seems like she would have an appreciation for Blackness.

Group Leader B: Sounds like you are angry. I noticed during session that you were really pushing Anzella to focus on her Blackness. I tried to reframe what you were saying to her but you were more powerful than I at that point. What was going on with you?

Group Leader A: Anzella reminds me of myself. I too lived in a predominantly White environment and found that for a large part of my life the Blacks that I was around seemed jealous of me and my family. I come from a family of light-skinned people too, but as I said, my father, even though light-skinned, was a proud African-American man who embraced values such as collective behavior and the importance of "self" in relation to others. I think I just lost focus and balance. I wanted to help Anzella love herself. She is a beautiful Black woman.

Group Leader B: Yeah, you and I know that we are beautiful people! We also know that we are human beings; thus, we struggle with each other for a variety of reasons. Let's agree that I will focus on Anzella in group until you and I can work through what you are dealing with right now. I appreciate the opportunity to help you in this way. You've helped me so many times in the past as I questioned my racial identity. It's great having you in my life. How can I support you in addition to taking the lead with Anzella for awhile?

Leaders who use an Afrocentric group approach will encourage active togetherness and mutual interdependence and again find themselves connected with group members (emotionally, psychologically, spiritually, and/or physically) whether the members share different or similar identities. Clearly, African-American group leaders share race and gender (Dimension A) with African-American group members. Yet, as African-American group leaders, they may come from a different social class (Dimension A) and geographic location (Dimension B). However, due to their value for an Afrocentric approach to life, they strive toward balance and promote mutual interdependence and active togetherness among group members as well as among themselves as co-leaders. This task is not easily accomplished and frequently calls for support and feedback.

A critical question undergirding the leaders' work is: "Through whose lenses am I looking?" Having to help others deal with issues that are not uncommon to personal life experiences, such as oppression, racism, and sexism, is a burden difficult to meet under the best of circumstances. Yet, the ways in which group leaders view and balance dimensions of self, their personal life experiences, and their personal worldviews are important to how they lead groups and to how they support other group leaders as they foster successful leadership behaviors and attitudes.

Group Leaders' Challenges: Leaders Need Support

African-American female group leaders, as females and members of the African-American community, tend to appreciate a relational connectedness life approach. As such, a dual perspective of self emerges. The self is viewed as an individual (a person distinct from other people by specific characteristics) and a member of a group (the female gender and the Black race). The following five conditions help group leaders identify and understand the impact of their beliefs, values, attitudes, self image, and worldview on group work while promoting their effectiveness with African-American females:

1. Planning and processing individual group sessions
2. Personal journaling
3. Videotaping to provide direct and immediate feedback
4. Being in therapy
5. Embracing the principles of Kwanzaa (Nguzo Saba)

Three of these conditions are discussed here: embracing the Nguzo Saba, planning and processing group sessions, and personal journaling. Suggestions to help group leaders identify and survive emotions and thoughts that emerge in their self-images and worldviews as they co-lead group sessions are offered.

Embracing the Nguzo Saba—An Afrocentric Guide to Daily Living

Dr. Maulana Karenga states that the principles of Nguzo Saba serve to guide daily living (Porter, 1991). As leaders lead, they bring to the groups their worldviews, their rules for living, and their ways of interpreting reality. Two principles, Kuumba and Ujima, are significant to group leaders working to maintain their personal and professional expertise as they espouse an Afrocentric group approach. Enacting these principles requires skill and can be viewed as an art. Fundamental to this skill/art is the ability to identify and understand worldviews as well as personal guidelines for daily living. In our work with African-American women, we have found that group leaders who use an Afrocentric group approach, and include the Nguzo Saba, must skillfully embrace collective work, responsibility, balance, and creativity.

It is important to keep in mind that as Afrocentric group leaders embrace collective work, responsibility, balance, and creativity, they simultaneously embrace Afrocentric values. One value that is clearly manifested among *Images of Me* group leaders and among leaders of groups similar to *Images of Me* is an appreciation for the worthiness of emotions in life. Emotions are a part of the core of their physical, spiritual, verbal, and nonverbal behaviors and life experiences. The exhibition of emotions presented here is not to be confused with a person who is emotionally focused to the degree that he or she loses perspective and simply reacts to life and its realities. The type of emotional behavior referred to here can be equated with an appreciation for the ability of humans to freely feel and experience life on a daily basis.

This type of emotional freedom and expression has many benefits, including the following:

1. The ability to understand the affective experience of life's realities around oppression, discrimination, and empowerment through faith and religion;
2. The ability and comfort to name and discuss personal privileges experienced in society because of their gender, race, and physical abilities;
3. A sense of enhanced comfort with others exhibiting emotions; and
4. An enhanced ability to recognize nonverbal behavior and the resultant value thereof.

At the same time, this type of emotional freedom has many challenges. For group leaders working with members who share similar personal identity dimensions, worldviews, and life experiences, challenges include, but are not limited to, the following:

1. A sense of powerlessness when hearing and feeling the realities expressed by group members;
2. A sense of confusion around an ability to see the influence of various dimensions of personal identity among group members and the leaders' role in promoting the cultural self-awareness of group members; and
3. A skewed perception of helping limitations.

Embracing the Nguzo Saba as a guide to daily living has the benefits and challenges just described. Thus, during the challenging times, group leaders need help and support. We encourage leaders to recognize these needs and seek balance within themselves as they create opportunities for group members to grow. One way to do so is to support each other. We present selected methods of support in more detail later in this chapter.

Creative Labor—Kuumba—Among Group Leaders

Kuumba is Swahili for creativity. One of the major roles of leaders who are guided by the principle of Kuumba is to continuously and creatively provide experiences and opportunities which create and affirm the physical, psychological, spiritual, and emotional beauty evident in the community. They do so by employing culturally competent helping behaviors that are consistent with the life experiences of group members. They operate from a helping system that embraces a multicultural worldview whereby each individual group member, the collective group members (i.e., the family), and external environmental factors work together to promote mental, spiritual, and emotional health. A fundamental goal of leaders is to build on the collective mentality and efforts of group members (i.e., we are sisters working to help sisters) to encourage change and build positive self-images. At the same time, leaders must differentiate their racial and gender identities from those of group members as they work toward affirmation and appreciation of the African-American community.

Of course, as leaders create and facilitate groups, they too have experiences. As previously mentioned, leaders experience emotions as they lead groups. A familiar emotion experienced by leaders of *Images of Me* is anger. Although anger may exist, it is important to remember that leaders possess skills to manage their anger and to promote their professionalism during group sessions. It is equally important to remember that emotional experiences are there; and that these emotions and subsequent experiences need to be addressed in order to promote group leaders' continued mental health and ensure their ongoing and effective leadership behavior. If not addressed, leaders may "burn out" and give up leading groups comprised of members who share similar identity dimensions and worldviews. If this happens, the number of services offered to engage African-American clients in a reasonable number of sessions to promote growth and change will diminish. This would be a travesty in that, to date, clients of color tend to remain in counseling for only a few sessions (Brown, Parham, & Yonker, 1996; Ivey, Ivey, & Simek-Morgan, 1993).

Images of Me leaders may become angered and frustrated as they experience their sisters (group members) struggling psychologically and emotionally to contend with questions like "Am I crazy, or is this what is going on?" These leaders sometimes become impatient with the levels of racial and gender identity exhibited by their sisters. As leaders, they may become restless with a group member who reflects a Pre-Encounter stage of racial consciousness and denies or avoids issues of race while racial issues seem evident if for no other reason than that the member elected to join a group specifically designed and advertised for and facilitated by African-American females. Further, leaders may become confused with the rate of the group's movement toward resolution of issues such as, "As a woman, I am responsible for the success of my relationship with my boyfriend," without regard for the actual power she may or may not have in the relationship.

As leaders hear the stories of oppression and experiences of racism and sexism encountered by other African-American females, they may find themselves angry and frustrated. At the same time, leaders have thoughts and psychological experiences that tap their personal and professional behaviors and energy. If taken into the group setting without proper processing, these thoughts and experiences may manifest themselves in the work and enthusiasm of the leader and influence the effectiveness of group process and outcome.

Leaders may break the yolk of emotions (e.g., anger, frustration), confusion, troubling thoughts, and psychological experiences by following a three-pronged approach—focus, feel, finish—to support. First, leaders must *focus;* after group sessions, leaders can support each other by identifying and focusing on personal concerns and issues stemming from the sessions and members. As a way to support each other, their primary task is to specifically and simply tell the other leader exactly what they want to happen in group and/or with a group member.

Group Leader A: I want Latifa to see the beauty in her dark
   brown skin and not let society sell her a bunch of crock!
   Even though images are becoming more diverse in the
   media, there still remains a consistent playing of White
   women against Black women in terms of what is considered
   beautiful. I get so angry when I see our sisters struggle with
   what, historically and still today, seems to say what we
   ought to look like if we want to be beautiful. There is this
   commercial on television that captures my attention and
   gives me hope. It is an African-American woman talking
   about aging. She says her concern/problem is not wrinkles
   but gravity. I like that because it acknowledges that our
   naturally oily skin can be an asset during the aging process.
   We tend not to wrinkle as quickly a White women. The realities of gravity and sagging skin are more of a problem for us.
   Visualizing and presenting oily skin as an asset is a very different image than visualizing and presenting oily skin as
   something to try to correct.

Second, leaders must *feel*. During this part of support, they creatively provides experiences and opportunities to affirm the spiritual and emotional beauty within the community as evidenced by themselves as leaders; after group sessions, leaders provide mutual support by freely expressing their emotions and compassion. They share with each other their deepest feelings about the suffering of group members, particularly as they relate to shared issues, experiences, and so on. Of significance during this sharing is that leaders focus on the actual helping abilities that they possess. We have found that calling on empowerment from one's spiritual life is one of many instrumental behaviors to use during support sessions.

Group Leader B: I need you to pray with me about the suffering group members are experiencing with working with White women. I know the pain and struggle to be heard! I also know the strength I receive from God and prayer as I deal with tough issues and tough times. Lord help me, this is so difficult to do! Yet I am committed and we will stay with this. We will help these women.

Third, leaders must *finish;* that is, they must finish their task and stretch themselves until the job is done. They must "lock/ground" themselves into something to give them the strength and motivation to utilize their formal leadership skills and intentionally and actively provide the services necessary for the development of group members. We suggest that leaders lock/ground themselves in the Afrocentric value system and approach to life, including, but are not limited to the following:

- Call on a spiritual leader for support and wisdom as they deal with personal issues, confusions, and feelings.
- Surround themselves with African-American females who are coping positively with issues and experiences of group members.
- Read and discuss inspirational passages from African-American female writers such as Iyanla Vanzant; recommended works include *Acts of Faith* and *The Value in the Valley: A Black Woman's Guide Through Life's Dilemmas.*
- Interact with women of diverse populations (Asian-American and Pacific Islanders, European-American, Latin-American, Native-American) who are sensitive to and knowledgeable about racism, sexism, and oppression issues.

As stated throughout this book, some traditional helping theories, strategies, and interventions have proven helpful with clients of color. Clearly, these could also be used as tools to help group leaders support themselves as they lead groups. For example, a traditional theoretical orientation that could be used to help group leaders reach the "lock/ground" goal is the Rational Emotive Therapeutic (RET) approach to helping. The RET approach espouses helping clients decide their desires based on personal and logical reasons that are harmonious with their emotions. Emotions are so central to change that if not addressed along with cognitions, change may not occur (Ivey et al., 1993). Thus, as group leaders address thoughts, feelings, and experiences related to surmounting discrimination, prejudice, and unfairness, they too must generate a more realistic cognitive view of self and their ability to change situations, in this case related to helping African-American female group members. Following are two examples of dysfunctional ideas that group leaders who have experienced similar life realities and share worldviews consistent with group members may hold:

1. I must always be thoroughly competent, adequate, and achieving if I am to be a good group leader: "It's my fault if group members do not change while working with me."
2. It is catastrophic if group members are not aware of and/or receptive to their African heritage: "Isn't it terrible that someone would join a group for African-American females, led by an African-American female, and not be able to see and/or respect her African values?"

As group leaders support each other and promote leadership effectiveness, we encourage them to collaborate in generating additional dysfunctional beliefs. Leaders do so in order to enhance their abilities to recognize their individual and collective irrational thoughts. In particular, they want to tap those verbal behaviors that directly or indirectly send the message that what they, as leaders, are saying in group is "all or nothing" for group members. Once these behaviors are tapped, leaders support each other in disputing these beliefs and in generating more rational beliefs to enhance their personal experience in group and promote leadership sensitivity and effectiveness.

Leaders not only experience emotions while leading groups, they also have thoughts and psychological experiences that tap their personal and professional behaviors and energy. A common thought among *Images of Me* leaders is: "I am excited about working with my sisters, yet I am saddened when I experience a sister who has no idea of who she is as a woman or who she is as an African-American." Such thoughts, if taken into the group setting without proper processing, manifest themselves in the work and enthusiasm of the leader and influence the effectiveness of group process and outcome.

Building Community and Responsibility—Ujima

Leaders can remain available and productive for group members by seeking balance within themselves. A tool to facilitate achievement of balance is to build and maintain community in a unified manner (*Ujima*). Until now, we have talked about unity within and among group members, but group leaders can support each other as they temporarily make their sisters' burdens their own, and as they promote mutual interdependence and active togetherness within the group. Immediately after group sessions, the leaders can begin the balancing process by informing each other of specific and thematic physical, emotional, and psychological leadership behaviors evident during group. For example, she may say:

Co-leader: You know as Jan was struggling with being able to see the limits of the influence she has on her relationship with her husband, you seemed to get upset and become more involved than usual. I know you value women taking responsibility for themselves and you take care of yourself well, but Jan is at a different level than you. Let's talk about how you and I can help you help Jan to grow at her own rate?

As leaders seek mutual balance, they are challenged to recognize the knowledge they have about the group members with whom they are working, the influence of that knowledge on themselves as individuals and as leaders, and the need for support as they lead groups.

Leader Awareness: Do I Need Therapeutic Support?

From birth on, an African-American woman's gender and race are significant contributors to her identity. When she looks at another African-American female, she sees a person who physically (in terms of gender and often race) exibits qualities similar to her own. She also sees a person who shares a race and gender history not uncommon to her own. Given this physical likeness and similar history, when an African-Amerian female sees another African-American female in many ways she sees herself and may even think, "When I look at you, I see myself." An outcome of this image of physical and historical similarity is often a sense of connection, a linking with one another because of some familiar trait. In addition, there is a sense of connectedness, a spiritual and psychological sense of being united in some way. From this connection and connectedness we have found that African-American women in the *Images of Me* group experience a spiritual, psychological, and emotional reality that sends the message, "When I look at you, I feel connected and I see my sister—I am my sister."—A similar image and sense of connection and connectedness seem to emerge when a woman (regardless of race or ethnic heritage) sees another woman, in part, because as females they too share a familiar history and physical characteristics.

Images of Me, as it is currently designed, is co-led by African-American females. The connection and connectedness felt by group members is more often than not also enjoyed by the leaders. There are benefits to the experience of connection and connectedness; generally, there is an immediate sense of comfort among group members. To illustrate, members have frequently said "I am glad this group exists because I can be who I am and not have to explain my behaviors and thoughts." Often group members experience an immediate sense of comfort with group leaders, "I feel more comfortable because Shari (a group leader) has also questioned whether she is crazy or whether what is happening in her life is real." Finally, there is a familiarity among leaders and members with the physical (real) and the psychological (mental) experiences of racism and sexism: "As African-American females, we have had to learn the rules and values of the dominant culture to survive."

In the midst of advantages, disadvantages and negative experiences exist. For group leaders these disadvantages and negative realities include discomfort, fatigue, and frustration. It is not uncommon to hear group leaders say, "It is very hard to hear African-American women question whether we, as Black women, will ever get ahead." There's a sense of frustration with those sisters who seem to be unaware of the influence of race and gender on their lives when their underlying messages clearly indicate that race and gender issues are alive and well in their lives. Fatigue is a by-product of work around "isms" and overcoming oppression. Inherent to these frustrations are the thoughts, feelings, attitudes, beliefs, and assumptions that are related to their gender and Afrocentric worldviews, which group leaders bring to the group. As such, questions about the psychological and emotional experiences and needs of the leaders working with other African-American females emanate.

> Do African-American female group leaders need therapeutic support as they co-lead groups for African-American females?
>
> Do African-American female group leaders need to be assisted in the process of remaining separate while connected with their African-American sisters?
>
> Do African-American female group leaders need to be assisted in respecting their personal and group boundaries while leading a group comprised of their sisters?

Clearly, the potential for unproductive behaviors, such as countertransference and overidentification, is present. Yes, therapeutic support (help in remaining separate while connected and respecting boundaries) for group leaders is necessary to counter unproductive therapeutic behaviors and to promote productive therapeutic behaviors. More important, therapeutic support is necessary to help group leaders position themselves so that they are better able to help group members work through their issues and live more productive lives.

A first step to effective therapeutic support is to enhance the group leader's awareness of personal issues, biases, stereotypes, and attitudes around her images of African-American females. A recommendation to help group leaders enhance their personal awareness and begin the discrimination process related to their images of African-American females is to pose and respond to questions such as the following:

- Why do light-skinned African-American females get better opportunities in life than dark-skinned African-American females (i.e., a light-skinned sister is tough competition for a dark-skinned sister)?
- What influence does the color of my complexion have on my work with the light- and dark-skinned African-American

females in group (i.e., a light-skinned sister turns me off; a dark-skinned sister generates empathy within me)?
- What is my perception of a well-adjusted and productive African-American female (i.e., a sister who has an idea of what is going on)?
- What is my perception of a poorly adjusted and nonproductive African-American female (i.e., a sister who has no idea of what's going on)?

As the leaders mature in identifying their general perceptions and images of African-American females, the next step is to identify the relationship and intersections of their perceptions to the images of African-American females reflected within the group. Leaders are encouraged to use cognitive/behavioral approaches to generate tools that can promote self-empowerment, modify biases, and facilitate group leadership. Posing and responding to strategic questions helps identify specific cultural influences on the leaders' daily living and beliefs that may inhibit Kuumba, Ujima, and group leadership. The following questions might be included:

- How intensely did I experience the group and individual group members? For example, "Group was intense. We were animated and took care of business!"
- What motivated my level of experience with the group and with individual group members? For example, "I felt angry with Binta because she was too meek. African-American females don't take no stuff!"
- What thematic verbal messages did I send to the group and/or individual group members? For example, "We are all sisters."
- What thematic thoughts did I carry from group? For example, "This group seems ready to work, they are sharing thoughts and feelings early in the group process."

During the question-and-response process, we recommend couching the discussion around personal perceptions and images of African-American females. Such discussions build a foundation for what belongs to group leaders and what is specific to group members. Through honest canvassing, leaders are encouraged to identify and restructure their problematic thoughts, beliefs, and attitudes around African-American female images. They then support each other in recognizing the need to be helpful and their reasons for group leadership.

A leader decides to lead groups for a variety of reasons. Because leaders simultaneously strive to connect to and remain separate from group members, it is important (for them as well as group members) that they understand their reasons for wanting to lead a group for African-American women. Some do so because they recognize a need and have a commitment to provide culturally responsive services. In addition to these reasons, others have the added impetus of wanting to give back to or to do something for the African-American community and their African-American sisters. Still others lead groups for African-American females because they are forced to do so: They fit the physical criteria (they are African-American and female) and, therefore, are best qualified to lead such a group.

Culturally competent group leaders, regardless of the reasons for leading a group for African-American females, realize the influence of such a decision on group process, dynamics, and outcome; they have a working knowledge of their racial and gender identities and are open to monitoring both. Culturally competent leaders possess well-defined knowledge of the psychological, emotional, and spiritual realities of African-Americans, females, and, in particular, African-American females and are aware of the influence of such factors on effective leadership. They understand institutional barriers that inhibit the advancement and maturation of African-American females and realize the parallel of such barriers on effective leadership. These leaders recognize the conditions, tools, and attitudes that promote the mental health of African-American females and are prepared to professionally and therapeutically offer a service.

As culturally competent leaders, they are guided by the elimination of inappropriate perceptions and beliefs that may cloud the lenses that they wear to make interpretations and diagnoses about African-American females. Their leadership is guided by the question: "Through whose lenses am I looking as I work with group members?" Leaders engage in a number of activities to ensure that their lenses are reflective of the perceptions and beliefs of group members. They assist each other in assessing personal methods of viewing and interacting with the world by pondering questions like, "As I look at the world of African-American women, what qualities am I looking for?" and "Am I looking through my lenses or the lenses of individual group members as I hear their words, feelings, and experiences?"

The leaders who are competent spend time identifying personal assumptions about African-American women and ask, "As I look through my lenses, what have I been taught about being an African-American and a woman?" and "How do my teachings and assumptions about African-American women influence my observation and experience of group members, particularly those who think, feel, and believe differently than I?" They use this information to keep them conscious of how their views and beliefs (their lenses) influence their ability to see, hear, and relate to the views and beliefs of group members (lenses of group members). Thus, to enhance their personal and professional effectiveness, upon completion of each session, as co-leaders, they support and help each other to identify and stay abreast of what each knows about African-American females and how this knowledge influences their individual and collective group leadership. Yet each leader must begin with a working understanding of her own worldview.

A requisite to effectively helping others is knowedge of self and appreciation for the influence of self-knowledge on life's tasks. As group leaders prepare for and facilitate groups, they are encouraged to grasp individual and mutual attitudes, beliefs, values, and assumptions. Of significance are those worldview directives that dictate daily emotional, psychological, and spiritual behaviors and influence abilities to promote balance, mutual interdependence, active togetherness (Ujima), creativity, and creative labor (Kuumba). As leaders support each other in providing effective group service, "What do I know?" becomes a focal point.

Planning and Processing Group Sessions: Knowledge—What Do I Know?

Regardless of the race and/or gender of group participants, careful planning and processing of group sessions cannot be overemphasized. Corey (1990) shared this: "If you want a group to be successful, you need to devote considerable time to planning" (p. 86). Generally there are two types of planning. First, as leaders formulate groups, they plan how to best structure the total group experience. Second, as they lead groups, leaders plan how to best structure each group session. Significant to planning is processing—spending time after sessions to discuss thoughts, feelings, beliefs, values, and attitudes that emerged during group.

When leading groups for African-American females, both planning and processing necessitate an accurate knowledge base and understanding of the individual and collective world-views and life experiences of group members. Equally important is that group leaders possess an accurate knowledge base and understanding of their own and their co-leader's world-view and life experiences. Thus, after each group session, leaders are encouraged to discuss and revisit thoughts, feelings, and ideas shared by group members and encountered by group leaders as the leaders diagnose the session.

Three factors instrumental to building a culturally accurate knowledge base within *Images of Me* groups are thematic attitudes, values, and beliefs that underscore the African-American community, African-American females in general, and individual African-American female group members. Of significance to differentiating among the three factors is awareness, knowledge, and appreciation for the history and sociopolitical realities of African-Americans and African-American females in the United States. Leaders need to recognize the ongoing influence of racism and sexism on the current life experiences of the community and the group, as well as on themselves. They should use this awareness and knowledge to assist in identifying and separating biases, prejudices, and stereotypes which influence attitudes, values, and beliefs exhibited during group planning and processing.

Group leaders support each other in planning and processing. They do so first by assessing the accuracy of their knowledge base and the subsequent influence of this knowledge on their effectiveness as group leaders. To illustrate, a group leader has a strong knowledge base about the historical realities and consequences of oppression for African-American females. She has not, however, clearly identified the lines of demarcation around oppression between her boundaries and those of the group. Although she genuinely desires to help her sisters move beyond unproductive resolutions of oppression, the leader's professional vision of oppression (e.g., "While oppression is a common and real experience of African-American females, each addresses oppression differently and there are different ways to be effective.") becomes clouded by her personal vision of oppression (e.g., "Black women must stand up and fight for women's and African-American's rights."). The leader needs support in order to separate her professional self from her personal self to more appropriately take what she knows about oppression and African-American females and enhance the mental health of group members.

Another area in which group leaders are encouraged to question what they know and to support each other is in the area of ethics and group behavior. Principle number seven "e" of the *Ethical Guidelines for Group Counselors* says that group counselors need to be aware of their own values and assumptions and how these apply in a multicultural context (Jacobs, Harvill, & Masson, 1994, p. 421). Even though ethical behavior is a critically important guiding force for group work, sometimes, because of specific conditions, cultural philosophies and behaviors, what is ethical becomes confused or inaccurate. To this end, professional organizations, such as the Association for Specialists in Group Work and the American Counseling Association, are reevaluating and rewriting ethical guidelines to reflect the influence of culture, race, gender, and other factors on culturally appropriate ethical behavior (Corey, Corey, & Callahan, 1993; Jacobs et al., 1994; Wehrly, B., 1991).

Ethical leaders of African-American female groups are skilled in recognizing and understanding their own worldviews and in leading groups from an accurate historical and contemporary race and gender knowledge base. In addition, these leaders are skilled in recognizing their own racial and gender identities. However, identity development is not a static process. Thus, group leaders' racial and gender identity is evolving continuously. Although their levels of identity are presumed to be more advanced than those of group members, as leaders they too are evolving in their sense of identity with the African-American community and in how they define themselves as females. Thus, as leaders plan for and process group sessions, they need support in the evolution of their racial and gender identities and the subsequent effects of both on group process, dynamics, and outcome.

To illustrate: A group leader may be in the Immersion stage of racial identity and, as the group discusses relationships between Black women and White men, the leader becomes angered. She recognizes that several members see no problem with Black women becoming emotionally involved with White men (the very people who are at the base of racial oppression) and displaces her anger. Even though she genuinely strives to engage in effective group leadership, she becomes more intense in her leadership approach. The leader is less empathic, almost hostile, toward members who deny life's racial realities and, yet, send messages that race is a life issue; thus, a cognitive and emotional imbalance is apparent.

Leaders must be prepared to lead groups in ways that are functional for group members. As they promote the mental, spiritual, and emotional health of members, leaders who share a racial and gender history and similar racial and gender experiences as group members often need emotional, psychological, and spiritual support. Their skills in coping with life experiences are, however, deemed better than those of group members. At the same time, as leaders they must identify and utilize ways to keep their coping skills sharp and decrease the possibility of unproductive leadership. As leaders prone to experience a racial and gender connection and connectedness with group members, they may feel the brunt of oppression and yet not fully understand the implications and origin. As they struggle to identify "What they know," leaders may find it helpful to process their psychological and emotional group experiences. Asking and answering discussion questions like the following may be helpful:

- What racial and gender issues are mine?
- Which racial and gender issues are real and which are imagined?
- How have I dealt with my racial and gender issues?
- How are my racial and gender issues emerging in my work with group members?
- How is the group addressing race and gender?
- Is there a group theme around race and gender? What is the theme?
- Which group member(s) most affects me when race and gender emerge?
- How do my experiences and attitude about race and gender merge with the group's experiences and attitudes about race to promote forward movement of group members?
- What thoughts, feelings, values, and experiences do I need to leave outside of the group environment?
- How do oppression and discrimination affect me in general?
- What influence do my experiences with oppression and discrimination have on my work with group members?

- Where am I in terms of my personal racial and womanist identity? What influence does this have on group dynamics, group process, and group outcome?
- Am I comfortable with the differences that exist between myself and the members of *Images of Me*? If not, how do I reach and practice a more productive level of comfort?
- What formal training do I have that prepares me to competently lead a support/therapy group for African-American females?
- What knowledge do I have about the mental health and mental disorders of African-American females?
- Outside of group, what interactions do I have with African-American females across socioeconomic levels and diverse educational backgrounds? What influence do these interactions have on my work with group members?
- How have religion and spirituality influenced my life? How do my spirituality and religion impact on my behavior as a leader ?

Personal Journaling to Promote Leaders' Emotional Health

A tool to quickly facilitate identification of feelings and provide therapeutic release of emotions is journaling. Once the thematic feelings become evident, group leaders can support each other in dealing with emotional experiences while effectively leading group sessions. Leaders may write about specific aspects of the group in journals. A primary objective of keeping a journal is to create another tool that promotes both personal and professional growth while working with a population that shares a similar history, life experience, and value system. They journal, for example, to identify areas in which they, as leaders, need emotional support. Each leader uses this knowledge to structure interventions that promote a more congruent self-definition of their African-American heritage, life experiences, and value system. Each strives to diminish the emotional struggles experienced when internal conflicts emerge during group. In fact, each broadens her knowledge about emotional effects related to experiencing bicultural behavior exhibited among themselves and group members.

A case in point is a leader who reviews her journal and discovers she is often frustrated when group members place value on themselves (i.e., self as an individual) more than on the extended self (i.e., self as a member of a group). Athough the leader does not impose her frustration on group members while leading the group, she realizes that her journal entries reflect intensity about this issue. She shares this conflict with her co-leader and they identify an intervention, such as cognitive/behavioral strategies, to help change how she thinks about the world and consequently her feelings about people who think and feel differently. Critical to this process is changing how she thinks about the world when promoting the growth of group members sharing a similar history and life experiences.

A second objective of journaling is to assist leaders in identifying their fundamental value system, particularly those values that relate to the African and female cultures. As co-leaders develop a solid understanding of their value system, they become better equipped to help each other establish direction and meaning in group process and dynamics. Further, with a sound knowledge base about values, leaders are better positioned to encourage each other and group members to use Nguzo Saba to enhance positive individual and collective images. For example, a leader may write about her experience with group members as the members share and work on issues of race and gender. Specific thoughts and feelings are highlighted as the leader experiences group members' stories of isolation, pain, and anger associated with being the only African-American female in a particular setting such as a college classroom, a corporate meeting, or an industrial assembly line. She writes this in her journal:

Leader: There's that familiar message of feeling isolated because we are the only, or one of few, African-American female(s). All we need is a WFDO (a White folk's day off), a day off from White folks and their cultural nonsense.

As leaders share and review thematic journal messages, the WFDO message becomes evident. Yet each leader holds in high esteem a philosophy of collective responsibility as she supports others in becoming effective group leaders. A thread woven throughout their belief system is, "I am because we are, we are therefore I am." This thread serves to validate and reaffirm their sense of interconnection and interdependence. Thus, as connected and dependent people, they identify and challenge personal worldviews; reveal and encourage emotional, spiritual, and psychological behaviors and experiences; and work to eradicate personal and professional issues, attitudes, and approaches to racism, sexism, and oppression that may inhibit the forward movement of the group.

Afrocentric Guiding Forces

A common emotional experience among *Images of Me* leaders has been fatigue often associated with the intensity of pain and simultaneous vitality reflected in group members. Yet, as leaders strive to ensure openness and professionalism while leading groups, a motivator for mutual sharing and processing of thematic experiences is to promote and maintain balance and active togetherness (Ujima) among themselves as leaders and among group members. They further promote Ujima as they build and maintain the African-American community by sharing the burdens of their African-American sisters and therapeutically becoming a part of their sisters' physical, emotional, spiritual, and psychological journeys. As leaders, they use an Afrocentric approach to processing and fostering the Afrocentric worldview by creatively (Kuumba) upholding collective survival (a "we" mentality) and emotional vitality (frequent and animated expression of feelings). Again, important guiding forces include mutual interdependence, active togetherness, and creative labor (Kuumba) while they, as leaders, prepare for group sessions.

Of equal importance is that these guiding forces serve to help group leaders effectively provide experiences that enable African-American females to evaluate, define, validate, and endorse their individual and collective images. Group members are empowered to determine for themselves the value of their philosophies and their perspectives relative to who they are as women and who they are as African-American women.

Summary

Race and gender are critical to our relationships. We share a "sisterhood"—we are related—that makes us one. We share a sisterhood with members of *Images of Me* that also makes us one with members (our sisters) of the group. We, as African-American women, are interconnected in ways such as a shared

276 THERAPEUTIC SUPPORT OF GROUP FACILITATORS

racial and gender history, worldviews, and life experiences. We are intentionally connected and support each other through out belief in and the blood of our Creator. We are joined by the principles of Ujima (balance, mutual interdependence, active togetherness) and Kuumba (creativity and creative labor) as we lead groups. This joining gives us freedom to "be" (exist), to be Black (African-American) and female, and to be *both* similar *and* different. As effective group leaders, we walk in unity and work cooperatively. We are family and we act as one for the growth of the group.

The above message undergirds the efforts of leaders of *Images of Me* as they address the need for support among themselves and promote the mental health and general life experiences of African-American females. For this message to be effective, group leaders need to be aware of, knowledgeable about, and skillful in putting into practice the Nguzo Saba as guides to their work with *Images of Me* groups. We emphasize the principles of Kuumba and Ujima as leaders work to effectively lead and serve groups. Regardless of the race and/or gender of group leaders or of group members, we propose that the principles of Ujima and Kuumba can be effective guides for living and leading groups. As culturally competent group leaders, the following characteristics are critical: (1) awareness of self (biases, prejudices, and so on), (2) knowledge of the culture of group members (worldviews, values, attitudes, and so on), and (3) use of culturally appropriate group skills (e.g., an Afrocentric group approach).

References

Arredondo, P., Toporek, R., Brown, S., Jones, J., Locke, D., Sanchez, J., & Stadler, H. (1996). Operationalization of the multicultural counseling competencies—A monograph. Alexandria, VA: The Association for Multicultural Counseling and Development, a division of the American Counseling Association.

Brown, S., Parham, T. A., & Yonker, R. (1996). Influence of a cross-cultural training course on racial identity attitudes of White women and men. *Journal of Counseling and Development, 74*(5), 510–517.

Corey, G. (1990). *The theory and practice of group counseling* (3rd ed.). Pacific Grove, CA: Brooks/Cole.

Corey, G., Corey, M. S., & Callahan, P. (1993). *Issues and ethics in the helping professions.* Pacific Grove, CA: Brooks/ Cole.

Ivey, A. E., Ivey, M. B., & Simek-Morgan, L. (1993). *Counseling and psychotherapy: A multicultural perspective.* Needham Heights, MA: Allyn and Bacon.

Jacobs, E. E., Harvill, R. L., & Masson, R. L. (1994). *Group counseling: Strategies and skills* (2nd ed.). Pacific Grove, CA: Brooks/Cole.

Newlon, B. J., & Arciniega, M. (1992). Group counseling: Cross-cultural considerations. In Capuzzi, D., & Gross, D. R. (Eds.), *Introduction to group counseling* (pp. 285–306). Denver: Love Publishing Company.

Porter, A. P. (1991). *Kwanzaa.* Minneapolis: Carolrhoda Books.

Sue, D. W., Arredondo, P., & McDavis, R. J. (1992). Multicultural counseling competencies and standards: A call to the profession. *Journal of Multicultural Counseling and Development, 20,* 64–80.

Sue, D. W., & Sue, D. (1990). *Counseling the culturally different.* New York: John Wiley and Sons.

Wehrly, B. (1991). Preparing multicultural counselors. *Counseling and Human Development, 23,* 1–24.

Glossary

advocated feminism The shift, suggested by bell hooks (1984), from "I am a feminist" to "I advocate feminism" could serve as a useful strategy for eliminating the focus on identity and lifestyle. It could serve as a way for women who are concerned about feminism as well as other political movements to express their support while avoiding linguistic structures that give primacy to one particular group. It could also encourage greater exploration of feminist theory.

African self-concept the self is defined in terms of the group, the family, or the collective body of Africans' experiences

bias a preference in the form of likes, dislikes, interests, and/or priorities

boundary management setting limits to ensure congruence among members, tasks, and purposes: There is a high positive correlation between effective boundary management and effective group outcome.

challenging to urge one to explore new options, perceptions, and behaviors

clinical paranoia an internalized, deep-seated, psychological condition

culture accumulated values and moral standards of society; patterns of learned thinking and behavior communicated across generations through traditions, language, and artifacts

cultural encapsulation process of disregarding variations among people, dogmatizing a technique orientation, allowing personal cultural values to become the integrating force in decision making

cultural values the totality of beliefs and behaviors common to a group of people, including language, customs, traditions, and so forth

directiveness a form of being confrontational; the act of the giver versus the receiver; being genuine and to the point

discrimination to show partiality or prejudice based on factors other than merit, which influences how a person treats another person or group of persons

diversity describes individual differences. In the context of organizational life, diversity reflects individual differences that can be drawn on and developed to promote the goals of the organization.

efficacy faith in one's ability to achieve a desired outcome

empowerment acknowledgment and appreciation of self as having power to take responsibility for accurate personal and psychological images; assume leadership in obtaining parity; and promote a strong foundation for cultural understanding, communication, and collaboration

ethnic group hereditary membership based on race and cultural distinctiveness

ethnicity a group classification in which the members share a unique social and cultural heritage, such as language, religion, morals, and/or race, which is passed on from one generation to another

ethnocentrism the development of standards that are based on the cultural background of a group; a belief that one's personal culture is "the right or the best" culture; a lack of flexibility about other approaches and/or worldviews

Eurocentric group approaches group interventions based on European-centered values and beliefs

functional paranoia a psychological reaction to an environmental condition or situation

gender female or male essence of self

group process the quality or nature of the relationship between or among people who interact with one another

human nature raw essence of being and behavior

immediacy dealing with what is occurring at the moment; being genuine in one's relationships; discussing current "here-and-now" occurrences

minority group those identified as such for political reasons because they are members of a group that is numerically less than that of other groups in the total population

multicultural generally refers to five major groups: African/Black, Asian, Caucasian/European, Hispanic/Latino, and Native American or indigenous people who, historically, have resided in the continental United States and its territories (see Arrendondo, Toporek, et al., 1996)

Nigrescence   Black racial identity theory; the process of becoming Black. Cross's "Negro-to-Black Conversion Experience" model was developed in the context of consequences and adjustments to interracial interaction.

oppression   coerced subordination of the powerless by the powerful

organization   such an entity serves human needs for comfort or camaraderie, inspiration or education, products or services—through people who perform some functional work (Harris & Morran, 1979, p. 123)

personal culture   the organized totality of a person's identity comprised of historical moments; unchangeable human factors; and a range of developmental, sociocultural, political, and economic dimensions, including religion, work experience, parental status, and so on. The interaction of the dimensions makes for a dynamic versus static personal culture and workplace.

race   a subgroup of people possessing a definite combination of physical characteristics of genetic origin, which to varying degrees distinguishes the subgroup from other subgroups of humankind through skin pigmentation, head form, facial features, color distribution, hair, and so on. *Note*: There is no scientific validity to the classification of races.

racial identity   the sense of group identity an individual has with a racial group based on the individual's perception of a shared or common heritage with a specific group

racism   the doctrine that race is the basic determinant of human abilities and that, therefore, the various racial groups constitute a hierarchy in which one group should properly be regarded as superior to other groups

rigid individualism   excessive focus on self and individual autonomy

role   the performance of expected acts and duties

self   the personal core of an individual's identity

self-esteem   the value we give to ourselves based on the feedback we receive and the experiences we have

sexism   exploitation and domination of one sex by the other, specifically of women by men—as "prejudice or discrimination against" women

socialization   developmental process characterized by the influence of external controls and the internalization of values

spirituality   an emphasis on the spirit as the essence of humanity

stages of group development   the life of the group process, including the initial, the transition, the working, and the termination stages

stereotype   a preconceived, standardized idea about the alleged essential nature of those making up a whole category of persons. Typically the idea is generalized to an entire group without regard to individual differences among those making up the category and is usually emotion-charged. Stereotypes have a controlling function.

sullenness   emotionally unexpressive

therapeutic forces   factors or qualities that help group members work through their difficulties, grow, and change

traditional theories   those group counseling approaches that are based on European, White, middle-class cultural values and beliefs

value   an individual or group of individual intrinsically desired objectives, services, and so on.

win/lose   a belief system that guides psychological, emotional, and spiritual behaviors and emanates from thinking; for example, "the way to the top is to step on whomever or whatever is in the way."

womanist identity   a sense of identity a woman has with members of the female gender; predicated on her individual definition of self which influences her perception of herself, and other women and of her connectedness to other women

worldview   consists of presuppositions/assumptions held about the makeup of the world; "how one perceives her or his personal relationship to the world" (nature, institutions, other people, things, and so on); culturally learned/based

Index